D1611851

STANIER '8Fs'
AT WORK

STANIER '8Fs' AT WORK

Alan Wilkinson

LONDON

IAN ALLAN LTD

To the enginemen of Northwich Depot who
so often showed me just what a Stanier '8F'
could do, and to the signalmen who allowed
me to see it in comfort.

To my parents with apologies for being
neither sportsman nor musician.

And to Margaret, for putting up with it all.

Acknowledgements

Given the wide ranging nature of the '8Fs' work, a
comprehensive account of their activities would have been
impossible without the assistance of many professional
railwaymen, enthusiasts and historians. I am especially
grateful to Mr A. J. Powell for his help with mechanical
aspects and his contribution to Chapter 3, and to Mr
J. W. P. Rowledge without whose painstaking research
into '8F' affairs abroad Chapter 5 would have been much
bereft of detail. Andrew Biwandi has been most
considerate in allowing access to his photographic
material, whilst Vic Forster has been a mine of
information and help with '8F' work on the Midland
Division. At the National Railway Museum Philip Atkins
and John Edgington have pointed the way to much
previously unpublished official material on the Stanier
'8Fs' for which I am most grateful. Extensive reference
has also been made to the *Railway Observer, SLS Journal,
Railway Magazine, Trains Illustrated* and *Modern
Railways* in the period from 1935 until the untimely
demise of the Stanier 2-8-0s in 1968. Sincere thanks are
also due to the many photographers, operating under a
great variety of environments and conditions, whose
activities have made such a complete photographic record
of the '8Fs' at Work possible.

In addition to those whose names appear in the text, I
should also like to thank Messrs S. G. Abbott, A. G.
Blackman, J. P. Bond, D. Bradford Barton Ltd, H. C.
Burgess, Col K. R. M. Cameron, D. H. Cardew, J. F.
Clay, E. S. Cox, J. Davenport, A. Draycott, K. Fairey,
J. Foreman, H. A. Gamble, F. Gale, R. S. Greenwood,
C. H. Gledhill, Maj E. Howell, J. W. T. House, E. J. M.
Hayward, L. C. Jacks, D. G. Jones, P. M. Kalla-Bishop,
Maj W. Kirby, G. Knight, E. A. Langridge, M. McDo-
nald, P. J. Negus, New Zealand Railway Society, B. D.
Palmer, Col C. R. L. Rice, L. Rowbotham, Col C. F.
Ryan, K. Slattery, B. Stephenson, K. Stokes, S. Summer-
son, D. Tyreman, J. A. Waite and A. V. Wilson, who
have all given much appreciated assistance in producing
this portrait of my second favourite locomotive class.

First published 1986

ISBN 0 7110 1603 8

Published by Ian Allan Ltd, Shepperton, Surrey; and printed by Ian
Allan Printing Ltd at their works at Coombelands in Runnymede,
England

Contents

Workshops of origin

The Stanier '8Fs' were produced by no fewer than 11
workshops. An indication is given in the photographic
captions of individual locomotive origins. Thus No 8000
(C35) denotes 'built Crewe 1935'. Hence:

A Ashford SR
B Brighton SR
BP Beyer Peacock Ltd
C Crewe LMSR
D Darlington LNER
Dn Doncaster LNER
E Eastleigh SR
H Horwich LMSR
NB North British Locomotive Co Ltd
S Swindon GWR
VF Vulcan Foundry Ltd

Title page

**No 48694 (B44) bursts out of Red Hill Tunnel, south of
Trent Junction, with a Toton-Brent freight on 24 March
1950.** *J. C. Flemons*

Front endpaper

**The Glory of the Settle & Carlisle. The autumn sun
highlights the scene as Heaton Mersey's '8F' No 48074
(VF36) storms away from Ribblehead Viaduct towards
Blea Moor with a Manchester-Carlisle freight on
4 November 1967.** *G. W. Morrison*

Rear endpapers

**Buxton's No 48744 (D46) was probably the last '8F' to
receive an overhaul at Crewe in November 1966. In a
Christmas card setting, she is seen leaving Grindleford
on the Hope Valley line with a down ballast special on
8 January 1967.** *L. A. Nixon*

Preface

To those of us who grew up in the London Midland panorama of the postwar years, the sight and sound of Stanier's '8Fs' hard at work on a great variety of duties was not the most glamorous, but certainly an essential part of the bustling railway scene. Whether with limestone from the Peak district, coal and iron ore for Midlands industry, or oil from Stanlow, the 2-8-0s with their heavy trains provided a constant background to the passenger 'fliers'. The scene was not that much changed from the 1930s, for the postwar recovery was heavily based on previous technology and, with certain notable exceptions, the long loose-coupled freight train remained the order of the day. Previously, the '8Fs' had carved another distinctive niche for themselves in foreign spheres — chased by German fighters in the Western Desert, attacking Iran's soaring mountain barriers with Russian supplies, and working in Middle Eastern countries after the war. They had also endeared themselves to footplatemen and maintenance staff alike for their willing performance and rugged reliability. The Stanier '8F' was a highly versatile freight locomotive; it could be hammered relentlessly on heavy freight work, whilst its modern front end and free-running qualities allowed fitted freight, parcels and even slower passenger workings to be tackled without qualm. It effectively broke the impasse in LMS freight locomotive design and had an important influence on subsequent design paths through the 'Austerity' 2-8-0 and 2-10-0 locomotives.

The '8Fs' were the largest class of Stanier locomotives, and with 852 examples, the fourth largest class of British locomotive, being produced by eight railway workshops and those of three contractors. By 1939, only 126 had been built but the '8F' was selected as the early War Department standard design for overseas service, 208 being ordered from the North British Locomotive Company and Beyer Peacock including 27 sent to Turkey to fulfil a commercial export order. A further 51 locomotives requisitioned from the LMS saw 205 '8Fs' sent abroad to Egypt, Iran, Palestine, the Lebanon and Italy. Others operated in Iraq and Israel after the war. At home, the Ministry of War Transport selected the '8F' as the standard wartime freight locomotive, 450 being built by all the British railways at Crewe, Horwich, Swindon, Darlington, Doncaster, Ashford, Brighton, Eastleigh, and by North British. The LNER ordered a further 68 locomotives for its own use, built at Brighton, Doncaster and Darlington.

Eventually, 42 locomotives returned from overseas, giving 666 at work on British Railways. The class was concentrated mainly on the London Midland Region, but as only the Southern Region lacked a permanent allocation, they could be seen at work in many parts of the country.

Then came modernisation, the Beeching cuts and route rationalisation; The '8Fs' lasted well, for early in 1965 there were still 638 engines in service. Massive withdrawals followed in the next three years, but the '8Fs' were there to the last, working hard into steam's final hours. Dirty, unkempt and generally run down, they were still capable of good performances in the evening of their days.

I remember a wild winter's night in January 1966; rain and wind lashing the windows of Hartford East box perched high on the embankment beyond the Weaver viaduct at Northwich. A mile away at the foot of the 1 in 100 gradient a fountain of sparks and exhaust was staining the night sky and the stentorian voice of a hard-worked '8F' was clearly audible above the howl of the wind. A break in the clouds revealed the exhaust shooting 20ft into the air before being flung in wraiths of steam across the town. With the wind catching the heavy train of slack broadside, the engine plugged on gamely across the viaduct as the fireman shot another round into the firebox, the glare from the fire doors staining the exhaust an angry crimson. Working flat out at 25mph No 48074 thumped her Woolley Colliery-Hartford North coal haul off the viaduct and pounded past the box in a riot of sound, curving hard on to the 1 in 80 of the Winnington Branch. With the engine losing her feet slightly, 40 minerals thundered past, and then silence as the regulator was closed and the train dipped down the 1 in 50 to Oakleigh sidings, buffers closing up and big ends ringing. The ever willing workhorse — that is what the Stanier '8Fs' at Work were all about.

It is now difficult to picture the days when 50 or 60 '8Fs' could be found congregated at Toton or Kirkby, or when there was heavy freight to be hauled manfully over the mountains of Central Wales or the Settle & Carlisle. As heavy industry has declined so the routes that the '8Fs' worked, the industries they served, are but shadows of their former selves or have disappeared completely. Today, we use very little home iron ore, the domestic and export coal trades are greatly reduced. Loose coupled mineral trains have disappeared in favour of 'Merry-go-Rounds' and the Speedlink service has superseded the 'Maltese', as the partially-fitted through freight was known. It is a very different and rationalised railway system today.

Perhaps the Stanier '8Fs' were never really fully appreciated until their last glorious years in the North

Amidst a typical Pennine Landscape of factory chimneys and cottaged hillsides, No 48519 (Dn44) banks a westbound coal haul across Lydgate Viaduct on the climb to Copy Pit summit on 18 May 1968. *B. Lister*

West from 1966-68. Hopefully this book will help to redress the balance, and also reflect the views of those who had to work with the engines. The steam locomotive was a very human machine but without skill and dedication both on the footplate and in the running shed the difference between potential and actual performance could be very wide indeed.

It would be quite impossible — and I am not certain that preservationists should try — to recreate the halcyon days of the '30s and '50s. Happily the sight of No 8233 at work on the Severn Valley Railway and No 8431 busy on the Keighley & Worth Valley Railway should remind us of much more illustrious efforts in years past, and perhaps they will be joined before too long by Nos 48151, 48305 and 48624.

In conclusion I should like to thank the very large number of people who have so willingly helped me in the production of this volume; without their assistance such a detailed account of '8F' activities would have been quite impossible. I must also pay tribute to the very considerable patience of my wife Margaret, who has not only had to live with No 8233 for eight years of marriage, but has had to cope with the whole class of '8Fs' as well during the preparation of this book.

Alan Wilkinson

Sutton Coldfield
West Midlands
September 1986

6

1
False Starts

The formation of the London Midland and Scottish Railway at the Grouping in 1923 saw an impressive combination of railways, many of whom were prodigious freight carriers. The LNWR served thriving industrial areas in the Midlands and North West with a significant foray into South Wales; the Midland reigned supreme in the movement of coal from the North Midlands to the capital; the Lancashire and Yorkshire's wealth was based on the movement of Trans-Pennine coal and merchandise whilst the Caledonian was firmly established in the Scottish industrial belt. Even in depressed 1934, freight traffic accounted for 58% of the receipts of the LMS, with coal accounting for no less than 20% of that total. Four years later, the LMS was running 16,000 freight trains per day and yet, 12 years after its formation, the company had still to produce a thoroughly reliable and versatile heavy freight locomotive. Modern 2-8-0s, 4-6-0s and 2-6-0s could be seen on other railways' principal freight services, but on the LMS, with the honourable exception of the Horwich 'Crabs', it was a different story. Heavy reliance was placed on a varied range of Pre-Grouping types and a smaller number of new standard designs which were already exhibiting disturbing mechanical shortcomings.

The need for a powerful locomotive for the Toton-Brent coal hauls and also for a machine capable of taking heavier loads with greater versatility throughout the general range of freight duties had long been appreciated. However, on the LMS the Chief Mechanical Engineer (CME) was not master in his own house, and locomotive development remained stifled in the birth pangs of the new company. Not until the importation of William Stanier from Swindon as CME in 1932 were the warring factions in the Operating and Motive Power Departments finally quelled and real progress made.

In the 1920s, the Toton-Brent situation was critical. Two Midland proposals for 0-8-0s had been vetoed by the Civil Engineer, and the constant double heading with moderately sized 0-6-0s was very expensive. Under George Hughes (the CME at the time), the Horwich Drawing Office proposed a four-cylinder Pacific for passenger work with a parallel 2-8-2 for freight traffic, each having a common boiler and other components.

By 1924, the 2-8-2 had become a three-cylinder proposal, but it was difficult to comply with existing dimensional and axle-loading restrictions. Consideration was given to an 0-6-6-0 Mallet, but in March 1925 Hughes approached Beyer Peacock with a proposal for a 2-6-0+0-6-2 Garratt. Had it been built in accordance with the Manchester company's normal design practice, there is every reason to believe that a thoroughly satisfactory design would have transpired. Unfortunately, Hughes' retirement in 1925 effectively killed both the Garratt and the 2-8-2 proposals.

Meanwhile, Anderson, the Superintendent of Motive Power at Derby had made an entirely separate approach to Beyer Peacock which resulted in the Garratt which eventually appeared in 1927. Crippled by slavish adherence to Midland axlebox design, short lap valves and other features the class was soon detested by footplate and maintenance staff alike. Rarely capable of running more than 25,000 miles between shoppings, at the end of their short and eventful lives they had become 'virtually unmaintainable' (A. J. Powell — *Living with London Midland Locomotives*).

Sir Henry Fowler who became CME in 1925 was soon directing design towards a three-cylinder compound Pacific and parallel freight 2-8-2. However, the operating hierarchy was now in the ascendant; Anderson's trials of *Launceston Castle* in 1926 demolished the Pacific proposal and with it, the 2-8-2 freight locomotive.

The need for a heavy freight locomotive was now urgent; the Somerset & Dorset 2-8-0 design was examined but found to be too wide over the cylinders for acceptance as an all-line standard. This was fortuitous, for its inefficient front end and relative susceptibility to hot axleboxes would have meant trouble away from the enclave of the S&DJR where the class was justifiably popular. Recourse was then made to the existing 0-8-0 designs. Despite their mechanical shortcomings, the LNWR 'G2A' 0-8-0s were effective traffic machines, with good Belpaire boilers as fitted to them under Hughes' direction. This boiler design, restayed for 200lb pressure, was therefore married to a new 0-8-0 chassis in the form of the 'Austin Seven' standard goods locomotive of 1928. Alas, despite a good boiler and modern front end with long lap valves, the engines were afflicted with atrocious running gear. Undersized Midland '4F' axleboxes were quite unable to withstand the piston thrusts of large inside cylinders; heavy wear in axleboxes, motion and springs resulted in a mechanical disaster. In 1930, the 103 engines in service had 53 hot boxes — an appalling record involving great expense and hard manual labour to correct the situation.

On the departure of Sir Henry Fowler in 1930, it was realised that the way forward did not lie with another 0-8-0 and its inherent piston thrust problems. The new CME E. J. H. Lemon instructed his Locomotive Assistant S. J. Symes to investigate the situation and he proposed a two-cylinder 2-8-0 using the successful boiler and mechanical features of the Horwich 'Crab' 2-6-0. Here was a locomotive which, had it been built, would have been in no way inferior to the eventual '8F'.

Unfortunately, Crewe and Derby were still vying with each other, for in the same year H. P. M. Beames (the Deputy CME at Crewe) put forward an outside cylinder 4-8-0 version of the Derby 0-8-0 as a means of overcoming its mechanical problems! Shortly afterwards the LMS Board decided upon the appointment in (Sir) William Stanier, of a strong personality from outside the company as the only means of ensuring effective locomotive design policy. The machinations of the previous nine years had indeed left a very serious situation and the freight locomotive position in 1932 may be summarised as follows:

Garratt 2-6-0 + 0-6-2s
Poor front end design, therefore heavy on coal. Mechanically poor, largely confined to Toton-Brent workings.

Standard 0-8-0s
Capable of good work, economical, but suffered from rapid mechanical deterioration, and thus unsuitable for future construction for all-line use.

LNWR 0-8-0s
Old design dating back in basics to the Webb era. Satisfactory front end and good boiler in Belpaire form, but with mechanical weaknesses. Performance controversial — especially on the Midland Division!

L&Y 0-8-0s
Performance satisfactory, but poor mechanically and with some boiler problems.

Horwich 2-6-0s
Thorough going mixed traffic locomotive. Popular, generally good mechanically. Not enough of them.

Midland '4F' 0-6-0s
Universally foisted on the system for want of anything better. Temperamental steamers, not really big enough for the job, mechanically suspect.

Pre-Grouping 0-6-0s, 2-6-0s and 4-6-0s
A large and greatly varied collection of designs, especially in Scotland. Boiler, front end and mechanical design often left much to be desired. Rapidly demoted or scrapped with the arrival of the 'Black Fives' and '8Fs'.

At this point, the Garratts had solved the problem of double heading on the Midland Division, and the 0-8-0s were able to provide adequate power for general freight traffic. The Motive Power Department was however, increasingly concerned with the large amount of heavy maintenance work at both works and sheds which was necessary to keep the freight locomotive stud at work. The urgent need was not for greater speed — although this was an undoubted bonus of the Stanier '8F' — but to rid the railway of the racking piston thrusts of inside cylinders and their effects on mechanical performance.

The first 1932 scheme for a Stanier 2-8-0 involved three-cylinder propulsion and a low-slung boiler, very much akin to the GWR '28xx' 2-8-0, a class which undoubtedly provided the original design concept for the Stanier '8F'. It was soon realised that the benefits of three cylinders (if any) did not justify the increased cost and the initial diagrams issued from Euston by Stanier's Technical Assistant E. S. Cox showed two cylinders. Between 1932 and 1934 the design was radically developed by Chief Draughtsman T. F. Coleman in such a way as to remove any last vestiges of the '28xx' design, 'coffee pot' safety valve cover and all. Stanier had no wish to see his work as simply a copy of Great Western practice and Coleman ultimately produced a finely balanced design with the boiler mounted forward by 2ft to avoid the 'back end heavy' appearance of the '28xx'. As the original tubeplate and backplate depths were adhered to, the boiler centre line had to be raised to keep the firebox foundation ring clear of the driving axlebox guides. The characteristically neat and balanced 'Stanier look' of both the 'Black Five' and '8F' owe much to Coleman's work and there was no doubting the 1935 opinion of the Stephenson Locomotive Society Journal that 'No 8000 looks as if she means business'. The LMS had a thoroughly modern, independently designed heavy freight locomotive at last.

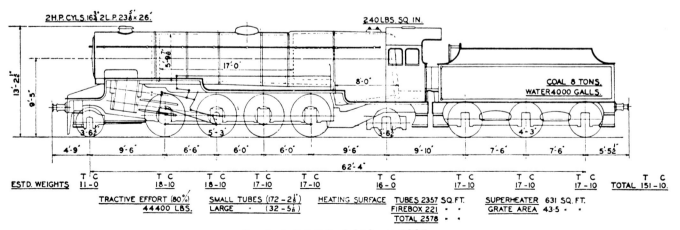

Fowler's 2-8-2 Freight Loco 1925.

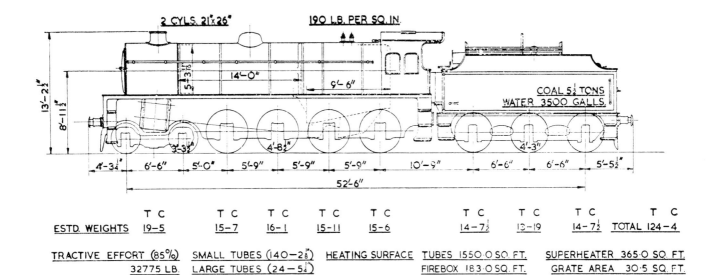

2 CYLS. 21″×26″ 190 LB. PER SQ. IN.

13′-2½″ 8′-11½″ 5′-3⅜″ 14′-0″ 9′-6″

COAL 5½ TONS
WATER 3500 GALLS.

3′-3½″ 4′-8½″ 4′-3″

4′-3¼″ 6′-6″ 5′-0″ 5′-9″ 5′-9″ 5′-9″ 10′-9″ 6′-6″ 6′-6″ 5′-5½″

52′-6″

	T C		T C	T C	T C	T C		T C	T C		T C	T C
ESTD. WEIGHTS	19–5		15–7	16–1	15–11	15–6		14–7½	13–19		14–7½	TOTAL 124–4

TRACTIVE EFFORT (85%)	SMALL TUBES (140–2⅛″)	HEATING SURFACE	TUBES 1550·0 SQ. FT.	SUPERHEATER 365·0 SQ. FT.
32775 LB.	LARGE TUBES (24–5¼″)		FIREBOX 183·0 SQ. FT.	GRATE AREA 30·5 SQ. FT.
			TOTAL 1733·0 SQ. FT.	

BEAMES' PROPOSED 4-8-0 FREIGHT ENGINE

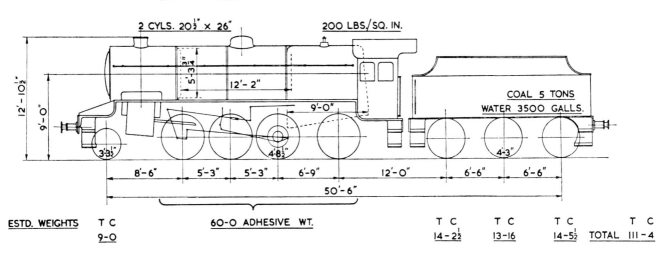

2 CYLS. 20½″ × 26″ 200 LBS./SQ. IN.

12′-10½″ 9′-0″ 5′-3¾″ 12′-2″ 9′-0″

COAL 5 TONS
WATER 3500 GALLS.

3′-3½″ 4′-8½″ 4′-3″

8′-6″ 5′-3″ 5′-3″ 6′-9″ 12′-0″ 6′-6″ 6′-6″

50′-6″

ESTD. WEIGHTS	T C	60–0 ADHESIVE WT.				T C	T C		T C	T C
	9–0					14–2½	13–16		14–5½	TOTAL 111–4

TRACTIVE EFFORT (85%)	SMALL TUBES (161–1⅞″)	HEATING SURFACE	TUBES 1345 SQ. FT.	SUPERHEATER 307 SQ. FT.
32900 LBS.	LARGE TUBES (24–5⅝″)		FIREBOX 160 SQ. FT.	GRATE AREA 27·5 SQ. FT.
			TOTAL 1505 SQ. FT.	

SYMES' PROPOSED 2-8-0 ENGINE.

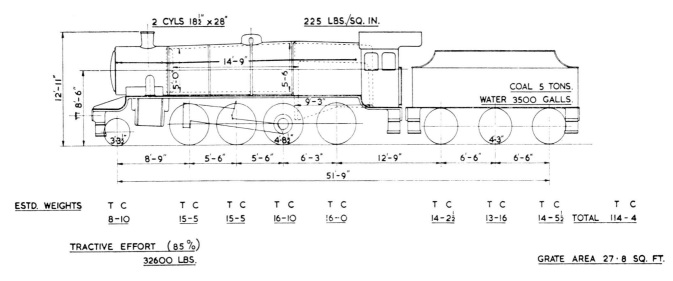

2 CYLS. 18½″×28″ 225 LBS./SQ. IN.

12′-11″ 8′-6″ 5′-0″ 14′-9″ 5′-6″ 9′-3″

COAL 5 TONS.
WATER 3500 GALLS.

3′-3½″ 4′-8½″ 4′-3″

8′-9″ 5′-6″ 5′-6″ 6′-3″ 12′-9″ 6′-6″ 6′-6″

51′-9″

	T C		T C	T C	T C	T C		T C	T C		T C	T C
ESTD. WEIGHTS	8–10		15–5	15–5	16–10	16–0		14–2½	13–16		14–5½	TOTAL 114–4

TRACTIVE EFFORT (85%)		
32600 LBS.		GRATE AREA 27·8 SQ. FT.

Stanier's proposed 2 cylinder 2-8-0 freight engine of 1932.

Above:
**Horwich 'Crab' 2-6-0
No 13002 heads a through
freight over Dillicar
troughs in the 1920s.**
Real Photos (6971)

Above right:
**The Old Order on the
Midland; '3F' 0-6-0
No 3580 pilots '4F'
No 3966 with a heavily-
laden up mineral train near
Radlett in the early
1930s.** *Real Photos (1500)*

Centre right:
**LMS Garratt No 4999
restarts a typically heavy
freight from a signal check
at Radlett on 3 May 1930.
Alas, the mechanical price
for such gargantuan
efforts was a very high
one.** *Wethersett Collection/
Ian Allan Library*

Right:
**Fowler '7F' No 9505 heads
a short mixed freight past
Bushey troughs.**
Ian Allan Library

Above right:
S&DJR 2-8-0 No 13809 tackles a very heavy load on a Bath-Templecombe freight, crossing the Western Region main line near Cole, on 8 July 1949.
P. M. Alexander

Centre right:
A period scene at Shap Summit as ex-LNWR 'G2A' 0-8-0 No 8907 completes the climb from Carlisle with an up through freight in early LMS days.
Real Photos (7224)

Below:
Hughes L&Y large boilered 0-8-0 No 1626 rolls a northbound coal train downhill from Farington towards Preston in 1924.
Real Photos (16808)

2
Design and Operation

The Stanier '8F' formed an essential part of what has been described as Sir William Stanier's 'mighty re-stocking of the LMS[1]'. The 1,694 'Black Fives' and '8Fs' represented well over half the total of Stanier locomotives, and brought about a degree of successful standardisation rarely seen on British railways.

The 2-8-0 wheel arrangement gave better riding and was kinder to the track than its 0-8-0 predecessors; there was a significant increase in tractive effort to 32,438lb but more importantly, drawbar horsepower at all speeds was considerably increased. A 22% increase in grate area, allied to the improved taper boiler and thoroughly modern front end, made for a powerful yet economical locomotive. Moreover, the '8F' was a willing machine in every sense of the word and few railways have produced such a versatile heavy freight locomotive. With a maximum axle loading of 18 tons on the tender, and only 16 tons on the locomotive, the '8Fs' enjoyed a wide route

availability and could negotiate a 4½-chain curve at slow speed. These were assets amply demonstrated on lightly laid foreign metals during the war.

The principal dimensions of the '8Fs' are given in the accompanying diagrams. Maximum steam production was about 23,000lb/hr with a corresponding superheat temperature of about 360°C. The maximum drawbar horsepower (DBHP) was about 1,300, these figures being based on test plant results for the 'Black Fives' which had identical cylinders and valve gear, but a boiler with a barrel 1ft longer. In practice, the shorter '8F' boiler steamed every bit as well.

Mechanical Description — Locomotive

Frames
These were of 1in thick, high tensile steel plates well braced at the front buffer beam, pony truck bearer and

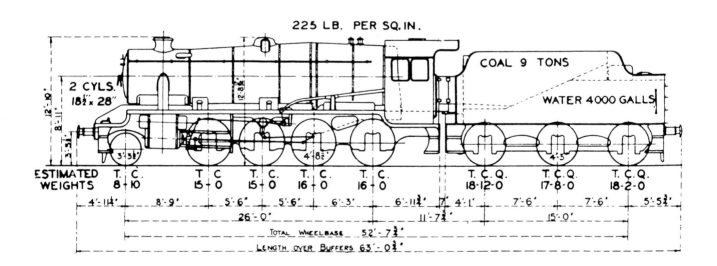

Fig 2
The Stanier '8F' 2-8-0 as originally introduced with domeless boiler (Nos 8000-11). Vacuum equipment was fitted from new to Nos 8006-11.

DESCRIPTION
Boiler: Barrel 12' 10$^{1}/_{16}$" diameter outside 5' 0" increasing to 5' 8⅜"
Firebox: Outside 9' 3"×4' 0". Inside 8' 4$^{12}/_{16}$"×3' 2⅛". Height: (outer) 8' 9$^{17}/_{32}$" and 7' 2$^{17}/_{32}$"

Tubes: Superheater elements (21) 1⅛" diameter outside×11swg. Large tubes (21) 5⅛" diameter outside×7swg. Small tubes (136) 2" diameter outside×11swg 13' 3" between tube plates

Heating surface: Tubes 1,300sq ft. Firebox 155sq ft. Total 1,455sq ft. Superheater 235sq ft
Grate Area: 27.8sq ft
Tractive effort: At 85% BP 32,438lb
Adhesion factor: 4.28

12

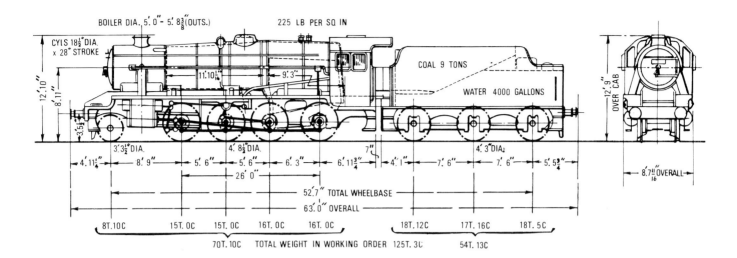

BOILER DIA. 5' 0"- 5' 8⅜"(OUTS.)   225 LB PER SQ IN

CYLS 18½"DIA.
x 28" STROKE

COAL 9 TONS

WATER 4000 GALLONS

12' 10"

8' 11"

11' 10¼"   9' 3"

3' 5½"

12' 9" OVER CAB

3' 3½" DIA.   4' 8½" DIA.   4' 3" DIA.

4' 11¼"   8' 9"   5' 6"   5' 6"   6' 3"   6' 11¾"   7"   4' 1"   7' 6"   7' 6"   5' 5¼"

26' 0"

52' 7" TOTAL WHEELBASE

63' 0" OVERALL

8.7/16" OVERALL

8T.10C   15T. 0C   15T. 0C   16T. 0C   16T. 0C   18T.12C   17T. 16C   18T. 5C

70T. 10C   TOTAL WEIGHT IN WORKING ORDER 125T. 3C   54T. 13C

Fig 3
The standard '8F' design as built from No 8012 onwards.
DESCRIPTION
Boiler: Barrel 12' 3⁹/₁₆" diameter outside 5' 0" increasing to 5' 8⅜"

Firebox: Outside 9' 3"×4' 0" Inside 8' 6⁷/₁₆"×3' 3⅝". Height (inner) 6' 8²¹/₃₂" and 5' 1¹¹/₁₆". Superheater elements (21), 1¼" diameter outside, 11swg
Tubes: Large tubes (21) 5⅛"

diameter outside×7swg. Small tubes (202) 1¾" diameter outside×11swg, 12' 2⅞" between tubeplates.
Heating surface: Tubes 1,479sq ft. Firebox 171.3sq ft Total 1,650.3sq ft

Superheater 245sq ft.
Grate area: 28.65sq ft
Tractive effort: at 85%BP 32,438lb
Adhesion factor: 4.28

smokebox saddle. Further cross stretchers were to be found, one in line with the motion brackets and two others between that point and the firebox. A substantial trailing dragbox was fitted under the cab.

Cylinders and Motion
Two outside cylinders of cast iron, 18½in diameter by 28in stroke were fitted. Piston valves 10in diameter with a travel of 6½in were actuated by Walschaerts valve gear. The slidebars were of the double bar type. Coupling and connecting rods were of high tensile molybdenum steel, with connecting rods of fluted section. Lubrication of the motion was largely by oil wells feeding through restrictors to felt pads for the crankpins, little ends and return

crankpins and through trimmings on other parts of the motion. A Silvertown mechanical lubricator mounted on the RH platform and driven from the expansion link provided lubrication for the valves and cylinders. A further lubricator mounted in the same position and driven in the same way, looked after the axleboxes. Steam atomisation was provided for the two points of oil delivery on each steam chest, but oil to piston rod packings (which were of segmental cast iron rings) valve spindle bushes and cylinders was supplied 'solid'. The steam supply to the atomiser was controlled from the cylinder drain cock operating mechanism, which when open (ie when the engine was stationary) closed the steam valve to the atomiser.

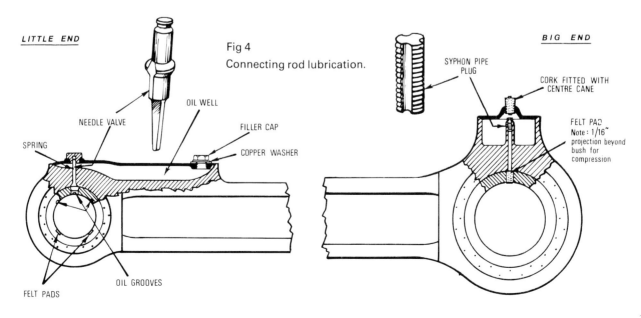

LITTLE END

BIG END

Fig 4
Connecting rod lubrication.

OIL WELL

NEEDLE VALVE

FILLER CAP

SPRING

COPPER WASHER

SYPHON PIPE PLUG

CORK FITTED WITH CENTRE CANE

FELT PAD
Note: 1/16" projection beyond bush for compression

FELT PADS

OIL GROOVES

Fig 4 Table of valve events

Forward Gear

Notch % Cut-off	Notch Angle	Travel Inches	Lead (inches) FP	BP	Diff	Port opening (inches) FP	BP	Diff	Cut off % FP	BP	Diff	Expansion % FP	BP	Diff	Release % FP	BP	Diff	Angle of release FP	BP	Diff	Compression % FP	BP	Diff	Exhaust travel (inches) FP	BP	Diff	Slip of die Inches
Full	27¼°	6.4765	0.2735	0.2265	0.047	1.6718	1.8047	0.1329	76.0	72.5	3.5	15.75	17.25	1.5	91.75	89.75	2.0	145.0°	144.5°	0.5°	90.75	92.5	1.75	3.3672	3.2343	0.1329	0.718
70	23½°	5.8906	0.2735	0.2265	0.047	1.3906	1.5	0.1094	71.0	67.75	3.25	19.0	20.0	1.0	90.0	87.75	2.25	141.5°	141.0°	0.5°	89.0	91.0	2.0	3.0625	2.9531	0.1094	0.594
60	18°	5.0625	0.2735	0.2265	0.047	0.9843	1.0781	0.0938	60.75	58.5	2.25	25.25	25.0	0.25	86.0	83.5	2.5	134.25°	134.25°	—	85.0	87.5	2.5	2.6406	2.5468	0.0938	0.445
50	14¼°	4.5468	0.2735	0.2265	0.047	0.75	0.7968	0.0468	50.25	49.5	0.75	31.75	29.75	2.0	82.0	79.25	2.75	128.0°	128.0°	—	81.25	84.0	2.75	2.3593	2.3125	0.0468	0.336
40	11¼°	4.1874	0.2735	0.2265	0.047	0.5937	0.5937	—	40.5	40.5	—	37.0	34.5	2.5	77.5	75.0	2.5	121.25°	122.0°	0.75°	77.25	79.75	2.5	2.1562	2.1562	—	0.259
30	8½°	3.9064	0.2735	0.2265	0.047	0.4532	0.4532	—	30.5	30.5	—	41.5	39.5	2.0	72.0	70.0	2.0	114.0°	116.0°	2.0°	72.5	74.75	2.25	2.0157	2.0157	—	0.187
20	5½°	3.6874	0.2735	0.2265	0.047	0.3515	0.3359	0.0156	20.25	20.25	—	44.25	42.75	1.5	64.5	63.0	1.5	104.5°	107.75°	3.25°	66.0	67.75	1.75	1.8984	1.9140	0.0156	0.101
10	1¾°	3.2534	0.2735	0.2265	0.047	0.2812	0.2422	0.039	10.75	10.0	0.75	42.75	43.0	0.25	53.5	53.0	0.5	91.25°	96.0°	4.75°	56.25	56.75	0.5	1.8047	1.8437	0.039	0.0156
Mid	—	3.5	0.2735	0.2265	0.047	0.2735	0.2265	0.047	8.0	6.75	1.25	40.25	41.0	0.75	48.25	47.75	0.5	85.25°	90.0°	4.75°	51.25	51.75	0.5	1.7890	1.8360	0.047	0.025

Backward Gear

Notch % Cut-off	Notch Angle	Travel Inches	Lead (inches) FP	BP	Diff	Port opening (inches) FP	BP	Diff	Cut off % FP	BP	Diff	Expansion % FP	BP	Diff	Release % FP	BP	Diff	Angle of release FP	BP	Diff	Compression % FP	BP	Diff	Exhaust travel (inches) FP	BP	Diff	Slip of die Inches
Full	27¼°	6.3905	0.2735	0.2265	0.047	1.5937	1.7968	0.2031	76.0	74.0	2.0	15.75	16.0	0.25	91.75	90.0	1.75	145.25°	145.25°	—	91.25	92.75	1.5	3.3593	3.1562	0.2031	0.828
70	23½°	5.8125	0.2735	0.2265	0.047	1.3125	1.5	0.1875	71.25	69.5	1.75	18.75	19.0	0.25	90.0	88.5	1.5	141.75°	141.75°	—	89.75	91.25	1.5	3.0625	2.8750	0.1875	0.710
60	18°	5.0234	0.2735	0.2265	0.047	0.9531	1.0703	0.1172	60.75	60.25	0.5	25.75	24.0	1.75	86.5	84.25	2.25	135.0°	135.25°	0.25°	86.0	88.0	2.0	2.6328	2.5156	0.1172	0.562
50	14¼°	4.5078	0.2735	0.2265	0.047	0.7187	0.7891	0.0704	50.5	50.75	0.25	32.0	29.75	2.25	82.5	80.5	2.0	128.5°	129.5°	1.0°	82.25	84.25	2.0	2.3516	2.2812	0.0704	0.437
40	11¼°	4.1718	0.2735	0.2265	0.047	0.5781	0.5937	0.0156	40.0	41.25	1.25	38.0	34.75	3.25	78.0	76.0	2.0	122.0°	123.5°	1.5°	78.25	80.25	2.0	2.1562	2.1406	0.0156	0.343
30	8½°	3.9062	0.2735	0.2265	0.047	0.4531	0.4531	—	30.25	31.5	1.25	42.75	39.75	3.0	73.0	71.25	1.75	115.0°	117.5°	2.5°	73.75	75.25	1.5	2.0156	2.0156	—	0.281
20	5½°	3.6718	0.2735	0.2265	0.047	0.3437	0.3281	0.0156	20.25	20.5	0.25	45.0	43.75	1.25	65.25	64.25	1.0	105.25°	109.0°	3.75°	67.25	68.25	1.0	1.8906	1.9062	0.0156	0.181
10	1¾°	3.5312	0.2735	0.2265	0.047	0.2812	0.25	0.0312	11.0	10.0	1.0	43.25	43.75	0.5	54.25	53.75	0.5	92.25°	97.0°	4.75°	57.0	57.5	0.5	1.8125	1.8437	0.0312	0.078
Mid	—	3.5	0.2735	0.2265	0.047	0.2735	0.2265	0.047	8.0	7.0	1.0	41.0	41.25	0.25	49.0	48.25	0.75	86.0°	91.0°	5.0°	51.5	52.0	0.5	1.7890	1.8360	0.047	0.025

Fig 5
Arrangement of atomised
cylinder lubrication.

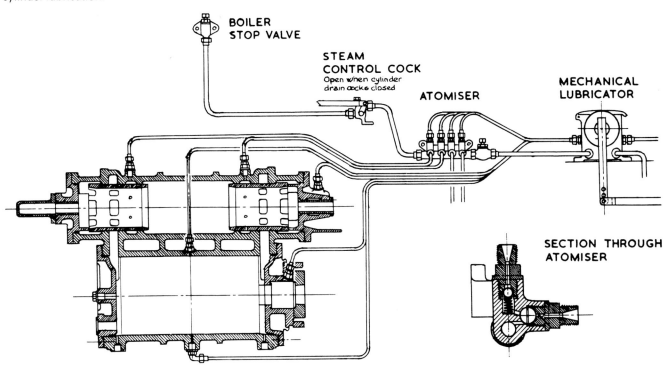

BOILER
STOP VALVE

STEAM
CONTROL COCK
Open when cylinder
drain cocks closed

ATOMISER

MECHANICAL
LUBRICATOR

SECTION THROUGH
ATOMISER

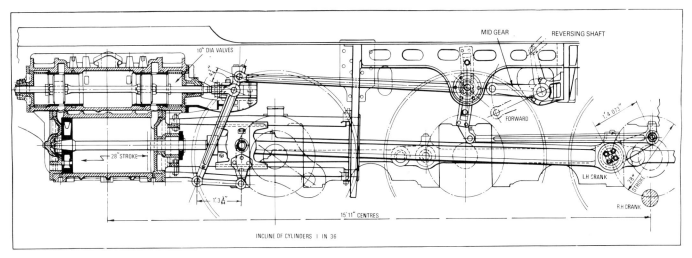

Fig 6

Wheels and Axles

The leading bissel truck was anchored to a stretcher beneath the smokebox 6ft 7¾in behind the axle centre, the weight of the front end being transferred by side bolsters with check springs to ensure steady riding. The wheels themselves were of steel, with triangular section rims and tyres retained by Gibson rings. The balance weights on the 4ft 8½in coupled wheels were of built up form. Coupled axle journals were generously proportioned — 8½in diameter by 11in long. The axleboxes were of cast steel, amply proportioned, with horse shoe brasses pressed in, featuring a continuous whitemetal bearing surface. The oil feed from the lubricator was fed in by grooves on the horizontal centre line of the journal. Further lubrication was provided from pads spring-loaded to the underside of the journal from an underkeep which

could be easily drained or slid out for inspection, whilst the horn checks were lubricated from conventional oil boxes with trimmings. This design was outstandingly free from heating problems.

Springs

All the laminated springs for both engine and tender were of silico-manganese steel. Nine plates of ribbed section with dimple fixing in the buckle applied to the coupled wheels, whilst a cotter type fixing in the buckle was employed on the pony truck. The spring links were screwed to allow adjustment.

Fig 7
'8F' coupled axlebox.

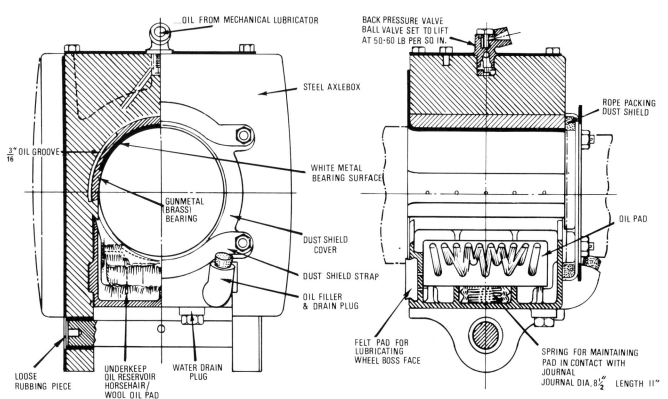

Brakes

Nos 8000-8005 originally appeared with steam brakes only, vacuum brakes being fitted later. The engine brake cylinder was mounted vertically from the dragbox under the cab, the piston actuating single pull rods to the brake cross-stretchers between the frames, connecting in turn with the brake hangers. The tender had a separate brake cylinder, fed by a flexible connection from the driver's brake valve. Separate lubrication cups were provided in the cab for both engine and tender brake cylinder supplies, whilst most of the brake gear itself was grease lubricated. The tender brake had dual pull rods to the brake stretchers, connected to the brake piston via the main brakeshaft and also to the tender handbrake.

Nos 8012-8176 and Nos 8226-63 (before shipment abroad) had a single-cone vacuum ejector, and the standard combined vacuum steam brake valve together with an independent steam brake valve. This arrangement confirmed that at first the '8Fs' were expected to do little vacuum-fitted work, and the single-cone ejector was quite adequate for partially braked trains. This position soon changed with the engines being used on express freight, parcels and even some passenger work. The independent steam brake valve disappeared from most engines by the 1960s, but many went to the scrap heap with their single-cone ejectors.

Standard brake equipment consisted of the two-cone ejector with separate steam supply valves for the large and small cones, and the standard Driver's Brake Application Valve, normally vacuum controlled, but which with some ingenuity could — and often was — used as an independent steam brake.

Sanding Gear

Originally Nos 8000-8011 had 'trickle' (gravity) sanding to the leading coupled wheels and to the front and rear of the

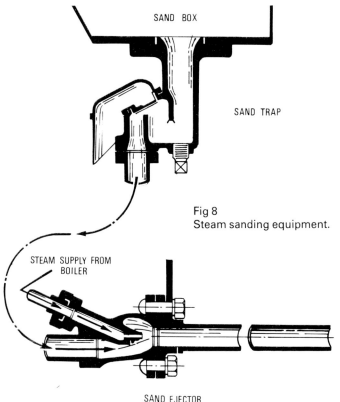

Fig 8
Steam sanding equipment.

driving axle. Three small steam cylinders controlled the supply, one to each pair of sandboxes. Water de-sanding was also provided, the rails being cleaned by water jets after the sand had been used, to prevent any interference with track circuits. The LMS standard steam sanding arrangements, whereby a jet of steam guided the sand directly on to the rails under the wheels was soon preferred. Water de-sanding was not then required.

Boilers

Nos 8000-8011 carried vertical throatplate, domeless taper boilers which were a direct import of Great Western practice to the LMS. Stanier was firmly committed to the taper principle, which gave more space on the firebox tubeplate and produced more steam capacity where evaporation was greatest. There was also a marginal advantage in output-to-weight ratio but it was in locomotives larger than the '8F' that these advantages were most marked.

The original '8F' boilers had smokebox regulators, a GWR feature which proved unpopular on the LMS. Their other weakness, along with other early Stanier boilers, lay in incorrect tube and element sizes. While the total free area through the tube bank was fully adequate, the proportions of the 2in diameter firetubes and the 1⅛in diameter superheater elements in standard 5⅛in diameter flues left something to be desired and allowed heat to be lost to the chimney which could have been better used. Fortunately with the '8Fs', the problem was not compounded by the very low superheat that beset the early 'Jubilee' and, to a lesser extent, 'Black Five' boilers with 14-element superheaters.

The standard '3C' boiler fitted to No 8012 onwards saw the A/S ratio (boiler free gas/grate area) brought down from 15.8% to 15.5% with the use of a larger number of smaller firetubes of 1¾in diameter, but the 21-element superheater was never enlarged to the 24 or 28-element versions carried by the later series of 'Black Fives'. The relatively moderate superheat on the '8F' does not seem to have been any handicap in everyday service, but the boilers might have been more efficient if fitted with larger superheaters. The other major change was the inclusion of a sloping throatplate which shortened the distance between the tubeplates by 1ft, making for a very free steaming boiler. The main changes in '8F' boiler dimensions are shown in the accompanying table.

Matching its steam producing qualities, this boiler's maintenance costs were remarkably low. LMS boilers were very well built, and the Belpaire firebox as successively developed on the GWR and under Stanier was very good indeed. Stay leakage was negligible and breakage rare whilst the copper inner fireboxes, apart from new tubeplates and some welded inserts, frequently lasted the life of the boilers. In the case of the '8Fs', the last few spare boilers were built as long ago as 1953. It was intended to fit Nos 8000-8011 with the standard sloping-throatplate boilers eventually, but only No 8003 underwent the frame modifications required. This created a spare vertical-throatplate boiler for the remainder, and they kept their original boilers to the end.

The standard boiler consisted of a three ring, mild steel barrel, the second and third rings of which were tapered. The top feed was positioned on the second ring, just in

Stanier '8F' 2-8-0 Boiler Specifications
Dimensions

Measurement	1935 Type 3C Vertical Throatplate	1936 Type 3C Sloping Throatplate
Outside Diameter – Front	5ft	5ft
Outside Diameter – Throatplate	5ft 8⅜in	5t 8⅜in
Barrel length	12ft 10¹/₁₆in*	12ft 3⁹/₁₆in*
Outside firebox	9ft 3in×4ft	9ft 3in×4ft
Between tubeplates	13ft 3in	12ft 3in†
Grate area	27.8sq ft	28.65sq ft‡

*From 8012 taper on second ring was therefore steeper.
†Shortened by ⅛in from 1938-9 when copper tubeplate was made ⅛in thicker, decreasing heating surface by 1.4sq ft.
‡Enlarged grate area due to reduction in width of water spaces.

Heating Surfaces

Locomotive Nos	Tubes	Tube Heating Surface sq ft	Firebox Area sq ft	Grate Area sq ft
8000-1	138×2in O/D+21×5⅛in O/D	1,322	155	27¾
8002-11*	136×2in O/D+21×5⅛in O/D	1,308	155	27¾
8012 onwards†	202×1¾in O/D+21×5⅛in O/D	1,479	171	28½

*Two tubes replaced by washout plugs to improve accessibility at washouts.
†Distance between tubeplates reduced to 12ft 2⁷/₈in, heating surface (tubes) reduced to 1,478sq ft

Superheater Elements

Diagram	222	222a	222B	222C	222D	222E	222F	222G
Element diameter	1⅛in	1⅛in	1⅛in	1⅛in	1¼in	1¼in	1¼in	1³/₈in
Element SWG	11	13	11	11	11	11	11	9
Heating surface sq ft	235	248	215	215	245	245	230	241
	(1)	(2)	(3)	(4)	(5)	(6)	(7)	(8)

All locomotives were fitted with a 21-element superheater

(1) Nos 8000-11
(2) Nos 8012 onwards
(3) Change of SWG

(4) ⅛in off tube length
(5) Change of element diameter
(6) WD diagram

(7) Alteration to elements
(8) BR change to 1³/₈in

front of the dome, consisting of clackboxes with three-stud flanges and spherical joint rings on a steel manhole cover containing reversible clack valves working in a cage. A four-stud flange and spherical joint ring secured the injector delivery pipe. The feed water was originally directed on to trays on either side of the main steam pipe, but during the war this was altered to a simple deflector plate guiding the water down the barrel sides. The dome regulator, mounted horizontally, gave better accessibility than the smokebox version. It consisted of a slide valve with pilot valve, giving differential action on opening and closing. The main steam pipe was cone jointed to the regulator head casting, and expanded and ferruled into the smokebox tubeplate, where it joined the superheater header.

The copper firebox was stayed to the outer wrapper with Monel metal and steel stays, being nutted inside the firebox to protect the ends. The firebox roof was stayed to the outside wrapper with vertical stays screwed through the plates and fitted with nuts on the outside. Three rows of stays were riveted at the front and back of the firebox to the underside of the firebox crown to facilitate the removal of the tubeplate or backplate. The outer and inner wrapper plates were very carefully made in flowing curves to reduce the problems of stay breakage from differential expansion, and to allow good water circulation. A relatively weak point was the brick arch. Some arches lasted as little as two weeks, although much greater success was obtained with concrete arches in BR days.

Boiler tubes consisted of 21 steel superheater tubes of 5⅛in outside diameter, (O/D), 7 SWG (0.176in), and 202 steel firctubes of 1¾in O/D, 12 SWG (0.104in). The superheater flues were swelled out at the smokebox end to 5⁷/₃₂in O/D, and screwed 4⁵/₁₆ O/D into the firebox tubeplate, afterwards being expanded and beaded over. The firetubes were swelled to 1¹³/₁₆in O/D for a distance of

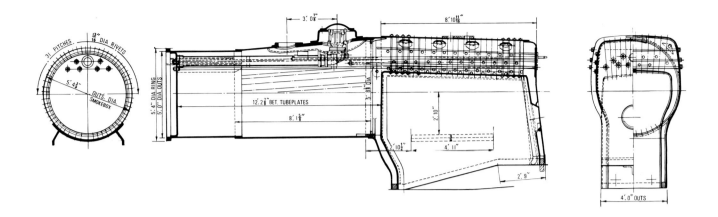

Fig 9
'8F' boiler arrangement

Fig 10
Stanier smokebox showing
location of deflector plates:
1. Deflector top plate;
2. Deflector bottom plate;
3. Locking lever and stops (A);
4. Locking lever support;
5. Locking bar; 6. Catch;

7. Blast pipe jumper; 8. Hinge
bar; 9. Lever fulcrums (to help
raise top plate).

Fig 11
Regulator valve — horizontal
dome type.

Fig 12
Original top feed
arrangement (with trays in
boiler, later discarded).

3¼in at the smokebox tubeplate before being expanded
in. At the firebox the tubes were reduced to 1⅝in for a
distance of 2in expanded and beaded over, but not
ferruled. The bottom three rows of tubes at the smokebox
end were also beaded over for protection against
corrosion.

The circular smokebox resting on a saddle was a great
improvement on the Midland pattern, and virtually ended
the problem of air leakage as mileage built up. The
smokebox door was held as a tight metal-to-metal fit by
the screwed dart fixing, making entry of air, causing burnt
smokebox doors, a great rarity. The smokebox tubeplate
was of the drumhead type. Attached to it was the
superheater header from which three rows of superheater
elements led into the flue tubes. These were of the
bifurcated type originally, but during the war the return
loop type was standardised. The spherical element ends
were held in place by clamps and nuts to the superheater
header — a much more accessible arrangement than on
many contemporary designs. The steam pipes from the
header were of solid drawn steel, with semi-spherical
joints at the header and three-stud, face to face joints at
the cylinders. Originally, deflector plates were fitted to
reduce spark emission and to balance the draught across
the tubeplate. In practice, they interfered with tube
cleaning and were soon discarded. The blastpipe was
originally a direct import from Swindon complete with
jumper top. This did not impress on the LMS and was also
discarded. In BR days, the blastpipe diameter was
reduced from 5⅛in to 4⅞in.

The boiler was fed by two injectors. A Gresham and
Craven 10mm Live Steam injector on the driver's side,
mounted behind the cab steps. The Exhaust Steam
Injector on the fireman's side was the Davies and Metcalf
type 'H'. A continuous blow down valve was fitted,

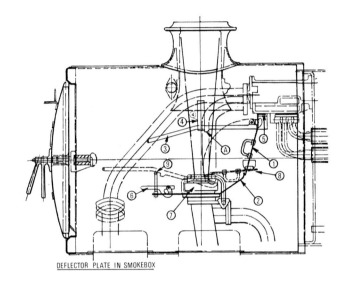

DEFLECTOR PLATE IN SMOKEBOX

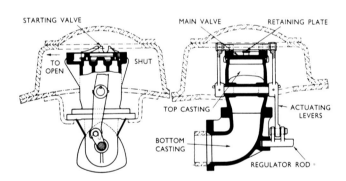

REGULATOR VALVE HORIZONTAL DOME TYPE

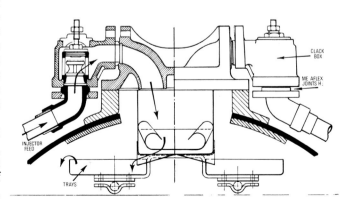

discharging a small amount (2gal/min) of water from the boiler whenever the regulator was open; this prevented the build up of soluble salts in the boiler water which would otherwise cause priming, thus greatly increasing the periods between boiler washouts. The water was originally discharged on to the ballast via a cooling coil in the tender tank but was latterly diverted to discharge into the ashpan following corrosion damage to the right hand rail and its fastenings, resulting in a derailment in Watford Tunnel in 1954. Two 2½in Ross 'pop' safety valves were fitted to the rear of the firebox, set at 225lb/sq in. Steam feed to all auxiliaries was via a main steam manifold fixed in the cab on the firebox backplate. Steam for the blower valve was from an internal pipe from the dome, whilst the supply for the steam lance fitting was taken from the superheater header on the right-hand side of the smokebox. A similar connection on the left-hand side under a pear-shaped cover provided steam for the atomiser.

Mechanical Description — Tender

The Stanier standard high-sided tender carrying 4,000gal of water and 9 tons of coal was fitted, having a three-axle fixed wheelbase of 15ft. This came in two varieties — Mk 1 with a riveted structure, and Mk 2 of welded construction. The coal bunker was designed to be self-trimming as far as possible, and many tenders were fitted with water spray pipes in the coal space. Access to the coal space was by large double doors which could be swung open when the coal supply got well back. A large locker was provided for the crew on the left-hand side, whilst the fireirons were carried in a long tunnel on the right-hand side of the coal space. Handles for the handbrake and water scoop were arranged on the right-hand and left-hand side of the tender doors respectively, being arranged vertically with bevel wheels transmitting motion to the respective mechanisms. Water was taken on through a filler hole on the rear, and delivered via a well tank between the frames, through sieves and flexible hoses to the injectors.

The tender frames were robustly constructed (they were in fact double, the inner ones being shallow), with substantial dragboxes at each end and two large bracing stretchers between the wheelsets. The front dragbox carried the vertical steam brake cylinder and inboard bearings for the brake shafts, which also had bearings in the main frames. Double pull rods, one each side of the water scoop linked the shaft to the brake crossbeams and hangers. Intermediate drawgear consisted of a main drawbar, supplemented by a smaller safety link on either side, secured by cotter pins through the engine and tender dragboxes. Small buffers on the front tender dragbox bore on rubbing plates on the engine dragbox to stabilise the drawgear.

The War Department 'Austerity' 2-8-0s

The cost of a newly constructed '8F' was around £12,000 when the bulk of the class was being built during World War 2. Many '8Fs' were being built as preparations for the invasion of Europe were going ahead and there was a serious shortage of labour in railway workshops. The '8F' design also included 17 tons of steel castings and 16 tons of forgings in its 92 tons of empty weight, and these items were in competition with escalating armaments requirements. Large numbers of locomotives were required for the liberation of Europe, and R. A. Riddles, the LMS engineer then responsible for War Department (WD) locomotive requirements, decided that a simplification of the '8F' design was needed. He was assisted in this aim by T. F. Coleman, and the result was the well known WD 'Austerity' 2-8-0.

The main changes included a round top parallel boiler, the elimination of most steel castings and some forgings by fabricated items (or by substitution of cast iron for steel where possible), mechanical lubrication replaced by trimmings and hydrostatic lubrication for cylinders, Laird-type crossheads (the Stanier arrangement having worn excessively under desert conditions), simplified cylinder design and simple basic facilities on the tender and cab. This saved 6,000 man-hours (almost 20%) and produced a rugged basic locomotive which could go anywhere, but which because of its lack of refinement was not loved by its crews, especially when it was still in service 20 years later! On test steam raising capacity was about 16% inferior to that of the '8F', maximum drawbar horsepower was down by 22%, and fuel and water consumption up by around 14%. Of the 935 WD 2-8-0s built, 733 eventually saw service on British Railways.

[1] *Master Builders of Steam*, H.A.V. Bulleid; Ian Allan 1963.

Working With The '8Fs' — The Maintenance Viewpoint

One experienced London Midland Motive Power Officer has said of the '8Fs': 'They were lovely machines with long-lap motion, large axleboxes, excellent front end and trouble free fireboxes. They had very few troubles.'[1] Another LM engineer who had extensive experience of the class at Wellingborough, Willesden and Derby has written: 'Any Shedmaster with a depot full of "Black Fives" and "8Fs" had every reason to be a very happy man.'[2]

With this reputation added to sprightly performance and reasonable working conditions in the roomy Stanier cabs, it is not surprising that the 2-8-0s received a welcome reception from locomotivemen and fitters accustomed to inside cylinder 0-6-0s and 0-8-0s, let alone the Garratts. In 1939, not a single hot '8F' axlebox was recorded, whilst 748 were generated from the 1,235 '4F' and '7F' standard freight locomotives. To quote E. S. Cox 'The saving in cost, man hours and hard, slogging work was simply colossal'.[3]

This reputation for minimum maintenance on the shed remained with the '8Fs' for the rest of their careers, and is well illustrated by the availability figures for the 1950s. Beware however, that shedmasters knew how to 'play the system' — a locomotive could come on shed at 00.01 on Monday, be under repair and go off shed at 22.00 on Tuesday, having been 'in service' on both days. Hence some of the 'Black Sheep' of the flock — Garratts and 'Austin Sevens' for example — could return remarkably respectable figures. The consistently high availability of the '8Fs' is obvious however, notwithstanding the fact that they were also the second largest freight locomotive class at work on the system. From 1950 to 1957, with the sole exception of the Western Region allocation in 1955, '8F' availability was consistently above 80%. Admittedly

Comparison of locomotive class availability 1950

| | | | OUT OF SERVICE | | | | | IN SERVICE | |
| | | | Repairs | | | | | | |
Type	Stock	Average Mileage	Classified Shop and Shed	Running and Exams	Total Repairs	Not Reqd	Total Out	No	% of Total Possible
'8F'*	315	24,423	13	31	44	4	48	262	85
'WD'†	173	19,121	8	38	46	29	75	235	76
'G2A'	213	19,533	16	33	49	6	55	255	82
'G3'	67	18,372	15	42	57	7	64	246	79
S&D '7F'	11	25,631	19	37	57	5	62	247	79
Garratt	33	18,770	49	36	85	3	88	222	72
'28xx'	167	32,416	18	47	65	3	68	242	78
'47xx'	8	36,159	24	67	91	2	93	217	70
'O1'	58	25,107	16	36	52	4	56	254	81
'O2'	66	22,057	12	40	52	11	63	247	79
'O4'	271	22,302	15	33	48	6	54	256	82
ROD	29	23,124	16	63	79	5	84	226	72

*LMS built engines in LMR stock.
† LMR stock

Comparison of locomotive class availability 1954

| | | | OUT OF SERVICE | | | | | IN SERVICE | |
| | | | Repairs | | | | | | |
Type	Stock	Average Mileage	Classified Shop and Shed	Running and Exams	Total Repairs	Not Reqd	Total Out	No	% of Total Possible
'8F'	316	24,246	12	34	46	3	49	260	84
'WD'	240	20,926	10	29	39	14	53	256	83
'G2A'	185	19.095	14	40	54	6	60	249	81
'G3'	41	18,784	16	38	54	12	66	243	79
S&D '7F'	11	26,262	19	41	60	8	68	241	78
Garratt	33	20,295	48	44	92	3	95	214	69
'28xx'	167	30,428	15	37	52	4	56	253	82
'47xx'	9	37,001	11	43	54	10	64	245	79
'O1'	58	26,952	37	36	73	5	78	231	75
'O2'	66	22,375	15	31	46	10	56	253	82
'O4'	266	20,957	17	29	46	4	59	259	84
ROD	23	18,653	20	77	97	6	103	206	67

mileages were fairly modest — only the Western Region seemed able to keep its freight locomotives on reasonably high-mileage jobs. A large proportion of '8F' work was always taken up with colliery or heavy trip workings which inherently gave low daily mileages, and arguably utilisation could have been better. At the end of the war many Scottish engines were covering up to 40,000 miles per year.

Workshop Repairs and Modifications
The average '8F' accumulated 20-25,000 miles per year.

At 50-60,000 miles the condition of the axlebox thrust faces would demand an Intermediate Overhaul, probably 2-2½ years after the previous General Overhaul. Another 2-2½ years in traffic would see the 5-yearly boiler lift due at the next General or Heavy Intermediate repair. In latter years, the dispensation to extend the boiler overhaul period to seven years was used to advantage, many '8Fs' in service in 1968 having had two intermediate repairs since the last boiler lift.

An early problem with Nos 8000-8011 was an accumulation of waste water in the exhaust injector steampipe in

Comparison of locomotive class availability 1956

Type	Stock	Average Mileage	OUT OF SERVICE					IN SERVICE	
			Repairs						
			Classified Shop and Shed	Running and Exams	Total Repairs	Not Reqd	Total Out	No	% of Total Possible
'9F'	51	24,831	7	64	71	7	78	231	75
'8F'	316	21,559	12	34	46	5	51	258	83
'WD'	263	21,089	12	29	41	12	53	256	83
'G2A'	181	23,440	15	43	58	7	65	244	79
'G3'	32	18,522	11	34	45	16	61	248	80
S&D '7F'	11	23,601	19	49	68	21	89	220	71
Garratt	13	20,493	18	48	66	8	74	235	76
'28xx'	167	30,708	17	37	54	4	58	251	81
'47xx'	9	32,837	50	32	82	5	87	222	72
'01'	58	26,996	30	36	66	5	71	238	77
'02'	66	21,539	14	34	48	12	60	249	81
'04'	266	19,174	20	28	48	5	53	256	83
'ROD'	6	18,540	32	53	85	12	97	212	69

the smokebox saddle, which caused corrosion; the pipework was modified to prevent this.

Some trouble was experienced initially with derailments of the pony trucks. This was traced to the binding of the check spring guides on their spindles. Greater clearance was provided from June 1941, Nos 8000-8125 being modified retrospectively.

A fair amount of trouble was experienced with cracking of the early 1in-thick frames, an average of 1.7 cracks per engine appearing every 10 years. The most vulnerable point was from the top corners of the driving horn gaps, where the situation may have been made worse by the proximity of a gap in the frame giving access to the washout plugs in the bottom corners of the firebox. From No 8096 the frames were increased to 1$\frac{1}{16}$in thickness and from 1945 authority was given to fit strengthening patches around the driving horn gaps. However the long coupled wheelbase meant that the driving wheelsets needed a fair amount of sideplay, and this led to the wheel centres rubbing on the patches. The practice of fitting frame patches was discontinued in 1947 in favour of welding in new inserts in susceptible areas of the frameplates.

The '8Fs' were all built by 1945/6, and so did not get the benefits of the Ivatt frame improvements in the form of horse-shoe horn blocks, tension spring links with 'mutton chop' brackets with cottered adjustment, and the 'Horwich' hornstay bolted to the frameplate extension 'legs'. With shopping periods at around 50,000 miles perhaps this was not too serious, but a run down '8F' with axlebox play, weak springs and spring links out of vertical, could be quite a rough proposition.

Whilst the Stanier axlebox was remarkably free from heating problems, there is no doubt that considerable wear could develop in the thrust faces. Here the whitemetal bearing surface, whilst easy to machine and fit, was subject to substantial wear under the pounding it got and fore and aft play of up to 0.60in could develop giving

thoroughly uncomfortable axlebox 'thump', reduced spring life and accelerated wear on motion bushes, coupling rod and joint pins. In 1954 authority was given to fit up to 50 '8Fs' with manganese steel liners to the horn faces. On the 'Black Fives' this had allowed the elimination of one Intermediate repair between Generals and mileages of up to 100,000 between overhauls. With the '8Fs' the advantage was not quite so obvious; the 2-8-0s could not, by the nature of their work, build up such high mileages between boiler lifts and, being a long wheelbased locomotive running into numerous sharply curved sidings and yards, tyre wear was likely to demand shopping at lower mileages than the axleboxes. Although some '8Fs' did receive manganese liners, the experiment was not pursued after 1962.

An important modification from No 8126 onwards, and also on the WD engines, was the shortening of the connecting rods by 5in from 11ft 3in to 10ft 10in with the piston rods and slidebars lengthened accordingly. This allowed the piston heads to be slid clear of the front cylinder cover studs for ring changing without breaking the piston rod/crosshead assembly. Unfortunately, the crossheads usually needed re-metalling at the 20-24,000 mile examination so the piston rod joint would have needed breaking anyway. It could be that a reduction of weight was intended by shortening the connecting rods — Stanier motion was certainly not light!

Early in World War 2, the Stanier method of piston head fastening (a direct import from the GWR) was modified. The head was screwed directly on to the piston rod, giving a simple box section head with flat faces, no nuts and flat cylinder covers. Fatigue fractures tended to start from the roots of the piston rod threads just inside the head, with eventually disastrous results. Ivatt devised an arrangement with a collar on the piston rod, the head bored plain, and two units with LH and RH threads respectively and a heavy tab washer in between them

21

Comparison of Stanier '8F' availability performance by year

| | | | | OUT OF SERVICE | | | | | IN SERVICE | |
| | | | | Repairs | | | | | | |
Year	Type*	No	Average Mileage	Classified Shop and Shed	Running and Exams	Total Repairs	Not Reqd	Total Out	No	% of Total Possible
1950	'8F' STD	315	24,423	13	31	44	4	48	262	85
	'8F' HMG	22	22,972	9	34	43	11	54	256	83
	'8F' ORC	234	23,368	10	32	42	6	48	262	85
	'8F' ScR	15	22,413	11	31	42	5	47	263	85
	'8F' ER	42	21,032	11	34	45	7	52	258	83
	'8F' WR(ORC)	7	25,222							
	'8F' WR(ex-LMS)	11	29,034	13	29	42	5	47	263	85
	'8F' WR(ex-LNER)	11	22,148							
1954	'8F' STD	316	24,246	12	34	46	3	49	260	84
	'8F' HMG	22	25,021	10	34	44	4	48	261	84
	'8F' ORC	285	23,817	12	33	45	4	49	260	84
	'8F' WR	9	33,181	18	37	55	3	58	251	81
1955	'8F' STD	316	23,165	13	33	46	11	57	252	82
	'8F' HMG	22	22,771	17	35	52	9	61	248	80
	'8F' ORC	275	22,977	12	33	45	12	57	252	82
	'8F' WR	42	30,202	18	36	54	21	75	234	76
1956	'8F' STD	316	21,559	12	34	46	5	51	258	83
	'8F' HMG	22	22,312	13	33	46	4	50	259	84
	'8F' ORC	265	23,304	12	33	45	4	49	260	84
	'8F' WR	52	31,348	13	37	50	11	61	248	80
1957	'8F' STD	287	22,709	13	32	45	5	50	259	84
	'8F' HMG	17	22,599	14	29	43	5	48	261	84
	'8F' ORC	239	23,003	14	31	45	5	50	259	84
	'8F' WR	N/A	N/A	N/A	N/A	N/A	N/A	N/A	N/A	N/A

* STD — Standard
  HMG — Ex-HM Government
  ORC — Other Railways Construction
  ScR — Scottish Region
  ER — Eastern Region
  WR(ORC) — Western Region (ex-Other Railways Construction)
  WR(ex-LMS) Western Region (ex-LMS)
  WR(ex-LNER) — Western Region (ex-LNER)

hammered over the flats. New front covers were needed to accommodate the nuts.

Many '8Fs' built to REC orders were turned out without cylinder relief valves as an economy measure. This resulted in an increase in crosshead and piston defects, and the valves were fitted after 1945.

The question of coupled-wheel balancing on the '8Fs' is far too complex to allow detailed examination here; the normal Stanier practice was to provide either 66⅔ or 50% reciprocating balance, by plates rivetted to the wheel between which molten lead was poured. With non-ferrous metals in short supply, most REC-ordered '8Fs' had balance weights cast integral with the wheels giving a nil reciprocating balance, but all LMS-built wartime locomotives except Nos 8323-30 and 8332-82 had the 50% balance. In 1946, authority was given to bring the SR-built locomotives up to 40% balance, so that in BR days, three

degrees of balance, namely 50%, 40% and nil applied, the position being complicated because of wheel changes. In 1958, with the increasing use of the 2-8-0s on faster work, an attempt was made to identify those locomotives with 50% balance and therefore suitable for such jobs by painting a small star under the number on the cabside. Instructions were also issued to allow each type of balance to be recognised by examination of individual locomotives at the sheds. After about 1963, when '8Fs' were shopped at 'foreign' works, the star often disappeared on repainting, reliance then being placed on the individual engine records held at the sheds. A real oddity was No 48169, fitted with WD 'Austerity' style cast iron leading, intermediate and trailing wheels, and cast steel driving wheels giving nil reciprocating balance. Sheds usually managed to identify the balanced members of their allocation, which was just as well, as anything over

45mph with an unbalanced locomotive could lead to acute discomfort in the cab.

Boilers were normally lifted for overhaul every five years, each boiler lift constituting a General overhaul for the engine concerned. At intermediate repairs the boilers were left on the frames, but there was scope for a good deal of preventive maintenance at this time. The Stanier boilers were noted for low maintenance costs, but latterly they also operated in a world where copper welding techniques and improved water treatment meant that complete replacement of fireboxes, for example, was not so common as previously. The '8Fs' did not attain such high mileages between boiler lifts as did many of their passenger contemporaries — about 120,000 miles in five years being the maximum; lower average steaming rates also helped to keep repair costs low. In exceptional circumstances at the end of the steam era, some boilers remained with the same engine for up to eight or even nine years, following internal examinations during intermediate overhauls.

Most works repair work consisted of making good deterioration in the fireboxes, particularly those parts in direct contact with the fire. Wastage of the doorplate flanges was quite heavy, together with wastage of the plates at the back of the box where the fire was thickest. Here, a good deal of patch welding was necessary under the firehole, and welding in new three-quarter sections of firebox wrapper plate became a standard practice. The other area where inserts in the wrappers were often needed was in the vicinity of the copper tube plate below the brick arch. The flanges in this vicinity also needed periodic welding and rebuilding. New crownplates could be welded in, so it was rare indeed for a new inner firebox to be fitted.

The copper tubeplates needed fairly frequent replacement, mainly because the flue tube diameters were not allowed to exceed $4^9/_{16}$in after which the tubeplate was scrapped because of the reduced bridges between the flue tube holes. It was usually the top left-hand flue tube which reached the critical size first, and in practice a new tubeplate would be needed about every second General Overhaul.

The fireboxes were fitted with Monel metal and steel stays and from the early 1950s a major programme of stay replacement became necessary on many boilers built in the late 1930s. A policy of replacing at least one third of all the stays at each General Overhaul was instituted, the replacement material being Monel metal. All stays of over $7/_8$in diameter were replaced by copper stays, riveted over both externally and in the firebox itself.

At major boiler overhauls, the small tubes would be replaced. The flue tubes would be withdrawn for examination and either replaced, or have new ends welded on as required. Some new superheater elements would also probably be needed, although these could either be repaired by welding or replaced at the sheds as necessary.

The purpose of the Intermediate repair, both mechanically and in terms of boiler repairs, was to carry out sufficient work to allow the locomotive to cover approximately 50,000 miles to its next overhaul at the expiry of its boiler lifting period. The boiler would be examined before entering the works, and work required would probably consist of tube expanding, removing a number of small tubes for boiler cleaning, renewing stay rivets and welding firebox flanges as required. All the stays would be hammer tested and faulty ones renewed. It was also good policy to remove and replace all the stay nuts and recaulk the stays at this time.

Two modifications carried out in the 1950s were the alteration in the blow down operating mechanism so that steam was supplied from the injector steam pipes rather than the steam chest, and the removal of sandguns. The latter were rarely used and their continued maintenance was pointless.

Crewe, Horwich and Derby were the main works concerned with '8F' overhauls. Derby was responsible for 240 '8Fs' from 1952 to 1963, when dieselisation saw its commitment taken over by 'foreign' works, namely Eastleigh and Darlington. The latter had previously overhauled some of the '8Fs' which operated on the LNER, and Swindon could possibly have carried out some intermediate overhauls on the GWR '8Fs'. (Wolverhampton certainly did). Horwich works closed in 1964, its last repair being that of No 48756. Crewe continued with steam overhauls until March 1967 although the last '8F' overhaul is believed to have taken place in the autumn of 1966. Intermediate repairs, involving an overhaul of motion, axleboxes and wheels only, took place also at Bow works and at Rugby until the early 1950s whilst casual repairs to the 2-8-0s could even occur at places as unlikely as Oswestry and St Rollox.

1. *Living with London Midland Locomotives*, A. J. Powell; Ian Allan 1977.

2. A. V. Wilson — letter to author.

3. E. S. Cox — letter to author.

Running Shed Maintenance

From the fitter's viewpoint, the '8Fs' were good engines. Hot axleboxes and big ends were rare, and the Piston and Valve Examination at first fixed at 30-36,000 miles was progressively extended to 40-48,000 miles and finally to an as reported basis. Many locomotives went from one works repair to the next without having the cylinders opened up — a real achievement for a small-wheeled locomotive.

An early complaint about Stanier locomotives concerned leakage from the joint between the clack box and delivery pipe. It took several years to cure with the final use of Metaflex joints — a thick combination of asbestos and stainless steel. A small number of '8F' boilers received the Ivatt top feed in which the clack cages were inserted directly into housings in the top feed cover, abolishing the separate clack boxes.

At first, the coupled wheel horncheek stays had to be dropped before the pin could be removed to change the bearing springs, doubling the time involved. Reprofiling of the stays solved this problem.

There was some trouble in Central Wales with rough riding; this was attributed to excessive lateral wear in the leading coupled axleboxes, which were sometimes dropped for remetalling. This was not a general problem, and may have been caused by fast running on this sinuous route.

Remetalling of the side rod and big end bushes and the crossheads was often needed at the No 4 examination carried out after 20-24,000 miles. This was to be expected with a small-wheeled locomotive but it did mean heavy work for the fitters. Spring changing was another heavy job, and usually had to be done with portable jacks in the absence of a drop pit. The '8Fs' had a good record — each coupled wheel spring having an average life of 1.45 years, considerably better than many LMS standard classes. However, with much time spent on loose-coupled mineral jobs, brake block changing gave plenty of hard work.

No real cure seems to have been found for blowing cylinder drain valves, often caused by pieces of broken piston and valve ring finding their way into the valves and playing havoc with the seatings. Piston packings also needed a good deal of attention (although this was also a factor of crosshead wear); the spring clips holding the segmental packing rings often broke or became dislodged.

An unpopular task was changing the flexible oil pipes to the rear coupled axleboxes, which were situated under the ashpan; there was very little room to manoeuvre, and with a locomotive in steam there could be oil and water leaks and ash blowing around. Add a draught blowing through the pit, and the need to work by feel much of the time in hot and confined surroundings, and it can be easily understood why this was considered as a duty to be avoided if at all possible.

A fair amount of time was taken up in dealing with injector problems. Injectors on Stanier locomotives were certainly indifferent; The Exhaust Steam Injector was prone to a variety of defects, and as the '8Fs' spent only a comparatively small amount of their time under conditions of continuous steaming, it is very doubtful if the 8% fuel economy claimed for the use of exhaust steam matched the additional maintenance costs involved. Jammed water regulators and wear in the change-over or shuttle valves were the main problems. There was rarely time to deal with these defects properly, except at the 'X' (out of steam) examination. The '8F' exhaust injectors were by no means the worst, but latterly about half the class had the exhaust side of the injectors blanked off to save maintenance costs. The Live Steam Injector could be a fickle device, attracting much adverse comment from 'foreign' crews. It figured prominently in driver's repair cards, and also absorbed a good deal of fitters' time.

The first 12 engines with smokebox regulators were generally more troublesome. Access to the regulator was difficult and dirty, and the regulator valves were difficult to keep steam-tight. No 8011 was fairly typical — within weeks of shopping the regulator would start to blow through and get progressively worse until the engine would start a 40-wagon train with the regulator shut! Then came the unenviable task of scraping up the face in the superheater header and fitting new valves. The headers themselves were more prone to cracking than the standard fittings — this was another Great Western import which was not successful on the LMS.

Boiler maintenance was usually organised around the washout period, originally at intervals of 12-16 days, but latterly with improved water treatment these were extended to 18-24 days. After washing out, the boilers would be examined and any necessary repairs undertaken. Strict control was exercised through the six-monthly inspections of the Divisional Boiler Inspectors, and any work required here was closely adhered to. Careful

attention was paid to the condition of water spaces, lead plugs, tubes and stays. The '8Fs' were not unduly demanding, and most work was confined to stay nut changing — there was little stay breakage, and seam caulking. Major mechanical examinations coincided with washout days.

Less popular jobs on the boiler concerned grinding in the regulator valves and element changing. The former job was much more accessible with the dome regulators, but it was still quite a difficult task and care had to be exercised not to drop tools into the boiler. The elements could be a trial at times. Working conditions in the smokebox were cramped and dirty, and if tube cleaning had been skimped and the elements became firmly stuck in the flue tubes, then a good deal of 'persuasion' from the firebox end might also be necessary. Clack valves also needed fairly frequent cleaning together with attention to their seatings depending on water quality.

A small amount of tube replacement was sometimes undertaken at the sheds. This was usually because some small tubes had been removed for boiler cleaning, but any work on the flue tubes was strictly a works job. Some expanding of tubes might also become necessary.

One of the most unpopular jobs on Stanier engines was the six-monthly tank and float examination on the tenders. There was very little headroom in the baffle plate apertures, and even less in the vicinity of the float and front well tank while the tank base invariably retained pools of water.

However, the overall picture of the '8Fs' is that they were a popular locomotive with the maintenance staff, rugged, reliable and free from major time consuming and difficult maintenance tasks. They were amongst the best of British locomotives in this respect and this is fully reflected in their availability record.

Working with the '8Fs' — The Footplate View
Generally, the '8Fs' were well liked by footplate staff. They would steam on indifferent coal, respond to a variety of firing methods, and they would pull and run. The roomy Stanier cabs with conveniently placed controls added to their popularity; the wooden tip up seats were surprisingly comfortable, and folded out of the way easily when required. The shelf over the firedoors was useful for the billy can, convenient for a 'feet up' in quiet moments, or for oil bottles in winter. There was adequate protection against the elements without being too enclosed in summer, the large ventilator in the cab roof helping here.

There were a few vices; The blower valve over the firedoors was badly placed in the event of a blow back. The injector steam valve handles were often stiff and sometimes needed a clout with the coal pick to open. The ratchet damper controls often vibrated shut and had to be jammed open with spanners, and the injector water regulators were not well placed under the seats, especially in view of the amount of re-setting that was sometimes necessary.

For the Driver, the '8F' was an easy engine to prepare. All the motion and oil cups for the axlebox horns were outside the frames and easily accessible, although extra care was needed in oiling the front coupling rod bushes, and in ensuring that the little end reservoirs were full. Draining and topping up the axleboxes was normally fitter's work; access to the underkeeps meant going underneath the engine, but they could be attended to without bother, except for the trailing coupled boxes under the ashpan. Here it was a case of working in cramped, hot and sometimes wet surroundings, pushing a feeder above the head with the fingers a couple of inches away from a hot ashpan. The pony oil spouts were not large enough and were inconveniently placed — quite a lot of oil going to waste on the floor in consequence. The filling of mechanical lubricators was allocated to the fitters at certain depots, but it was always good practice to give these a good manual turning before leaving the shed. In the cab, the steam brake reservoir needed patience to fill. This job was usually done first and the steam brake then left on to allow the oil to vapourise in the brake cylinders. There was usually no difficulty in preparing an '8F' in the 60min allowed.

The engines responded to most methods of driving, the partially open regulator technique with the valve gear pulled up to about 25% for fast running being the favoured method. If necessary, they would stand being hammered on full regulator and 55% for long periods. The LMS brake valve sometimes took a bit of getting used to, but artistry was possible once familiarity was established. Coming down from Peak Forest with 'The Hoppers', Northwich men would set the vacuum at 15in by jamming the brake lever on the quadrant with a spanner before entering Dove Holes Tunnel, and would go most of the way to Cheadle Heath like this, any additional braking being achieved by pulling on the fulcrum rod to give more steam to the steam brake on the engine. The independent steam brake valve, where fitted, was not liked except for shunting purposes, and was little used when a more sensitive, vacuum-controlled steam brake was available.

The '8Fs' usually rode well — drivers often asserting that the higher the speed the better they rode — but the ride deteriorated as mileage built up and play in the axleboxes developed. This gave rise to thoroughly uncomfortable conditions on the footplate, with constant thumping in the trailing axle boxes. Those engines without 50% balancing were also prone to 'shuttling' between the engine and tender at much over 30mph, again creating very uncomfortable conditions and when braking there was violent bucking between engine and tenders which would quickly move coal from the tender onto the footplate. Usually, engines in run down condition were confined to slower work, but this was not always possible.

From the Fireman's viewpoint, the '8Fs' had a spacious cab and there was room to fire from both sides. The engines were not over-sensitive to different firing methods. The usual practice for average work was a fire of even thickness, tapering off towards the front with a tump to keep the back corners well filled. Firing was mainly along the sides, and topping up at the back, with just a sprinkling at the front to keep the bars covered.

If there was real work to be done, with good Yorkshire lump coal, then the box would be filled right up, half way up the firedoors, and down under the arch, the coal packed in but still tapering towards the front. Then an engine could go from Cheadle Heath up to Peak Forest, from Cricklewood to Sharnbrook, or Carlisle to well beyond Appleby on one firing, but the fireman had to know the coal with which he was dealing, a clear road was needed, and an assumption that nothing was going to go wrong which involved dropping the fire!

With soft Welsh coal, care was needed to avoid over-firing, the fire needing to be thin and bright. The classical 'little and often' technique worked well, as related by Inspector K. Stokes of Sheffield:

'8278, 09.25 Grimesthorpe-Gowhole, some heavy climbing with a heavy train. Taking advantage of the shut off through Sheffield, a quick round of coal all over the box, back corners well filled, tapering down to the front, back damper wide open, firedoors partially open for the all-important secondary air and the 1 in 90/100 to Totley could be tackled with a full head of steam. Every 2 min, half a dozen half-shovel fulls over the combustion flap kept her on the mark with only a faint discolouring at the chimney top'.

The '8Fs' could carry a high level of water in the boiler without risk of priming, but it was good practice to aim for an indication of about ½ to ¾ of a glass. The '8F' injectors were fickle devices; the exhaust injector would sometimes fail to pick up the water and the regulators were often jammed. The live steam injector regulator was under the driver's seat. This could be inconvenient as the injectors rarely restarted themselves if disturbed (which was quite frequently). Normally, the water regulators were fixed in a position where the injector worked, and the feed valves in the tender used to shut off the flow of water. The delivery from the live steam injector was slow, and not sufficient for the largest efforts, so that if the exhaust injector, normally used, was playing up, performance would suffer. The saving grace of the live steam injector was its ability to work on less than 50lb of steam — a boon during disposal duties. Quite why Stanier locomotives were saddled with such relatively poor injectors remains a mystery.

The Stanier 4,000gal tender gave a steady ride, with coal and water for the longest diagrams. It was not self-trimming in practice, a lot of dragging coal from the back of the bunker taking place. The double doors gave good access to the coal space, but did not prevent small coals from spilling all over the footplate, or the odd large lump jamming steadfastly and defying all efforts with the coal pick. The fire iron tunnel was on the right-hand side, but the 10ft-long rake took some handling within the loading gauge whilst on the move, and a fire iron tunnel on the footplating in front of the cab would have been much better. The high sides of the tender restricted visibility when travelling tender first — quite a lot of '8F' work was done in this mode — but overall it was a good tender design, much more popular than the Midland 3,500gal version foisted on some '8Fs' in tender exchanges with 'Jubilees' in the late 1950s.

Disposing an '8F' could be an onerous task. The firebox was over 9ft long, and except for a few experimental installations, there were no rocking grates. It was this difficulty in dealing with the 2-8-0s that persuaded Ivatt to try a rocking grate on No 8490 in 1945, the forerunner of many on Ivatt locomotives, but no 2-8-0s were fitted retrospectively. Some of the LNER-built locomotives may have had drop grates for a while, but these were soon replaced with standard firebars.

The usual method was to remove three or four firebars and push the remains of the fire into the ashpan with a long rake for removal through the front damper door. First, a bent dart was needed to clear the clinker and old fire from the back corners, then a long rake or chisel bar would be used to break up the clinker on the grate, the good fire having been moved to one side. Great dexterity was then called for in the use of a pair of huge tongs to remove the firebars — even more skill being needed to replace them afterwards without breakage caused by dropping them into the ashpan. After one side of the grate had been cleaned, the other side would be dealt with, the firebars replaced and the remains of the fire pulled back under the doors and banked up ready for the next duty. The alternative was to use a 10ft-long clinker shovel, a longer and perhaps less risky procedure but still hot and awkward when the red hot paddle had to be manhandled in the confines of the cab. The former method was generally preferred, and the fire could be cleaned in about 25min under favourable circumstances, but if badly clinkered, an hour's thankless toil could often result.

The smokebox and ashpan also had to be cleaned, and as the '8Fs' were not fitted with self-cleaning smokeboxes, the char could sometimes be level with the crossbar after a long and hard run. All this amounted to hard, gritty, and unrewarding work.

Steam locomotive performance was always the subject of controversy. Consensus was rare, and here a selection of footplatemen give their opinion of the Stanier '8F' and its rivals.

Driver D. Speight, Wakefield: 'I well remember the "8Fs" taking over from the L&Y 0-8-0s and also the Midland "7Fs" on the Dearne Valley coal trains. The "8Fs" gave far better protection, they were easier to fire and you were not working in a cramped well, with a high and difficult firedoor, blistered on one side with Arctic winds whipping across the tender on the other. We did a lot of tender-first running, and this mattered. They could be prepared in reasonable comfort — a much easier job than the old engines. The "8Fs" were very good coal engines — so were the "Austerities", but they were not nearly such good runners, and the tender was poor in comparison with the "8Fs". Both classes had the coal and water for long diagrams, but you didn't have to go mountaineering to reach the coal on the "8F". The Stanier engines could handle all classes of freight work well. They were never short of steam, but rather lacked a "fifth gear" for passenger work, on which they would accelerate and climb the banks well, but were rather slow otherwise. A major failing with the "8F" was the lack of a rocking grate. Some of our engines would be out for 24hr, and cleaning a badly clinkered fire on an "8F" was no joke. The older drivers thought the blow down valve wasted water. After the war, I was involved with oil burning Nos 8385/86 working between Manchester and Wakefield with Newton Heath, Sowerby Bridge and Wakefield crews. They steamed very well and life was much easier for the fireman with no shovelling and disposal duties. The "8Fs" were used on all sorts of jobs for which they were never designed, both in this country and abroad. They still did anything that was asked of them and did it well'.

Inspector K. Stokes, Sheffield: 'I worked on the "8Fs" for years, and only once booked one for poor steaming. They were a first class engine, well liked by everyone. The exhaust injectors could be a nuisance. I have no idea why, since I did thousands of miles on Gresley Pacifics with no exhaust injector problems, perhaps maintenance was at fault. The "8F" had good brakes and we always felt confident dropping heavy limestone trains down into Sheffield. The Fowler "7Fs" were a disaster and very uncomfortable to work on — 'Roasting Sevens' we called them! Cab protection was virtually non-existent and the Central Division was welcome to them. The Garratts were coal gobblers and uncomfortable to work on, but the GC Robinson "04" could run an "8F" close. I have seen them sailing up to Woodhead with a heavy train, steaming well with a thin fire dancing on the firebars. The "9Fs" were a good loco, much better to ride on than an "8F", but heavy on coal.'

Driver D. Chalmers, St Margaret's: 'The "8Fs" were popular locos, and we liked them on fitted freight work. The cabs were far more comfortable than the NB types and the "Austerities", and the riding was usually much better than the average Gresley engine. They were not as strong as the "Austerities", but always steamed well'.

Fireman J. Downing, Cricklewood: 'They were a good all-round engine, reliable and comfortable to work on. They were never in trouble for steam, no matter how hard they were worked, although the Exhaust Steam Injector sometimes gave trouble, and the Live Steam Injector under the driver's seat was not popular'.

Driver F. Mellor, Buxton: 'They were much better than the "Super Ds" on the general range of freight work, but they were rather heavy on coal and lost their sparkle below 200lb pressure. A "D" would still be going on 150lb or less. The "D" and the "Austin Seven" were probably as strong as an "8F", but you wouldn't attempt much fast work with either! The "D" was a very good engine, once you got to know them, but those who did not have them regularly hated the sight of them. On the Buxton line we used big fires in the "8Fs", the smokeplate and door ring out, the fire made right up to the firedoor and under the brick arch — sometimes on top of it as well, although not by design! The "8F" was a smooth and fast runner, and would have been a good engine on suburban work. The "WD" was stronger than the "8F", but that was all — the riding was atrocious, with the footplate covered in coal. The "8F" cab layout was good — better than the "Standards", especially the reversers. The "9Fs" were good runners, but difficult to fire, you could not always get a deep enough fire all over the grate, and the injectors were very strong so that it wasn't easy to balance the steam and water. The brakes were not as good as the "8Fs", so on balance, we preferred the Stanier engines on jobs within their capacity'.

Driver W. Egerton, Northwich: 'When we got the "8Fs", the largest engine on the shed was a "J10", so we regarded them with some suspicion! If you could fire a "J10", you could tackle anything, and we LNER men would sometimes fire to Heaton Mersey drivers on the "Hoppers" until we got them in our own right in 1949. We thought the "8Fs" were heavy on water, but our GC engine didn't have Continuous Blow Down. The Stanier footplate was far better than an LNER engine — cleaner, more roomy, and the water sprays in the tender and the sand gun were real luxuries. The "8F" was a much better engine than a GC "Tiny" (O4), although there wasn't too much in it when it came to all out slogging. The "Tinies" would keep going on 80lb of steam, by which time the "8F" would have long expired, but they would also throw you all over the place at 30mph, with coal jiggered all over the footplate. I'm not admitting to some of the speeds we got out of the "8Fs", but they always rode very steadily. On the "Hoppers", we used a large fire, with both dampers open. The "8Fs" had to take some punishment — full regulator and 55% on most of the banks, and 65-70% getting round the curve at Hartford North. They were every bit as good as the "Black Fives", and could put up a fair show on passenger work. The "Austerity" wasn't a bad engine, not as smooth as the "8F", but with a good brake and strong. The "9Fs" were in a class apart, they rode well and could tackle anything — altogether bigger than the "8Fs" '.

Passed Fireman P. Smith, Branksome: 'The "8Fs" were a much better steaming engine than the S&D 2-8-0s, but they were not quite so strong and their brakes were not as good. The "7Fs" were very well suited to the conditions on the S&D, calling for fairly short all-out efforts and really certain braking characteristics. The S&D engines were prone to hot boxes, and would not have been such a useful all-round freight engine as the "8F". The "8Fs" were reliable and gave far better cab protection on the exposed Mendips but Bath had some very rough machines and this was possibly why they were not used on the summer Saturday extras in 1961/62. Some of them had so much play in the axleboxes that they were nearly as uncomfortable as the unbalanced S&D engines on faster work. The Bath Goods Link, never recognised any superiors to the S&D engines'.

Driver P. Johnson, Crewe: 'The "8Fs" could pull well, but the '28xx' had the edge on them, although not for steaming and cab comforts. Both types rode well until due for shops, when they could both get quite rough. The "Super D" was a strong engine, but had to be fired just right, and their footplate layout was a downright menace, the fireman was forever grazing his knuckles on the scoop handle. The Swindon-altered "ROD" 2-8-0s were a strong engine, but not the equal of an "8F" or "28xx". They would keep going on 50lb of steam — they had to for they were poor steamers, but the oscillation on the cab above 30mph had to be experienced to be believed. The "Austerities' had the same problem, but they were strong and free steaming. The "8Fs" could pull, steam and run. One day we failed a Class 40 at Chester with the morning Holyhead-Euston and got No 48601 in exchange. She waltzed the 13 coaches to Crewe, virtually keeping time. Most London Midland crews liked the "8Fs", and some LNW die-hards might say they preferred a "Super D", but

few Crewe men had the privilege of working on a "28xx" '.

Mr D. J. Flemming, recorded the views of Bristol drivers: 'The Barrow Road men worshipped the "8Fs", but at St Phillip's Marsh it was a different story. The injectors were very unreliable, care had to be taken not to over-fire them with the soft Welsh coal as the blast was softer than on GW locos. The position of the handbrake meant that you could not get the leverage on it that was possible with the GW vertically mounted brake, and they were driven from the wrong side! The general feeling of the fitting staff was, in a word, rubbish! They were not as strong as a "Hall" or "Grange" on fitted freight work, and no Western man thought them the equal of a "28xx" '.

Driver L. C. Jacks, Tyseley and Saltley: 'The "8Fs" came to Tyseley in 1959. They knocked and banged their way around the railway, the controls were stiff to operate, and steam leaked from various parts of their anatomy. They were not liked by the crews who preferred a "28xx", which was stronger, had more easily worked controls and better visibility when running tender first. The LMS injectors were poor, and the steam sanding was not as effective as the GW gravity system. The "8Fs" did not keep their feet as well as a "28xx" — and we had plenty of proof of this on the 1 in 45 through Snow Hill Tunnel — but they were a strong engine. The GW vacuum brake with its pump was better than the steam brake on other freight engines, since this became less effective if pressure dropped. Both the "28xx" and "8F" steamed well, and I also had a sneaking regard for the "ROD" 2-8-0s. The outside valve gear on an "8F" was no encouragement for men to examine the engine between the frames and things could be missed. The "Austerities" were strong, but slipped badly and rode atrociously. Their one saving grace was their excellent injectors — but the best thing about them was getting off them'.

Fireman T. Essery, Saltley: 'The "8Fs" steamed reliably and freely on almost any type of fuel, they were economical and had sufficient pulling power for the heaviest trains. The cab was comfortable and roomy to work in, whilst the Stanier tender was excellent with plenty of fuel and water capacity. I never heard an ex-LNW man say he preferred a "Super D" to an "8F", and the cab layout of the former was atrocious. The "WDs" were probably as strong as the "8Fs", but they didn't steam quite so freely and the riding over 20mph could be appalling, with an unpleasant buffeting oscillation between engine and tender when coasting. The "8Fs" and 'Black Fives' justly enjoyed wide acclaim, and I have even heard Great Western men grudgingly admit that they were good engines'.

Fireman Frank Buckley, Northwich: 'The "8Fs" were a willing loco which responded well to a variety of methods of driving and firing. They always steamed well with a large fire under the doors, tapering down to the front. The back damper gave enough primary air, and with smallish coal, firing over the flap was common. Many times I have wedged the deflector plate with a screw to prevent it stooping — it could be difficult to fill the back corners when that happened.

'On the "Hoppers", the trains would be brought down from Wallerscote and we would take over in the station. There would already be a big fire in the engine, but as there was climbing to do, I would soon be busy with the shovel as we got away to Lostock Gralam working in about 40% on the first valve. I would still be at it on the downhill stretch to Plumley with the engine now on 30% taking a run at the climb to Knutsford. Once over the top, we would drift through Mobberley and Ashley with the regulator just cracked and the cut-off in the "D" (drifting) position. Beyond Altrincham there was the short, sharp climb up to Skelton Junction and we usually took it fairly easily to Cheadle Heath.

'Here, the driver looked after the water column whilst the fireman was busy building up the fire for the climb to Peak Forest. We would have the measure of the engine by now, but it was very rare for an "8F" to be off form. Leaving Cheadle with a well prepared fire and the water bobbing in the top of the glass, you could have confidence in the climb ahead. Many tales were told of firemen filling the box at Cheadle and sitting down all the way to the summit, but I have my doubts even with the "8Fs"! The nearest I saw was with No 48735 when my driver, George Blease, was having a work out with the shovel. He filled the box before we set off, and gave her another good round at Hazel Grove and that was it! This was with the benefit of experience of course — George had spent 10-12 years in the Hopper Link and knew just what the "8Fs" were capable of.

'Hammering up the bank, a good exhaust injector was a boon as it could be set just right to deliver water to the boiler at the same rate that it was being used. The regulator would be well open on the main valve, and the cut-off at 40-45% for nearly 15 miles. There was a real sense of achievement in keeping the safety valves simmering and listening to the bark of the engine echoing from the hills. Special delights were in store in the passage of the long Disley and Dove Holes tunnels; if the engine started to slip it could be hair raising with the exhaust sucked back into the cab and the engine vibrating.

'After turning on the table at Peak Forest, nearly 1,000ft up, the fire would be cleaned and we would back down on to the loaded hoppers in Tunstead sidings. We would be banked up the 1 in 90 to Peak Forest, and then roll down to Cheadle Heath with the vacuum set at about 15in to keep our 1,000-ton train in check. Water was taken at Cheadle Heath where the fire was built up for some difficult work to come. We always had a 'guaranteed road' through Altrincham in view of the nasty 1 in 132 between Altrincham and Hale approached over two level crossings and with a nasty "S" bend in the middle of the bank. The engine would be flat out here with everyone praying that she wouldn't slip! The climbing continued beyond Hale, so it was back to the shovel, but once past Knutsford the fireman's day was done as she hustled them down the bank to Northwich. If heading for Wallerscote there was a final "hammer and tongs" session over the viaduct to Hartford Junction. The Northwich drivers, who were mostly ex-LNER men held the "8Fs" in high regard — they were great engines'.

Official photograph of Stanier Class 7F 2-8-0 No 8000 as she emerged from Crewe works in June 1935.
Real Photos

Above:

Class 8F No 8042, one of the main production series with improved boilers with dome regulators and vacuum brakes, produced from 1936 onwards. This example was built by the Vulcan Foundry in that year and the burnished motion, tyres and cylinder covers were a feature of '8Fs' built by that company. Requisitioned in 1941 as WD No 596, she was sent to Iran and subsequently ended her days in Israel. *BR (LMR)*

Below:

Crewe Works erecting shop, 1936. Work is proceeding on Lot 130, Nos 8012-36. The rear locomotive is about to be set on its wheels. *BR (LMR)*

Could this really be Swindon? In 1943, the erecting shop is seen full of Stanier '8F' parts. In the right foreground, cylinder castings are being matched to their cladding, to the left of these stands a recently fabricated smokebox saddle, frame stretchers lie across the pit, whilst to the left are newly cut frames on the finishing table. A pair of motion brackets lies to the right of the cylinders, whilst wheels await their frames in the background. A pannier tank gives an air of normality, contradicted by the naval guns in the top right-hand corner. *BR*

Right:
Frames of No 8233 at Bridgnorth, April 1981. On top of the trailing axleboxes in the foreground are the flexible oil connections from the lubricator, the driving axleboxes are protected by water shields, but the oil feed from the oil boxes on the running plate to the horn faces can be seen. Note the substantial horizontal bracing of the frames. Vacuum and steam heat pipes (RH) are visible, with the cylinder cock operating rod in the centre. The pipework on the smokebox saddle is to the steam heater for the cylinder lubricator, and the steam supply to the atomiser, the valve for which, operated by the cylinder cock rod, can be seen on the LH, leading sandbox. Note the blanked-off joint on the blastpipe for the exhaust steam injector supply pipe.
Author

Below:
A partially completed '8F' frame in the Southern Railway's Eastleigh works in 1943. Another set of frameplates can be seen behind. Some checking of cylinder and frame alignment is also taking place.
'8F' Society Collection

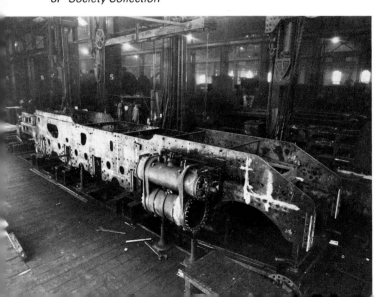

Left:
No 8233's boiler awaiting overhaul, 1981. The main steam manifold is prominent on the firebox backplate. The last remains of the cladding and its supporting crinoline can be seen. Note the riveted joints on the boiler barrel and the substantial nutted horizontal stays in the steam space above the inner firebox. The stays between the inner and outer firebox are a mixture of steel, Monel metal and riveted copper, the latter prominent in the lower areas. The bottom lines of rivets at the base of the firebox mark the location of the foundation ring. *Author*

Right:
Crewe Works was always responsible for large numbers of '8F' overhauls. No 8366 (H44) is being wheeled, probably after her first General Overhaul, in about 1947. Note that strengthening patches have been fitted around the driving axlebox horns, and also the proximity of the hole in the frame above the top of the horn gap, designed to give access to the front firebox washout plugs. The brake gear is substantially assembled, whilst the exhaust steam injector steam supply pipe lies in the foreground. *Fox Photographs/A. Biwandi Collection*

Below:
A rugged workhorse, devoid of frills, WD 'Austerity' 2-8-0 No 90491 clumps past Brentingby Junction, Melton Mowbray, with a substantial load of home iron ore bound for the furnaces of the North East in April 1964. *W. J. V. Anderson*

Above:
Along with Derby, Horwich was the other works mainly responsible for '8F' repairs. No 48756 (Dn45) is undergoing a full mechanical or 'Intermediate' repair with the boiler still in position, although some work is being undertaken on the regulator valves. This was the last locomotive to be overhauled at Horwich, 11 April 1964. *I. G. Holt*

Below:
Worn doorplate flanges in No 8233's firebox, bottom LH corner. The stays in the doorplate are of Monel metal, awaiting new nuts. Those in the wrapper plate are partially of riveted copper where the diameter has exceeded ⅞in and otherwise of steel. Many stays have been drilled out before a new copper insert is welded into the wrapper. All the remaining nutted stays are of Monel metal. *Author*

Below:
The firebox of No 8233 with copper tubeplate removed, looking towards the smokebox. Firebox crownplate at top of photograph, beyond lies the top of the barrel showing the main steam pipe with the regulator assembly removed. Trays for the top feed deliver water down the barrel sides. Also to be seen are the longitudinal stays between the front tubeplate and the backplate, and blower supply pipe from the dome. Throatplate in the foreground, drilled with stayholes and the two bottom mudholes for clearing out the foundation ring. Note the copper riveted stays in the RH wrapper at fire level with Monel metal stays above, together with three rows of riveted crownstays in the roof, the remainder being nutted. *Author*

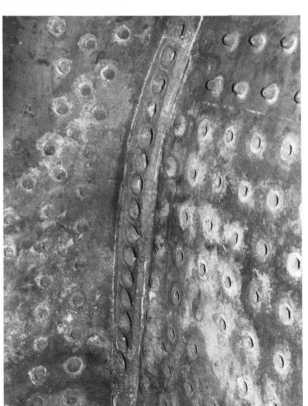

Right:
A view inside the boiler barrel of No 8233 (looking towards the firebox) shows the copper tubeplate and inner firebox stayed to the outer firebox. Main steam pipe, internal steam pipes and longitudinal stays above. Note the complex staying above the inner firebox with horizontal stays and roof stays from the crownplate. Palm stays attach the tubeplate to the barrel in the foreground.
Author

Centre right:
No 48517 (Dn44) is about to be outshopped from Darlington Works on 19 June 1965. Note the large numbers on the cabside and the absence of the power classification. The AWS magnet is suspended under the front bufferbeam. *J. R. P. Hunt*

Below:
Steam locomotives were traditionally maintained under fairly primitive conditions. No 48352 (H44) awaits her next duty at Leeds Holbeck, where fitters could at least count themselves fortunate to have a roof over their heads and fairly reasonable conditions under which to work.
Ian Alan Library

Right:

No 48666 (B44) is rerailed with jacks and packing at Rose Grove in 1968. Such items would be needed for spring changing without the use of a drop pit. There was little that was light or easy about steam locomotive maintenance! *R. J. Farrell*

Bottom:

Block and tackle being used to remove No 8233's superheater elements for inspection in 1971. Removed elements may be seen on the ground, and this job was fairly easy on a locomotive with regularly swept tubes. *Author*

Bottom right:

Cab layout of coal-fired locomotive No 8111. Key: 1 Water feed from tender to injector. 2 Water regulator for live steam injector. 3 Oil box for LH trailing coupled axlebox horn guides. 4 Oil box for engine steam brake cylinder. 5 Reverser. 6 Regulator handle. 7 Independent steam brake valve. 8 Sanding valve. 9 LMS standard Drivers Brake Valve (Vacuum brake application valve combined with vacuum controlled steam brake on locomotive). 10 Gauge lamp holder. 11 Steam valve to single-cone vacuum ejector. 12 Vacuum gauge. 12A Whistle handle. 13 Cab ventilator. 14 Main steam manifold. 15 Steam pressure gauge. 16 Injector steam valve handle. 17 Water gauge. 17A Try cock handle. 18 Continuous blowdown valve. 19 Blower valve. 20 Sandgun. 21 Oil box for RH trailing coupled axlebox horn guides. 22 Valve for water spray pipe. 23 Oil bottle locker. 24 Steam supply pipe to injector. 25 Sand hopper. 26 Water regulator for Exhaust Steam Injector. 27 Washout plug. 28 Oil box for damper controls. 29 Damper controls (only two dampers latterly). 30 Pins for drawbars. 31 Davies and Metcalfe Type H exhaust steam injector. 32 Vacuum bag. 33 Flexible connection to tender steam brake. 34 Gresham and Craven 10mm live steam injector. *BR(LMR)*

Left:

An '8F' 2-8-0 receiving attention from the Driver's feeder at Rose Grove, shortly before the end of steam working. The condition of the motion and wheels was quite typical of the external state of most '8Fs' in the last 10 years of their lives. *R. Wildsmith*

Below left:

Cab layout of oil-fired locomotive WD No 387. (Locomotive fitted with air, vacuum and graduable steam brakes).
Key: 1 Bottom of brake piston, and pull rod to brake cross beams. 2 Inspection/lighting up aperture in firehole door. 3 Westinghouse automatic air brake application valve. 4 LMS standard Driver's Brake Valve. 5 Graduable independent steam brake valve. 6 Large ejector steam valve. (Two-cone vacuum ejector). 7 Small ejector steam valve. (Two-cone vacuum ejector). 8 Air brake pressure gauge. 9 Vacuum gauge. 10 Steam supply cock, boiler to oil manifold. 11 Steam pressure gauge. 12 Auxiliary blower. 13 Steam to engine oil heater. 14 Auxiliary steam supply stop cock. 15 Steam for cleaning oil burner. 16 Steam to tender heating coil. 17 Burner steam control valve. 18 Sandgun — hand wheel for rotating nozzle. 19 Sandgun — steam valve wheel. 20 Control valve for oil supply to burner. 21 Oil pipe for tender buffer rubbing blocks. 22 Auxiliary drawbar. 23 Air brake pipes. 24 Engine brake return spring. 25 Vacuum pipe. *BR (LMR)*

Below:

No 48374 (H44) moves off the coaling stage at Kettering on 24 April 1965. Many freight depots had only rudimentary coaling facilities, in which tubs of coal were manhandled from wagon to tender. Coaling an '8F' under these circumstances could be a long process. In the foreground, a bent dart and rake lie on the ground. *K. Hughes*

Left:
At larger depots with mechanical coaling facilities the coal could be loaded much more quickly. LNER No 3548 of Heaton stands under the coaling plant at York as a wagonload of coal is hoisted into the hopper above on 29 June 1947. *C. C. B. Herbert*

Below left:
No 48753 (Dn45) stands on the disposal road, beside the coaling plant at Nuneaton MPD on 5 January 1966. The fireirons show ample signs of maltreatment and long use. A couple of very dilapidated clinker shovels lie on the fire iron rack. *B. Harris*

Top:
Very few '8F' enginemen enjoyed the luxury of a rocking grate and hopper ashpan for their disposal duties. Only No 8490 (H45) and a few others were so fitted. Here a locoman operates the handle to open the hopper doors before rocking out the remains of the fire into the pit below. June 1946. *Ian Allan Library*

Right:
No 48760 (Dn45) has just had its fire cleaned and ashpan raked clear at Bath Green Park MPD in February 1966. The old fire and clinker are then shovelled out of the pit. The water hydrant was very necessary to keep down the dust during this process. *R. I. D. Hoyle*

Below:
Preservationists find out what disposal duties are all about. No 8233 has its smokebox cleaned out at Bridgnorth in August 1971. *Author*

3

Stanier 2-8-0s On Test

Unfortunately, the '8F' design was never subjected to constant speed tests. However they did undergo dynamometer car tests between Toton and Brent with No 8000 in 1936 and with No 48400 during the 1948 Locomotive Exchanges. Unfortunately, this engine was in run down condition and No 48189 was substituted for the rest of the Exchanges. Similar tests had been carried out in LMS days with 'G2' and 'Austin Seven' 0-8-0s, an S&D '7F' 2-8-0 and a Garratt. Mr A. J. Powell has kindly produced this analysis of the various test results:

The 1948 Locomotive Exchanges
Although the '8F' did not prove to be the most outstanding design in the Exchanges, it did consistently occupy the middle ground amongst the freight loco-motives tested. As is well known, operating conditions in 1948 were appalling, and gave little opportunity to determine the optimum performance of which the engines were capable. The trials took place between Toton and Brent, Severn Tunnel Junction and Acton, Bristol and Eastleigh, and between Ferme Park and Peterborough. No 48189 was the '8F' used for most of the tests, and she steamed well throughout with the water level in the boiler being well maintained. She was driven with the partially-open regulator technique, and with cut-off between 18 and 45%.

The '8Fs' best work was between Stoke Gifford and Badminton, a distance of 17 miles uphill at a gradient of 1 in 300, with a time allowance of 55min. The '8F' cut this to 38min with a load of 1,065 tons, but the Eastern Region 'O1' managed in 3min less with a similar load. Pulling away from a signal check at Wootton Bassett, a steady drawbar pull of 11¾ tons at 5mph was recorded with the '8F'.

In examining the coal and water consumptions, it is perhaps appropriate to consider the overall figures for the three routes worked by all five engine designs (gauge restrictions barred the '28xx' from the Toton-Brent route). On this basis:

1. The low specific water consumption of the 'O1' undoubtedly reflects high superheat, with the '8F' not far behind. The curiosity is the '28xx', which returned the second lowest figure notwithstanding its low superheat. The two WD designs trailed well behind, with the 2-8-0 giving a figure 10% higher than the '8F', despite its 28-element superheater.
2. There was no significant difference in the evaporation rates for the four 2-8-0s (between 7.64 and 7.83lb/lb), but the 2-10-0, as would be expected, achieved a better figure of 8.12lb/lb, reflecting the lower firing rate.
3. Again the '28xx' returned a very low figure for specific coal consumption (3.42lb/DBHP h). The '8F' showed greater inter-Regional variation than the others, from a low of 3.17lb on ER to a high of 3.81lb on SR.

Undoubtedly different firing techniques, affecting the degree of superheat achieved, had a marked effect on the figures, as also did driver unfamiliarity. The good results with the '28xx' may have been influenced by the lead characteristics of the Stephenson valve gear at the low speeds predominating. There must be some doubt as to the condition of the WD 2-8-0 (No 77000) used on the WR and SR tests, which produced figures consistently worse than No 63169 on ER.

The 'star' of the 1948 Exchanges was possibly the '28xx' which returned some remarkable results for a design originating in 1903. The 'O1' and WD 2-10-0 showed up well overall, with the WD 2-8-0 trailing some way behind in efficiency and performance. The '8F' produced a thoroughly satisfactory result, and was also credited with providing by far the best ride. There was really little to choose between the freight locomotives; all were effective and efficient machines. Why did the '8F' outlast them all? It is likely that its reliability, low maintenance costs and versatility, together with its lively performance on the road were significant factors.

Comparison of freight locomotive performance — 1948 locomotive exchanges

Locomotive	Average coal consumption lb/DBHP hr	Average water consumption lb water/DBHP hr	Evaporation rate lb water/lb coal	Tractive effort lb	Adhesive weight lb	Adhesion factor	Piston valve diameter in	Piston valve travel in	Steam lap in	Blastpipe nozzle area	Cylinder clearance volume as % of swept volume
ER 01	3.40	26.22	7.70	35,518	147,504	4.15	10	6.66	1.625	20.63	7.7
WR 28xx	3.42	26.80	7.83	35,380	150,080	4.24	10	6.25	1.625	21.65	7.8
LMR 8F	3.55	27.11	7.64	32,438	141,344	4.35	10	6.47	1.500	21.65	9.5
WD 2-10-0	3.45	28.06	8.12	34,215	150,416	4.40	10	6.63	1.500	20.63	10.0
WD 2-8-0	3.90	29.12	7.64	34,215	137,200	4.01	10	6.63	1.500	20.63	10.0

NB: These figures do not include the Toton-Brent results which differed markedly from the test results elsewhere.

Dynamometer Car Tests with Mineral and Empty Wagon Trains: Toton to Brent

General Remarks

Dynamometer car tests were, by their very nature, relatively inaccurate and inconsistent, being based on a constantly varying workload at varying speeds, and subject in the freight field to unforeseen delays. They were also highly dependent on the skill of enginemen and the degree of control exercised over them. Day-to-day variations in coal and water consumptions of ±5% were commonplace. So on a general warning note, no weighty conclusions should be drawn from small differences in figures.

This is particularly important where testing was limited. A number of the tests referred to here were confined to a single run in each direction; in other cases, while two runs were made each way, delays and out-of-course stops on one or both were sufficiently frequent to invalidate the results. So again, figures for a single run are quoted in some cases; in more than one case this single run would normally have been excluded, but has been put in as the *least unsatisfactory* of the pair.

It has not been found possible to reconcile for comparative purposes the consumptions on prewar tests with those from the 1948 Interchange Trials. In general, conditions were very different; after World War 2 speeds were often markedly lower, partly by design and partly due to a multiplicity of operating and permanent way delays. Coals differed, and enginemen and operating staff had not yet recovered from wartime relaxations; on freight workings there was a tendency to regard the timetable more as a very broad guide than as a firm objective. It has therefore been considered better to separate the analysis and evaluation of prewar and 1948 results.

Characteristics of Trains

The task imposed on the engine can be broadly assessed for severity by the 'Ton-miles per Engine Hour' figure, using actual running times. Comparing on this basis:

Table A. Loaded mineral trains: Toton-Brent

		1927	1927	1930		1931	1936				Load 68×13-ton wagons, 1948 interchange trials			
	Year	Ex-LNWR G2 0-8-0*	S&D 2-8-0*	7F 0-8-0 Std		Garratt	Stanier 8F 2-8-0 8000				8F† 2-8-0	ER O1 2-8-0‡	WD 2-8-0‡	WD 2-10-0
	Engine			LS inj	ACFI		(1)‡	(2)	(3)					
Average load	(tons)	938	927	887	910	1,301	903	999	1,070		1,047	1,061	1,091	1,047
Train miles		127.5	127.3	128.0	127.9	128.5	127.8	127.5	127.6		127.7	127.8	128.0	127.9
Ton/miles	(excl eng)	119,593	118,019	113,630	116,339	167,144	115,455	127,436	136,517		133,691§	135,565§	139,622§	133,861§
Running time	(min)	434.9	435.1	381.5	393.9	346.9	362.2	388.2	401.1		484.7	440.3	440.7	514.1
Total time	(min)	515.8	511.2	442.3	447.9	417.6	436.0	465.5	478.4		614.5	490.5	525.0	664.6
Standing time	(min)	80.9	76.1	60.8	54.0	70.7	74.8	77.3	77.3		129.8	50.2	84.3	150.5
Delays (av)	checks	—	—	—	—	—	—	—	—		16	6	15	14
unbooked stops		—	—	—	—	—	—	—	—		6	4	2	6
Average speed	(mph)	17.6	17.6	20.1	19.5	22.2	21.2	19.7	19.1		15.8	17.4	17.4	14.9
Ton/miles/eng/hr		16,499	16,275	17,871	17,721	28,909	19,126	19,696	20,421		16,549	18,474	19,009	15,623
Work done, DBHP/hr		2,508	2,349	2,319	2,426	3,237	2,289	2,520	2,851		2,816	2,771	2,997	2,981
Average DBHP		346	324	365	370	560	379	389	426		349	378	408	348
DBHP/hr/train mile		19.7	18.4	18.1	19.0	26.7	17.9	19.8	22.3		22.1	21.7	23.4	23.3
DBHP/hr/ton mile		0.021	0.020	0.020	0.021	0.019	0.02	0.020	0.021		0.021	0.020	0.021	0.022
Coal burnt (lb)		10,088	10,267	6,202	5,929	11,879	6,615	7,360	8,463		10,182	9,824	10,807	11,144
lb/mile		79.0	80.6	48.4	46.4	92.4	51.7	57.7	66.3		79.7	73.0	84.4	87.1
lb/DBHP hr		4.02	4.37	2.67	2.44	3.46	2.89	2.92	3.03		3.62	3.37	3.60	3.74
lb/sq ft/hr (excl stops)		59	50	41	38	46	39	41	46		44	45	51	32
Water used (gal)		6,375	7,740	5,392	4,976	9,540	5,635	6,030	6,510		7,720	6,952	8,050	8,345
gal/mile		50.0	60.8	42.1	38.9	74.2	44.1	47.3	51.0		60.5	54.4	62.9	65.2
lb/DBHP hr		25.4	32.9	23.3	20.5	27.6	24.6	23.9	22.8		27.4	25.1	26.9	28.0
Evaporation lb/lb coal		6.32	7.54	8.69	8.39	7.91	8.52	8.19	7.69		7.59	7.46	7.45	7.49

* Single run only tested.
† Single run only: other test run invalidated by poor condition of engine.
‡ Single run only: other test run subject to serious delays.
§ Not quoted in report: calculated on approximate distance.

1 Loaded Trains

The easiest performances were made by the LNWR 'G2' 0-8-0 and S&D '7F' 2-8-0 engines, together with the '8F' 2-8-0 and WD 2-10-0 engines in 1948. Excluding the Garratt tests, which were a special case, the 1936 tests on the '8F' 2-8-0 built up to the hardest duty, with the WD 2-8-0 in 1948 following up closely.

2 Empty Trains

There was not a great variation, but again the 1936 tests on the '8F' 2-8-0 built up to the hardest duty; this fell short of that for the loaded trains, being limited by train handling and operating problems.

Speeds

1 Pre-war (loaded)

It is perhaps surprising that there should be such a wide variation in running speeds, from 17.6 to 22.2mph, representing over 1½hr of running time between Toton and Brent.

2 1948 Interchange Trials (loaded)

Running speeds were altogether lower, in the range 14.9-17.4mph. The best journey time was 5min to 6min longer than the slowest prewar. This in itself went a long way to invalidate comparisons.

Out-of-Course Delays

1 Detachment of Wagons en route

The great majority of loaded trains (12 out of 16 prewar and seven out of eight in 1948) were delayed by detaching wagons, presumably for hot boxes; in seven of these cases two separate stops were made for this purpose. In only two cases was this necessary with empty trains. Such was the problem with grease-lubricated wagon axle-boxes.

2 Signal Delays and Permanent Way Checks

No comprehensive details are available for prewar tests. In the 1948 trials such delays were extremely numerous in the loaded direction — in one case amounting to 19 checks and eight stops — and this clearly had a very adverse effect on efficiency. In the empty direction the situation was much better, though in one extreme instance the WD 2-8-0 suffered 20 checks and two stops.

Power Output Required

Average Drawbar Horsepower (DBHP), measured over the actual running times (not the time with steam on, which was about 70% of the running time loaded and about 89% empty) were higher for the

Table B. Empty wagon trains: Toton-Brent

| | | 1927 | 1927 | 1930 | | 1931 | 1936 | | | Load 84× empty wagons, 1948 interchange trials | | | |
| | | | | 7F 0-8-0 Std | | Garratt | Stanier 8F 2-8-0 8000 | | | | | | |
	Engine	G2 0-8-0*	S&D 2-8-0*	LS inj	ACFI		(1)	(2)†	(3)	8F 2-8-0	ER O1 2-8-0	WD 2-8-0†	WD 2-10-0†
Average load	(tons)	526	527	629	615	—	582	697	710	580	578	600	580
Train miles		127.2	126.8	127.4	127.5	—	126.8	126.8	127.1	126.8	127.0	127.0	126.6
Ton/miles	(excl eng)	66,958	66,827	80,166	78,476	—	73,330	88,380	90,332	73,544‡	73,432‡	76,200‡	73,428‡
Running time	(min)	346.4	336.3	371.3	380.8	—	354.0	378.0	367.1	346.9	357.8	336.2	351.9
Total time	(min)	370.0	360.1	446.1	440.6	—	401.3	414.1	418.2	378.5	430.3	371.2	406.0
Standing time	(min)	23.6	23.8	74.8	59.8	—	47.3	36.1	51.1	31.6	72.5	35.0	54.1
Delays (av)	checks	—	—	—	—	—	—	—	—	3.5	5.5	11	5
unbooked stops		—	—	—	—	—	—	—	—	3.5	3	1	4
Average speed	(mph)	22.0	22.6	20.6	20.1	—	21.5	20.1	20.8	21.9	21.3	22.7	21.6
Ton/miles/eng/hr		11,598	11,923	12,954	12,365	—	12,429	14,029	14,764	12,720	12,314	13,599	12,520
Work done, DBHP/hr		2,332	2,465	2,853	2,910	—	2,637	2,761	2,759	3,052	2,732	2,537	2,826
Average DBHP		404	440	461	459	—	447	438	451	528	458	453	482
DBHP/hr/train mile		18.3	19.4	22.4	22.8	—	20.8	21.8	21.7	24.1	21.5	20.0	22.3
DBHP/hr/ton mile		0.035	0.037	0.036	0.037	—	0.036	0.031	0.031	0.041	0.037	0.033	0.038
Coal burnt	(lb)	7,644	8,904	7,616	7,070	—	7,605	8,050	7,966	9,973	8,960	8,782	9,884
lb/mile		60.1	70.2	59.8	55.5	—	60.0	63.5	62.7	78.7	70.6	69.1	78.1
lb/DBHP hr		3.28	3.61	2.67	2.43	—	2.88	2.91	2.89	3.27	3.28	3.46	3.50
lb/sq ft/hr (excl stops)		56	56	52	47	—	46	46	47	60	54	55	42
Water used	(gal)	5,595	6,880	6,229	6,015	—	6,032	6,530	6,270	7,957	6,710	6,550	7,590
gal/mile		44.0	54.2	48.9	47.2	—	47.6	51.5	49.3	62.8	52.8	51.6	60.0
lb/DBHP hr		24.0	27.9	21.8	20.7	—	22.9	23.6	22.7	26.1	24.6	25.8	26.9
Evaporation lb/lb coal		7.32	7.73	8.18	8.51	—	7.93	8.11	7.87	7.98	7.49	7.46	7.68

* Single run only tested.
† One run only: other test run subject to serious delays.
‡ Not quoted in report: calculated on quoted distance.

Table C. Boiler ratios

| | Free gas areas (sq ft) | | | | Length between tubeplates | A/S ratios | | | Total FGA as % of grate area |
	Flues	Small tubes	Total	Flues as % of total		Flues*	Small tubes	Grate area	
G2 0-8-0	1.84	2.12	3.96	46.5%	14ft 10½in	1/483	1/438	23.6	16.8
S&D 2-8-0†	2.03	2.13	4.16	48.8%	12ft 3⅝in	1/424	1/363	28.4	14.6
7F 0-8-0 Std	1.84	2.05	3.89	47.3%	14ft 10½in	1/483	1/407	23.6	16.5
Garratt	2.71	3.56	6.27	43.2%	12ft 5in	1/430	1/340	44.5	14.1
8F 2-8-0 (1936)	2.03	2.35	4.38	46.3%	13ft 3in	1/323	1/365	27.8	15.8
8F 2-8-0 (1948)	1.89	2.54	4.43	42.7%	12ft 2⅞in	1/322	1/385	28.65	15.5
WD 2-8-0	2.32	2.50	4.82	48.1%	12ft 0in	1/344	1/377	28.65	16.8
ER Class O1 2-8-0	2.02	2.43	4.45	45.5%	13ft 11⅞in	1/445	1/383	27.9	15.9
WD 2-10-0	2.32	2.24	4.56	50.9%	15ft 8in	1/411	1/461	40.0	11.4

* Exact ratios cannot be calculated because the precise length and configuration of superheater elements at time of test is not known (except in the case of the WD 2-8-0). These values have been calculated on the *assumption* that element spear ends are 2ft from the firebox end of the flue and that the return loop is the full length of the flue to the front tubeplate.
† Fitted with large (5ft 3in dia) boiler.

empty trains (usually 400-460) than for the loaded ones (350-400), due to the higher running speeds. Allowing for coasting and running with light steam to keep drawgear taut etc, maxima were about twice these figures.

There is good consistency in the power demand figures for loaded trains in the range 0.019-0.022 DBHPhr/ton mile, though rather less for empty trains (0.031-0.041).

Water Consumption

The specific consumption (lb/DBHP hr) reflects both the efficiency of using steam (design of front end and valve events) and the degree of superheat obtained. On a modern locomotive it does not depend significantly on cut-off over a wide working range. In order of merit the figures were:

1 Prewar

Loaded

'7F'	0-8-0 (ACFI)	20.5
'8F'	2-8-0 (3)	22.8
'7F'	0-8-0 (LS inj)	23.3
'8F'	2-8-0 (2)	23.9
'8F'	2-8-0 (1)	24.6
'G2'	0-8-0	25.4
Garratt		27.6
'S&D'	2-8-0	32.9

Empty

'7F'	0-8-0 (ACFI)	20.7
'7F'	0-8-0 (LS inj)	21.8
'8F'	2-8-0 (3)	22.7
'8F'	2-8-0 (1)	22.9
'8F'	2-8-0 (2)	23.6
'G2'	0-8-0	24.0
'S&D'	2-8-0	27.9

The surprisingly low consumption for the '7F' 0-8-0 (using ACFI feed heater) partly arise from a fortuitous freedom from delay with loaded trains. This engine had a good front end with long-lap Walschaerts valve gear, but was certainly not superior to the '8F' 2-8-0 in this respect. The disparity between figures for ACFI and live steam injector, at 12%, appears excessive; it is doubtful whether this device produced as much as 8% water saving in normal service. By contrast, the very poor figures for the Garratt and S&D 2-8-0 faithfully reflect the abysmal front end design and steam distribution by very short lap valve gears.

2 1948 Exchange Trials

Loaded

'O1'	2-8-0	25.1
'WD'	2-8-0	26.9
'8F'	2-8-0	27.4
'WD'	2-10-0	28.0

Empty

'O1'	2-8-0	24.6
'WD'	2-8-0	25.8
'8F'	2-8-0	26.1*
'WD'	2-10-0	26.9

*Working on live steam injector; exhaust steam injector not picking up.

The consistently low consumption of the LNER 'O1' 2-8-0 was almost certainly due to high superheat at the rates of working which applied. The poorer consumption of the WD 2-10-0 as compared with that of the WD 2-8-0 can only be explained by the adverse effect on superheat of the very low firing rates on the grate due to the wide firebox — only 32lb/sq ft/hr on the loaded test.

Coal Consumption

The specific coal consumption (lb/DBHP/hr) derives from the specific water consumption and the evaporation rate (lb water/lb coal). The latter is influenced by the boiler efficiency — mainly a function of the combustion rate on the grate (lb/sq ft/hr) — and by the degree of superheat; about 4% extra heat is needed to raise steam temperature from 500° to 600°F.

(a) EVAPORATION RATES
In ascending order these were:

1 Prewar

Loaded

'G2'	0-8-0	6.32*
'S&D'	2-8-0	7.54*
'8F'	2-8-0 (3)	7.69
Garratt		7.91
'8F'	2-8-0 (2)	8.19
'7F'	0-8-0 (ACFI)	8.39
'8F'	2-8-0 (1)	8.52
'7F'	0-8-0 (LS inj)	8.69

Empty

'G2'	0-8-0	7.32*
'S&D'	2-8-0	7.73*
'8F'	2-8-0 (3)	7.87
'8F'	2-8-0 (1)	7.93
'8F'	2-8-0 (2)	8.11*
'7F'	0-8-0 (LS inj)	8.18
'7F'	0-8-0 (ACFI)	8.51

2 1948 Exchange Trials

Loaded

'WD'	2-8-0	7.45*
'O1'	2-8-0	7.46*
'WD'	2-10-0	7.49*
'8F'	2-8-0	7.59*

Empty

'WD'	2-8-0	7.46*
'O1'	2-8-0	7.49
'WD'	2-10-0	7.68*
'8F'	2-8-0	7.98

*Figure for a single run only.

There is a fair correlation on the loaded tests between evaporation rate and combustion rate for most engines, lying within the ±5% band previously mentioned. The figure of 6.32lb/lb for the 'G2' 0-8-0 loaded test, and the 7.49lb/lb for the WD 2-10-0 lie right outside this band, and appear therefore to be single test aberrations. All others are within these limits. It is nevertheless surprising that even in the empty tests the 'G2' 0-8-0 and the '7F' 0-8-0 should be at opposite ends of the spectrum, since they carried in effect the same boiler, only differing in working pressure. On the empty tests the scatter is rather larger, but only two tests were outside the ±5% band, namely the 1948 '8F' 2-8-0 (by a narrow margin) and the WD 2-10-0 (much wider of the mark).

(b) SUPERHEAT
Steam temperatures were not measured except in the 1936 tests on the '8F' 2-8-0, when even while working fairly hard on the climbs, they did not exceed a poor 500°F. The boiler proportions and ratios suggest that the cause was excessive free gas area through the flues due to inadequate superheater element diameter (1⅛in). Much of the hot gases would avoid surface contact, to provide superheat, and high smokebox temperatures could be expected. A careful study of Table C suggests that steam temperatures would have fallen into three broad bands with some overlapping:

Poor:	'8F'	2-8-0 (1936 tube layout)
Fair:	Garratt	
	'7F'	0-8-0
	'G2'	0-8-0
	'S&D'	2-8-0 (large boiler)
	'8F'	2-8-0 (1948 tube (layout)

Good:

    'O1'   2-8-0
    'WD' 2-8-0
    'WD' 2-10-0

Superheat temperatures are a function of the firing rate, and this would tend to depress that for the WD 2-10-0 at the working rates of the Interchange Trials.

(c) BOILER EFFICIENCY

At a typical combustion rate for loaded tests of 40-45lb/sq ft/hr a boiler efficiency of about 80-82% could be expected; the 'G2' 0-8-0 at 59lb/sq ft/hr on its relatively small grate could be expected to have a lower efficiency of about 76%, thus increasing coal consumption by perhaps 8% as compared with others, though higher superheat might offset some of this disadvantage. In contrast the very low combustion rate of 32lb/sq ft/hr for the WD 2-10-0 on loaded test should have given a boiler efficiency of the order of 85%, but superheat temperatures would be relatively low, giving a higher specific water consumption, as seen.

(d) SPECIFIC COAL CONSUMPTION

In merit order the figures were:

1 Prewar

Loaded

'7F'	0-8-0 (ACFI)	2.44
'7F'	0-8-0 (LS inj)	2.67
'8F'	2-8-0 (1)	2.89

'8F'	2-8-0 (2)	2.92
'8F'	2-8-0 (3)	3.03
Garratt		3.46
'G2'	0-8-0	4.02
'S&D'	2-8-0	4.37

Empty

'7F'	0-8-0 (ACFI)	2.43
'7F'	0-8-0 (LS inj)	2.67
'8F'	2-8-0 (1)	2.88
'8F'	2-8-0 (3)	2.89
'8F'	2-8-0 (2)	3.00
'G2'	0-8-0	3.28
'S&D'	2-8-0	3.61

In view of earlier remarks, a strong element of suspicion hangs over the '7F' 0-8-0 results. The Derby dynamometer car team were adept at this period at producing abnormally low test figures, as was seen in 1933/34 with the first tests on 'Princesses', 'Jubilees' and Class 5s; further tests immediately after showed specific consumptions more than 10% higher! Note also that in 1936 the '8F' was using Grimethorpe Grade 1 coal. In 1948 the coal used was Blidworth Grade 2. On this basis, the 1936 (2) figure should be 3.24 pro rata.

The average position of the Garratt in the 'league table' is perhaps rather higher than might be expected, given the shortcomings of its valve gear and its poor boiler ratios. The higher average speeds indicate a comparative freedom from out-of-course delays, which could only be beneficial to its figures.

2 1948 Interchange Trials

Loaded

'O1'	2-8-0	3.37
'WD'	2-8-0	3.60
'8F'	2-8-0	3.62
'WD'	2-10-0	3.74

Empty

'8F'	2-8-0	3.27
'O1'	2-8-0	3.28
'WD'	2-8-0	3.46
'WD'	2-10-0	3.50

Under the somewhat different conditions of the Trials there is little to choose between the three 2-8-0 designs. It must be remembered that the loaded 'O1' trial was particularly free from delays by comparison with the other three, and this appears to come through in the consumption figure. The WD 2-10-0 was clearly over-provided with grate area for the nature of the work it was expected to do on this occasion.

Conclusions

Subject to reservations about the apparent efficiency of the '7F' 0-8-0, the relevance of the consumption figures is very much what might be expected from a study of the relevant design features of each design. They establish the 'Stanier' '8F' 2-8-0 as one of the leaders in this general locomotive type. Further modification of the tube layout to improve superheat temperatures would probably have made it marginally more efficient than any of its three modern competitors.

No 8000 stands at Rugby with one of its first workings, a Toton-Willesden minerals haul in June 1935. *D. J. Montgomery Collection*

Above:
The Rivals: A Stanier '8F' and a Thompson '01' meet near Skelton Junction on the once busy CLC freight route through the south Manchester suburbs, shortly before nationalisation. *W. S. Garth*

Below:
No 48189, attached to the LMS Dynamometer Car, arrives at Hornsey sidings with the 12.15 freight from Peterborough during the Locomotive Exchanges on the Eastern Region. 18 August 1948. *Ian Allan Library*

Above:
The GWR '28xx' 2-8-0 was a very advanced design for its day. It success had much to do with the design concept of the '8F', and it performed very well indeed in the 1948 Exchanges. No 2839 was nearly 60 years old when heading this long van train off the Hereford line through Shrewsbury station on 28 January 1964. *Author*

Below:
In a class of its own: The BR Standard Class 9F 2-10-0 was altogether bigger and more versatile than any of its predecessors. No 92234 takes hold of a long tank train returning to the Wirral chemical factories, at Chester on 7 December 1963. *Author*

4
Forging a Reputation

The Prewar Period

The Stanier '8F' was originally intended purely as a mineral hauler of similar capacity to the Fowler '7F' 0-8-0, but without its mechanical vices. Nos 8000-8005 were accordingly delivered to the Midland Division in July 1935 without vacuum brakes and were classified '7F'. Nos 8006-11 followed shortly afterwards, but had vacuum brakes from new.

Initially, Nos 8000/02/03 were sent to Toton, No 8001 to Wellingborough and Nos 8004/05 to Willesden. Here, they replaced the 'Austin Sevens' on the heavy Toton to Willesden coal hauls, No 8001 also being transferred to Willesden by October. Early in 1936, the 12 locomotives in traffic had been equally divided between Toton and Willesden and already their potential ability had been recognised with the '8F' classification appearing on their cabsides.

The 1936 building programme envisaged 15 2-8-0s from Crewe, together with 69 from the Vulcan Foundry financed by the Government Guaranteed Loan Scheme which had been introduced in the wake of the Depression. These were of the new standard design incorporating the domed sloping-throatplate 3C boiler with improved tube proportions, and vacuum brakes. Although the '8Fs' spent 90% of their time on mineral work, their ability to work vacuum-fitted bulk loads, faster freight and empty coaching stock duties was soon realised, and the original six engines quickly received vacuum brakes from 1938.

In the spring of 1936, Nos 8003-05 transferred to Sheffield. and Nos 8003/04 moved to Coalville in the summer. In July, the Vulcan Foundry began to turn out Nos 8027-95 in pristine order with burnished coupling rods, wheel centres and cylinder covers. How long they remained thus with the rigours of freight operation is open to question! The new locomotives went mainly to Toton and Wellingborough, but Canklow, Royston, Kirkby, Derby and Saltley also received allocations. The Saltley engines soon disappeared to Staveley and Westhouses in December, and Leicester gained No 8005 on transfer.

Crewe belatedly delivered Nos 8012-26 early in 1937, Hasland, Peterborough, Normanton and Burton acquiring their first '8Fs' at this time. Throughout the year new engines appeared at the rate of five to six per month, all going exclusively to the Midland Division north of Wellingborough. Vulcan Foundry deliveries were complete by November 1937, but no '8Fs' were put into traffic at all in 1938, since Crewe did not start work on Nos 8096-8110 until December. These deliveries saw the dispersal of many of the Fowler '7Fs' to the Central Division, where they replaced the L&Y 0-8-0s.

Willesden and Northampton were the main recipients of new 2-8-0s in 1939, but Nos 8113-15 went surprisingly to the small depot at Warwick. The requirement for this allocation is uncertain, but iron ore traffic from the GWR destined for the North Midlands and North East could have been a possibility, or indeed the cement traffic from the works at Southam. In the meantime, Heaton Mersey had received five '8Fs' by transfer, and Crewe South had No 8116 on loan.

On the outbreak of war in 1939, the 126 locomotives in traffic were overwhelmingly concentrated on the Midland line south of Leeds, with only very small numbers

LMS prewar orders — building and allocation

Built	Locomotive Nos	Period into traffic	First allocation
Crewe	8000-11	8/35-11/35	Toton 4, Willesden 7, Wellingborough 1
Vulcan Foundry	8027-80	7/36-12/36	Toton 14, Wellingborough 13, Kirkby 6, Saltley 6, Canklow 8, Derby 1, Nottingham 5, Royston 1
Crewe	8012-14	13/36*	Normanton 1, Hasland 2
Vulcan Foundry	8081-95	1/37-2/37	Staveley 3, Westhouses 1, Normanton 4, Royston 2, Peterborough 1, Canklow 1, Kirkby 3
Crewe	8015-26	2/37-4/37	Royston 4, Normanton 1, Sheffield 1, Kirkby 1, Wellingborough 2, Burton 1, Stourton 1, Canklow 1
Crewe	8096/97	1/39†	Willesden
Crewe	8098-8125	1/39-7/39	Willesden 14, Northampton 13, Warwick 2

* 1936 Building programme   † 1938 Building programme.

elsewhere. On the Western Division, the LNWR 0-8-0s reigned supreme, with only occasional forays by Willesden and Northampton '8Fs' on traffic other than that destined for the Midland Division. Whilst Midland enginemen and fitters were welcoming the new arrivals with open arms, the prowess of the Stanier '8F' on all manner of freight work remained a mystery to most of the LMS system. How this picture was to change over the next few years, not only on the LMS but on many foreign railways as well!

The '8Fs' were at first used on the Toton to Willesden coal trains, and also on the Stonebridge Park coal hoppers. As deliveries to Toton increased in 1936, they began to share the Toton to Brent coal hauls with the Garratts, with the loadings reorganised around the maximum load for an '8F', much to the delight of the firemen who had had more than enough of the voracious Garratt appetites! Loadings for the '8Fs' were fixed at a maximum of 70 loaded wagons — the practical maximum if broken couplings were to be avoided, and the Garratt loads were often an embarrassment in this respect. Other '8F' activities encompassed the line to Peterborough via Stamford, traffic for March being handed over there to the LNER. The heavy trains from Beeston to Holwell Iron Works soon became an '8F' preserve, where previously Garratts had been unpopular and double heading of '3F' and '4F' 0-6-0s expensive. Southwards the '8Fs' worked to Washwood Heath via Trent and Stenson Junctions, whilst from a variety of depots from Stourton southwards they brought a continuous stream of coal trains into Toton Yard. These were the days when the goods lines between Clay Cross and Toton would be continuously occupied by mineral trains, perhaps 55% of them '8F'-hauled. Utilisation being the order of the day, the new 2-8-0s sometimes appeared on unusual fill-in jobs, and an evening excursion from Melton Mowbray to Nottingham was worked by No 8077 in between trips to Holwell Iron Works on at least one occasion in the summer of 1939.

The Coalville engines were used on the Desford to Wellingborough coal trains, which were sometimes worked through to Cricklewood, but normally Wellingborough '8Fs' worked forward to the capital. This was also true of Stourton and Kirkby engines working coal trains from Yorkshire and Nottinghamshire. The Kirkby allocation was mainly used on coal traffic to Manchester routed across the Pennines via Butterley and Ambergate to Gowhole, where Central Division 0-8-0s took over. Occasionally, the '8Fs' worked through to Preston with these trains.

The Heaton Mersey locomotives were used mainly on the 1,000-ton limestone hopper workings from the ICI quarries at Tunstead to the chemical works on the Cheshire saltfield at Northwich. It was here, along with the Toton to Brent coal hauls that the Stanier '8F' established its reputation as a willing and thoroughly reliable workhorse.

Before the war, '8Fs' were only rarely seen north of Leeds, for the Stourton allocation worked mostly to Cricklewood or Willesden. However, Normanton engines did have a diagram to Carnforth with the Snydale to Barrow coke workings.

In these years when home produced iron ore was used extensively, there was a heavy flow of traffic from Oxfordshire and Northamptonshire to the Teesside steel works, hence the early allocation to Northampton in 1939. The Midland main line between Wellingborough and Toton was emphatically *the* place to see '8Fs' at work, trailing long trains of wooden-bodied, loose-coupled wagons with grease-lubricated axleboxes. Much of the work was undertaken at slow speed, but there was no mistaking the '8F' bark when they were frequently worked at full regulator and 45% cut off over long stretches. With the exhaust steam injector singing away, deft work with the shovel would see steam pressure consistently close to the 'red mark' and a display from the chimney top which left no doubts at all that the Stanier '8Fs' could mean business. It was business that was to be repeated in an amazing variety of spheres over the next few years.

Allocation of Stanier '8F' 2-8-0s as at 1 January 1940

Shed Code	Depot	Total
1A	Willesden	15
2C	Northampton	14
2E	Warwick	1
15A	Wellingborough	20
15C	Leicester	2
16A	Nottingham	5
16C	Kirkby	6
17C	Coalville	3
18A	Toton	24
18B	Westhouses	7
18C	Hasland	1
18D	Staveley	6
19A	Sheffield	1
19C	Canklow	4
19D	Heaton Mersey	5
20C	Royston	5
20D	Normanton	6
21A	Saltley	1

'The Engines That Won the War'

In justice, this compliment should apply with equal force to the Gresley 'V2s', Stanier 'Black Fives' and quite a wide range of other locomotives, but there is no doubting the sterling contribution made by the '8Fs' to the war effort.

In 1940, there were a mere 126 '8Fs' in traffic. Munitions demands and WD orders for overseas meant that it was 1942 before there was sufficient capacity to build large numbers of locomotives for home use. With incessant demands on scarce resources, and with the prospect of a serious locomotive shortage as the war effort built up, the Ministry of War Transport was anxious to standardise on a single modern freight locomotive design capable of running on all main and most secondary routes in the country. The Stanier '8F' fitted the bill admirably.

At first the GWR, LNER and SR were aghast at the prospect of having to build '8Fs' and claimed that their own designs could be modified to a maximum width of 8ft 7⅝in and a 17-ton axle loading. All three railways refused to absorb the '8Fs' at the end of hostilities. Eventually, this opposition was overcome and in 1943 the LNER agreed 'in the national interest' to build '8Fs', being prepared to purchase up to 100. In 1944, the company asserted that the '8Fs' were not as powerful or

New Locomotives 1940-46

Year	LMS Orders	WD Orders to LMS/GWR → WD	WD Orders	Railway Executive Committee	LNER	Total
1940	—	53	23	—	—	76
1941	14	3	94	—	—	111
1942	68	24	11	—	—	103
1943	41	—	—	92	—	133
1944	58	—	—	107	25	190
1945	24	—	—	46	18	88
1946	—	—	—	—	25	25
	205	80	128	245	68	726

SR built   — 1943 105 for LMS (REC ordered)
               — 1944 25 for LNER (LNER ordered)   130

LNER built — 1943 — 1 on loan to LNER (REC ordered)
               — 1944 — 28 on loan to LNER (REC ordered)
               — 1945 — 31 on loan to LNER (REC ordered)   103
                       18 built for LNER
               — 1946 — 25 built for LNER

GWR built   — 1943 — 27
                 1944 — 38   on loan to GWR (REC ordered)   80
                 1945 — 15

economical as their own 2-8-0s (the '8Fs' cost £2,500 more on average, but they were new locomotives). In the event, the '8Fs' acquitted themselves well on foreign territory, and 'modified Wiltshire wisdom' was introduced in good measure to the confines of Swindon, Eastleigh, Brighton, Ashford, Doncaster and Darlington!

Nos 8400-79 and 8500-59 ordered on behalf of the Railway Executive Committee were regarded as being on loan for the duration of the war, after which they were to be absorbed into LMS stock. Nos 8705-8772 were actually built for the LNER, appearing in 1944-46 as LNER Class O6 Nos 3500-67. They were loaned to the LMS from 1947, not becoming London Midland Region stock until 1953.

With over 400 '8Fs' in home service at the end of the war, the class could be seen hauling their vital cargoes over large parts of the country from Scotland, through eastern and central England, the Midlands, South Wales and the West Country. Whether hauling ammunition for the fleet, constructional supplies for Wiltshire aerodromes, or coal and iron ore for Midlands industry the '8Fs' played a vital role in wartime transport.

Wartime on the LMS
The overwhelming use of the '8Fs' was on the Midland Division. The North Midlands coalfields supplied the North West, London and the West Midlands and locomotives from Kirkby, Westhouses, Toton, Stourton, Royston and Normanton were busily engaged with such traffic, as were those at 'staging point' depots such as Wellingborough, Leicester and Kettering. Cricklewood was a major '8F' base in the London area, as was Willesden, but the '8Fs' were practically absent from the Western Division in the early war years.

As well as coal, traffic in iron ore from Northamptonshire and Oxfordshire to the steel plants in the North East was very heavy. This reached the Midland at Bedford or Market Harborough, and almost any form of motive power could be rostered at times of pressure — two Midland 'Compounds' have been known. The '8Fs' avoided the need for double heading, and with their large tenders could work right through from Oxford or Bletchley to York, being remanned at Toton or Westhouses.

Another major traffic flow was that of ammunition and supplies from the North Midlands to Scotland for the fleets at Rosyth and Scapa. Initially, the Holbeck and Stourton '8F' allocations were augmented in 1940, and began to work to Carlisle. In 1941, long through workings to Scotland began, the Leeds engines alternating with others from Motherwell, Grangemouth, Polmadie and St Rollox, crews being changed at Carlisle.

During 1940, '8Fs' ordered by the War Department, which should have seen service in France, were put to work on the LMS and GWR. Although intended to become LMS stock at the end of the war, these engines, together with 51 existing LMS engines were requisitioned for use in Iran and Egypt in the summer of 1941.

A little known, short lived, '8F' foray was on to the Somerset and Dorset line. Three engines were sent to Bath late in 1940, but it was found that their braking characteristics with the heavy wartime loads on the steep gradients of the S&D were not as good as the native '7F' 2-8-0s, and the '8Fs' soon disappeared.

In the summer of 1942, Beyer Peacock and NBL delivered the last '8Fs' ordered by the War Department, not all of which could be sent abroad immediately. They were loaned to the LMS and ultimately became surplus to

LMS wartime orders — building and allocation

Built	Locomotive Nos	Period into traffic	First allocation
Crewe	8126-39	1/41-13/41	Toton 2, Leeds 7, Leicester 1, Nottingham 1, Heaton Mersey 1, Kettering 1, Normanton 1.
	8140-57*	1/42-13/42	Royston 1, Sheffield 1, Toton 2, Leeds 2, Kingmoor 6, Motherwell 6
	8158-75	1/43- 8/43	Motherwell 3, Kingmoor 5, Kirkby 1, Wellingborough 1, Toton 1, Royston 1, Nottingham 1, Willesden 5
	8301-16	10/43-13/43	Polmadie 1, Kingmoor 2, Westhouses 1, Leeds 2, Salop 3, Swansea 1, Perth 3, Sheffield 3
	8317-30	1/44- 5/44	Canklow 1, Perth 3, Motherwell 1, Polmadie 2, Swansea 2, Crewe S. 2, Speke Junction 1, Heaton Mersey 1, Toton 1
North British	8176-8225	2/42-10/42	Leeds 5, Coalville 2, Toton 10, Motherwell 6, Normanton 4, Royston 1, Wellingborough 4, Staveley 3, Nottingham 4, Canklow 2, Leicester 1, Westhouses 2, Derby 1, Sheffield 2, Kirkby 3
Horwich	8331-37	10/43-13/43	Polmadie 1, Kingmoor 1, Perth 2, Westhouses 1, Wellingborough 1, Swansea 1
	8338-81	1/44-13/44	Sheffield 1, Perth 2, Motherwell 1, Polmadie 1, Swansea 3, Crewe S. 9, Nottingham 3, Derby 2, Saltley 1, Royston 3, Westhouses 2, Stourton 1, Kettering 2, Normanton 1, Wellingborough 5, Toton 2, Willesden 3, Kirkby 2
	8382-99	1/45- 6/45	Toton 6, Derby 1, Kirkby 4, Westhouses 1, Normanton 3, Kettering 3
	8490-95	7/45- 8/45	Saltley 1, Kettering 1, Wellingborough 1, Staveley 1, Westhouses 2

*8143 carried 'Crewe 41' plates, 8146 'Crewe 42'.

WD requirements, entering LMS stock in 1943. In the meantime, their Westinghouse brakes and WD livery provided an unusual sight on the LMS until removed and replaced by LMS livery by 1944.

Deliveries from Crewe and NBL in 1941/42 were almost exclusively to the Midland Division. Motherwell, Kingmoor and Polmadie had their first '8Fs' in 1941 for the through workings to Leeds, while Kettering gained some 2-8-0s for iron ore and steel traffic at Corby. New ground was broken in September 1942, when No 8216 of Derby appeared on a northbound freight at Forres — a foretaste of the excellent work the '8Fs' were to do in the Highlands. Hellifield and Lancaster gained '8Fs' at this time for the heavy oil and coal traffic between Heysham and Yorkshire. In the North West the class was rarely seen, apart from the Heaton Mersey engines. Toton engines could be seen in Birmingham — often in the company of S&D '7F' 2-8-0s at Saltley — but only Northampton and Willesden on the Western Division had '8Fs' on their books.

Early in 1943, Grangemouth received Nos 8148-52 which replaced '4F' 0-6-0s on long haul work. With both Crewe and Horwich turning out the '83xx' series, the Scottish allocation was considerably expanded. Edinburgh acquired Nos 8160/61, whilst Motherwell engines began working to Aberdeen, and they sometimes penetrated as far south as Cricklewood. Grangemouth now had turns to Aviemore, Aberdeen and Carlisle, whilst Perth began to acquire the first of a substantial allocation.

In England, the Southern Railway began to deliver the first of the Railway Executive Committee-ordered 86xx series to Willesden, and the '8Fs' began to work once more to Crewe and the West Midlands. Shrewsbury and

WD Locomotives loaned to LMS 1940, returned 1941

Shed Code	Depot	Locomotives
1A	Willesden	8230/35
	Northampton	8228/46/97
18A	Toton	8232/33/34. WD 316/17
19A	Sheffield	WD 312/405
4A	Salop	WD 426/27. 8227/29/31/36/45
20A	Leeds	8247-51/54-56/58-60/98/9
	Royston	WD 324/26
	St Rollox	WD 423

WD Locomotives loaned to LMS 1942, into LMS Stock 1943

Shed Code	Depot	WD Locomotives
12A	Kingmoor	549-55
15A	Wellingborough	559/65
15B	Kettering	623
15C	Leicester	570
16A	Nottingham	566/69
18A	Toton	561-64/68, 407 (8293)
18B	Westhouses	560/67
20A	Leeds	558/71
27A	Polmadie	556/57, 604, 620/21
28A	Motherwell	602/03/15/16/18

These locomotives became LMS Nos 8264-85. WD Nos 602 (8079), 603 (8024), 604 (8080), 615 (8069), 616 (8078), 618 (8085), 620 (8088) and 621 (8093), requisitioned in 1941, reverted to their original numbers.

Swansea received some of the '83xx' series for work on the Central Wales line. WD 2-8-0s and 2-10-0s were tried here in 1944, but were unpopular and the '8Fs' reigned supreme. Both here and on the Highland line, their work with heavy trains on the long, steep banks was highly praised. Their oil-fired brethren in Iran were doing even greater work.

During 1944, both Crewe, Horwich and the SR works were delivering '8Fs' and in March the Western Division gained allocations at Crewe South and Speke Junction. They were soon busy over Shap on through freights to Carlisle and Glasgow. On the Midland Division, the already large allocation had been steadily expanded since 1942, one visitor to the Erewash Valley in 1944 describing it as being 'full of "8Fs" '. Life for the 2-8-0s in those years was hard; delays were interminable and the engines were sometimes on the road for days without servicing. Frank Mellor was transferred as a young Fireman from Buxton to Cricklewood from 1944-46 and recalls the situation:

'The "8Fs" took the full Garratt loads, so big fires were essential. The trains were kept on the move as far as possible and there was no room for a poor steaming engine. Problems arose when bombs were dropped on the track, and delays amounted to hours on end. In exceptional circumstances, engines had to be dragged off their trains with their fires a mass of clinker, very little steam and hardly any water in the boilers having been stuck for 24 hours in the same place. Sometimes, engines went for a week in extreme cases without having their fires cleaned properly. Life was certainly tough for the locomotives and their crews'.

Occasionally, in the chaotic wartime situation, the LMS was not beyond 'poaching' other company's '8Fs'. In January 1944, No 8416 spent some time on the Midland Division and had previously been seen marauding on the Great Central line. No doubt the Oxley Foreman had some difficulty in tracing his missing engine!

It was in the summer of 1944 that the '8Fs' began to establish a reputation as a passenger locomotive. They had a fair turn of speed, and could cope quite well with heavy loads on the wartime schedules. Once steam heat was no longer needed, they appeared quite frequently on Glasgow-Aberdeen workings in lieu of 'Black Fives', and also on the Highland line where some were fitted with tablet catchers. Soon the 2-8-0s were working turn about with the 5MTs on an almost regular basis. Not to be outdone, Swansea was also using its 2-8-0s on Central Wales passenger work.

In August, Brighton delivered the last of the REC-ordered '8Fs', No 8704. Unusual depots to acquire '8Fs' about this time were Dawsholme, Belle Vue and Dumfries. The latter had three or four until they were lost to Carlisle Kingmoor early in 1945, presumably for main line relief work as they were not officially allowed on the Stranraer line. During 1945 new deliveries continued from Horwich, mostly to the Midland Division, whilst the Dawsholme allocation moved to Kingmoor. In the Southwest, Bristol Barrow Road was seeing an increasing number of '8F' visitors, and Saltley had a permanent '8F' presence once more.

The cessation of hostilities found the Stanier 2-8-0 allocation on the LMS greatly increased from the 126 there had been at the start of the war, with 303 engines on the Midland Division, 68 on the Western Division, and 56 in Scotland. The class now had an important role to play in the postwar recovery, in a world that was to be an increasingly uncertain one for Britain's railways.

SR-built Stanier '8F' locomotives — building and allocation

Built	Locomotive Nos	Period into traffic	First allocation
Eastleigh	8600-9	2/43-11/43	Willesden 6, Toton 2, Kirkby 1, Staveley 1
	8650-60	11/43-13/43	Westhouses 1, Kingmoor 1, Carstairs 3, Willesden 6
	8661-62	6/44	Westhouses
Ashford	8610-12	4/43- 8/43	Willesden
	8618-24	10/43-13/43	Leeds 1, Stourton 1, Westhouses 2, Carstairs 1, Perth 1, Willesden 1
	8671	13/43	Sheffield
	8672-74	1/44- 4/44	Toton 1, Swansea 1, Crewe South 1
Brighton	8613-17	7/43-12/43	Willesden 1, Nottingham 1, Toton 1, Kirkby 1, Carstairs 1
	8625-49	4/43-13/43	Willesden 12, Nottingham 1, Toton 3, Leeds 2, Kirkby 1, Staveley 1, Carstairs 1, Kingmoor 1, St Rollox 2, Perth 1
	8663-70	2/44- 7/44	Staveley 1, Swansea 2, Nottingham 1, Heaton Mersey 1, Leicester 1, Saltley 1, Normanton 1
	8675-78	4/44- 6/44	Nottingham 1, Heaton Mersey 1, Royston 1, Wellingborough 1
	8679-80	13/43	Willesden 1, Sheffield 1
	8681-8704	1/44- 7/44	Toton 5, Canklow 1, Staveley 1, Shrewsbury 2, Swansea 3, Nottingham 3, Crewe South 1, Derby 2, Heaton Mersey 1, Leicester 1, Royston 2, Normanton 1, Kettering 1
	7651-75	6/44- 9/44	Mexborough 15, March 3, Aberdeen 2, Heaton 5, Dunfermline 1

'8Fs' on the Southern

The Southern Railway was primarily a passenger line and had no long-term use for large numbers of 2-8-0s. However, there were times — principally in the preparations for D-Day — when the SR did need heavy freight power and this was usually provided by WD 2-8-0s. There had been a very brief '8F' incursion into SR territory late in 1940, when LMS Nos 8251-55 (WD Nos 325-29) spent a couple of weeks working from Feltham. They were quickly transferred to the GWR in South Wales, before despatch abroad.

Although the Southern was adamant that it did not want any '8Fs', it did agree to build them for other railways on behalf of the Railway Executive Committee. Early in 1943, Nos 8600/01 appeared from Eastleigh Works sporting builders plates which read 'LMS built 1942 SR'. Naturally, the new engines were run in on Southern territory, and No 8600 was seen several times on Eastleigh to Bournemouth freights before being handed over to the LMS in a special ceremony at Charing Cross.

The engines appeared from the three Southern works in a rather haphazard fashion totally out of sequence with the number series. However, by the end of 1943 they were being turned out at the formidable rate of about 10 per month, 128 engines being produced in just 15½ months for both the LMS and LNER — an unprecedented rate of construction for an 'electric' railway. There was some help with boiler construction, as shown in the accompanying table, whilst those locomotives built for the LNER

(Class O6) were fitted with the LNER's standard 'Wakefield' mechanical lubricators rather than the 'Silvertown' type.

Newly constructed locomotives were worked away on SR freights via Southampton and Salisbury to the LMS and LNER, many Willesden engines reaching their new depot on transfer freights from Norwood Junction. The LNER locomotives were often similarly handed over at Neasden.

'8Fs' from the GWR continued to be frequent visitors to the Eastleigh and Southampton area with freight for the docks via the Didcot, Newbury & Southampton line or via Salisbury, but they were never regularly used on the Southern itself.

Wartime on the GWR

The first '8Fs' to work on the GWR between December 1940 and September 1941 were WD engines, ordered for service in France, but diverted instead to the LMS and subsequently loaned to the GWR. They were recalled in 1941 for service in Iran and Egypt. About 22 engines were stationed at Severn Tunnel Junction, Newport, Cardiff, Llanelly, Neath and Landore. Many parts of the GWR system were to see Stanier '8Fs' over the ensuing 25 years, but this initial allocation worked mainly between South Wales and London via the Severn Tunnel or Gloucester on heavy mineral work.

As has been recorded, the GWR had considerable reservations about having to build only '8Fs' for heavy

Boilers constructed to REC orders

| Built | Sent To | | | | | | | Total |
	Doncaster	Darlington	Swindon	Ashford	Brighton	Eastleigh	Crewe	
Gorton	1	4			5			10
Doncaster	29							29
Darlington		26						26
NBL				4	11	3	2*	20
Swindon			74					74
Brighton				5	44	4		53
Eastleigh			6	5	10	12		33
	30	30	80	14	70	19	2	245

*Two NBL boilers sent to Crewe (used on Nos 8174/5) to replace two Crewe boilers sent to Eastleigh (for Nos 8600/1)

GWR-built Stanier '8F' locomotives — building and allocation

Built	Locomotive Nos	Period into traffic	First allocation
Swindon	8400-26	6/43-12/43	Swindon 3, St Phillips Marsh 7, Didcot 3, Newton Abbot 3, Southall 1, Laira 1, Oxley 6, Exeter 2, Old Oak Common 1
Swindon	8427-64	1/44-12/44	Laira 1, Oxley 9, Newton Abbot 2, Taunton 2, Penzance 1, Croes Newydd 1, Chester 1, Birkenhead 1, Old Oak Common 3, Exeter 1, Didcot 1, Reading 3, Worcester 2, Newport 2, Cardiff 3, Tyseley 1
Swindon	8465-79	1/45- 7/45	Severn Tunnel Jct 2, Pontypool Rd 4, Newport 1, Cardiff 3, Tyseley 1, Reading 2, Paddington 1, Oxley 1

freight work, but there must surely have been some compensation in the name Stanier, and some LMS practice was absorbed in the design of the subsequent 'Modified Hall' and 'County' classes. Nos 8400/01 were turned out of Swindon in June 1943, sporting LMS livery, but without smokebox numberplates and with numbers painted on the bufferbeam instead in the very best GWR tradition.

The new locomotives were run in on local freights to Didcot, and then on through workings to London. Swindon, Didcot and St Phillips Marsh (Bristol) received the first examples, and they could be seen on a variety of duties to South Wales, Plymouth, Shrewsbury, the Midlands and Southampton. Subsequent deliveries were to Newton Abbott, Laira, Southall and St Phillips Marsh, until November when Oxley received an allocation. The class could therefore be seen at work on practically all the principal GWR routes. Early in 1944, Exeter and then Taunton received allocations, but more interesting was the despatch of No 8435 to Penzance, allegedly to help with the broccoli traffic. She spent 14 months on all types of freight work between Penzance and Tavistock Junction before being transferred to Laira.

In 1944 the railways were busy with preparations for the invasion of Europe, and massive freight trains were needed for military and airfield construction traffic. The '8Fs' worked on all the principal GWR main line and cross-country routes in the West Country and also on routes to the south coast ports, including the heavily graded Didcot, Newbury & Southampton line on which Bristol and Didcot engines did sterling work. The GWR enginemen acknowledged no peers to the Churchward '28xx', but they could find a good word for the '8Fs':

'They had a lot of Swindon in them, and they looked like an updated '28xx', so we forgave the left hand drive, 'pop' safety valves, and the injector handles which sometimes needed a coal pick to open them. They would steam and run well — we found we had a part Great Western locomotive after all'.[1]

The Stanier locomotives had now become established at Old Oak Common, Reading, Croes Newydd, Chester and Birkenhead, being frequently involved on top link work with the '28xxs'. Early in 1945, there were substantial numbers at Bristol, Old Oak Common, Tyseley, Newport, Cardiff, Severn Tunnel Junction, and Pontypool Road. Worcester had acquired two in September 1945 and the class was clearly involved in the heavy freight traffic from the West Midlands to the Channel ports. Parcels and empty coaching stock work was also tackled, and on August Bank Holiday Monday 1945, No 8433 worked the 'North Mail' the 11.05 Plymouth-Manchester, as far as Exeter. Clearly the engines were very much part of the GWR wartime scene and a visitor to London on 30 December 1945 described the situation as 'More like Toton than Old Oak Common' with 15 '8Fs' on shed.

The last GWR-built engine, No 8479, was delivered to Reading in August 1945. Transfers back to the LMS started in July 1946 with Nos 8453/54/55 from Oxley. Replacements for the '8Fs' were generally WD 2-8-0s which were almost universally disliked on the GWR. At Oxley, the replacements were '72xx' 2-8-2Ts — a very

retrograde step from the viewpoint of cab comfort. In the autumn of 1947, the departure of No 8467 from Severn Tunnel Junction and No 8477 from Old Oak Common left the GWR without any '8Fs'. They were to return in 1955.

'8Fs' on the LNER

The LNER was a reluctant user of '8Fs', and at first showed no great disposition to have large numbers of them; it took care also to run a series of trials against its own freight locomotives before taking substantial numbers of '8Fs' into traffic. No 8510 was the first locomotive to appear from Doncaster in June 1943. No 8500 which was next, did not appear from Darlington until February 1944. Much more rapid progress was made from mid-1944 onwards when both Doncaster and Darlington began quantity production, No 8559 finally appearing in September 1945.

In the meantime, the LNER had been persuaded to purchase 68 '8Fs', which were destined to become Class O6. The first, No 7651 appeared from the Southern Railway's Brighton Works in June 1944. In only 14 weeks, 15 others rapidly followed. Darlington continued the series with No 3125 in September 1945 (allocated numbers now being 3100-67 in anticipation of the 1946 renumbering scheme), Doncaster building Nos 3148-67. The last locomotive, No 3147, was delivered in October 1946, just as the first of the '85xx' series were returning to the LMS. In 1947, the 'O6s' were further renumbered 3500-67.

The new 2-8-0s were sorely needed on the LNER, where many Gresley locomotives were long overdue for shopping. The '8Fs' were allocated to depots dealing with heavy wartime traffic, and LNER enginemen were soon giving them an enthusiastic reception on a wide variety of duties — heavy mineral, merchandise, express freight, empty stock and even the occasional passenger job came their way.

In 1943 No 8510 first worked from Doncaster on main line freights to Newcastle. In October she moved to Tyne Dock, working regularly to Neville Hill, having some unusual pilots in the shape of 'C7' Atlantics over the steep grades to Wetherby. Doncaster had other '8Fs' for running in purposes, and these worked over the East Lincolnshire line through Louth, and on the Great Northern & Great Eastern joint line via Lincoln and Spalding with freights for Whitemoor. March had its own '8Fs' which worked mostly to Temple Mills and the London Docks. The class was not often seen on the GN main line out of London, but in May 1944 No 8513 ran trials against 'O1' No 6244 on New England to Ferme Park workings. Early in 1946, No 3150 was similarly tested against the rebuilt 'K5' 2-6-0. Ardsley depot acquired '8Fs' Nos 3154-58 from Mexborough in May 1946 to work LNER trans-Pennine freights diverted via Standedge during the relining of the Woodhead tunnels.

On the Great Central, Gorton gained No 8511 in March 1944 for trials over Woodhead against the first Thompson 'O1' No 6595. By early 1945, Gorton had 15 and they had replaced the GC 'O4s' on the principal mineral workings to Wath and Immingham. In May 1946, Gorton lost its '85xx' locomotives to Immingham as a means of keeping down their mileage before transfer back to the LMS. The Mexborough engines ranged widely to Annesley, Banbury, Woodford, Immingham and Whitemoor, on duties

LNER-built Stanier '8F' locomotives — building and allocation

Built	Locomotive Nos	Period into traffic	First allocation
Doncaster	8510	6/43	(Doncaster), Tyne Dock
	8511-25	2/44-12/44	Gorton 5, Heaton 4, Thornton Jct 4, Doncaster 1, March 1
	8526-39	1/45-10/45	Heaton 1, Dunfermline 3, Gorton 3, St Margarets 1, March 5, Thornton Jct 1
	3148-55	10/45-12/45	Heaton 2, Mexborough 5, Dunfermline 1
	3156-67	1/46- 6/46	Mexborough 8, Dunfermline 3, Heaton 1
Darlington	8500-09	1/44-12/44	Heaton 4, March 2, Thornton Jct 2, Gorton 2
	8540-42	12/44	Heaton 2, Darlington 1
	8543-59	1/45- 7/45	Aberdeen 1, Dunfermline 1, St Margarets 2, Heaton 4, Gorton 5, March 3, Thornton Jct 1
	3125-34	9/45-12/45	March 1, Dunfermline 2, Mexborough 4, Heaton 3
	3135-47	1/46-10/46	Dunfermline 4, Heaton 6, Thornton Jct 1, Mexborough 1, March 1

For LNER Nos 7651-75 (3100-25) see SR building programme

Maximum LNER allocation of Stanier '8F' locomotives — October 1946

Shed Code	Depot	Total
MAR	March	16
MEX	Mexborough	27
IMM	Immingham	16
ARD	Ardsley	5
TDK	Tyne Dock	4
HTN	Heaton	28
STM	St Margarets	8
DFU	Dunfermline	15
THJ	Thornton Jct	9

formerly taken by the 'O4s'. The southern area of the GC also saw newly delivered Southern built 'O6s' running in from Neasden where they helped to relieve the perpetual engine shortage.

In the Northeast Heaton had a substantial allocation of 15 '8Fs' and 17 'O6s' by June 1946. They were used on long-haul mineral and merchandise freight to Edinburgh and sometimes to York, Hull or Leeds. Crews were changed at Marshall Meadows or Tweedmouth. Tweedmouth men got the worst of the job between these two points, sometimes taking a whole shift to cover the distance, coping with badly clinkered fires before handing over to St Margarets or Heaton crews. The NE men took to the '8Fs' on these jobs, and many considered them better timekeepers than the 'O1s' on fitted and semi-fitted work.

In June 1944, '8F' No 8514 ran trials from Tyne Dock against 'O1' No 6334 in the Durham coalfield, No 8512 being later substituted due to collision damage. In July 1946, the Heaton engines went to Tyne Dock to reduce their mileage, and York became host to a batch of 17 'O6s' in April 1947.

The '8Fs' possibly did their best work in Scotland where their versatility was quickly recognised, and they took over a great deal of fitted freight work previously handled by 'K3' 2-6-0s. By 1946, the majority of through goods traffic was '8F' hauled in the Edinburgh area, and in addition the '8Fs' could be seen on empty stock, troop specials and some passenger work as well. The engines were based at St Margarets, Thornton Junction, Dunfermline and Aberdeen. They carried the main burden of freight traffic between Edinburgh, Fifeshire and Aberdeen, worked to Heaton, and to Carlisle over the Waverley route. Their use on Fife-Glasgow coal traffic and long distance work gave the footplate crews a distinct improvement in performance and comfort over the North British 0-6-0s previously used.

Naturally, the NB men had some qualms about working on what were termed 'Caley' locomotives, but the '8Fs' were justifiably popular as three St Margarets enginemen recall:

Charlie Meacher: 'They were free running, and well liked on fitted freights, despite indifferent injectors. They could digest the rubbish we had for coal and still maintain pressure on the testing gradients of the Waverley Route — the sharp exhaust on the banks was an audible indication that the "8Fs" thrived on hard labour, and their smallish wheels were no barrier to reasonable speed, especially south of Berwick'.

George White: 'I felt like a turncoat, admitting a "Caley" engine to be one of my favourites. They had a good cab, would steam well, and were more economical than many LNER types. This mattered at the end of a 15-hour shift coming back from Dundee to Edinburgh diverted via Dunfermline and the Alloa Bridge. We once waltzed a 16-coach troop special from Berwick over Grantshouse in spanking form. My driver was amazed to find at Portobello we had used only 1,500gal'.

Donald Chalmers: 'They usually rode well — what a change from jousting around on the "Austerities"! The firing technique was different from the LNER parallel boilers, and we had to get used to carrying a much higher level of water. With a large fire at the back, tapering to the front, firing "little and often" with proper use of the firedoor flap and deflector plate they would steam very well indeed, but No 8519 could hardly pass a signalbox without a blow up. One night we left Innerwick with a huge, bright fire and the boiler full to the whistle, blowing off hard. The pressure came back steadily all the way up to Grantshouse and I never had the injector on. We went over the top with 100lb on 'ie clock and the water almost out of sight'.

The loaned '8Fs' were recalled to the LMS between the autumn of 1946 and July 1947. The LNER also agreed to take surplus WD 2-8-0s in exchange for their own Class 'O6' locomotives which were transferred on loan to the LMS from October 1947. The last to leave, No 3554, was transferred as a BR locomotive in January 1948.

1 *Memories of a GW Fireman*, Harold Gasson; Oxford Publishing Co.

The Postwar Years (1945-1950)

This was an unusual and eventful period for the '8Fs'. Swindon and Horwich had turned out their last examples by September 1945, and the last engine to be built (LNER 'O6' No 3167) appeared in the following June. Within 12 months the LMS was in the happy position of receiving 208 modern and reliable freight locomotives from the GWR and LNER. A highly successful experiment with oil burning was followed by a rather less happy experience with water softening. The 1948 Locomotive Exchanges brought a little disappointment, but rapidly changing regional boundaries meant that the '8Fs' could be seen in some very unexpected places in these years. As 1950 dawned, 39 battle-weary survivors were repatriated from

abroad, some of them destined to soldier on until the bitter end in 1968.

The end of the war saw a gradual reduction in the '8F' allocation in Scotland — Belle Vue, Rose Grove and Crewe South receiving former Scottish engines, many from Perth. The most important change however was the mass infiltration of '8Fs' — the majority from other railways — on to the Central Division. No fewer than 101 '8Fs' were drafted in over 15 months, and whilst L&Y enginemen were exchanging their 0-8-0s of both L&Y and Midland origin for a superior product, LNER and GWR men were getting surplus WD 'Austerities' in exchange.

The accompanying table shows the extent of change in the motive power on Trans-Pennine routes, but notice also that substantial numbers of engines went to the Midland and Western Divisions. The Midland Division successfully rid itself of the 'Austin Seven' Class 7F 0-8-0s, and also the LNWR variety which were never popular with Midland men. The L&Y 0-8-0s were extinct by 1950, and their place as 'second string' units was taken by the 'Austin Sevens'. The '8Fs' in the meantime appeared in greater numbers on the Western Division (although large numbers of LNWR 0-8-0s remained here until the early 1960s). Buxton received its first 2-8-0s in September 1946. In the West of England the new Saltley allocation began working regularly to Bristol via both the main line and the Redditch branch.

Many of the engines from the LNER were delivered in steam, and renumbered at the receiving LMS depots — Peterborough for March, Farnley Junction for York and Canklow for Mexborough. Some sheds on the Central Division used their 2-8-0s on passenger work — No 8416

Allocation of Stanier '8F' 2-8-0s on 10 November 1945 LMS Depots			16A	Nottingham	19	20B	Stourton	6
			16C	Kirkby	38	20C	Royston	13
			16D	Mansfield	2	20D	Normanton	19
Shed			17A	Derby	6	20F	Skipton	1
Code	*Depot*	*Total*	17C	Coalville	3	20G	Hellifield	3
1A	Willesden	35	18A	Toton	53	20H	Lancaster	1
4A	Shrewsbury	11	18B	Westhouses	26	21A	Saltley	3
4B	Swansea	14	18D	Staveley	19	28A	Motherwell	15
5B	Crewe South	4	19A	Sheffield	8	28B	Edinburgh	2
8C	Speke Junction	4	19C	Canklow	6	28C	Carstairs	4
15A	Wellingborough	32	19D	Heaton Mersey	12	29A	Perth	27
15B	Kettering	5	19G	Trafford Park	2	31A	St Rollox	2
15C	Leicester	10	20A	Leeds	16	31D	Grangemouth	6

LNER Depots			GOR	Gorton	10	STM	St Margarets	8
Shed			HTN	Heaton	19	TDK	Tyne Dock	1
Code	*Depot*	*Total*	MAR	March	15	THJ	Thornton Jct	8
DFU	Dunfermline	6	MEX	Mexborough	22			

GWR Depots			EXE	Exeter	5	SVT	Severn Tunnel Jct	3
Shed			GLO	Gloucester	4	TYS	Tyseley	2
Code	*Depot*	*Total*	LA	Laira	3	Total in service 10 November 1945		612
BHD	Birkenhead	1	NA	Newton Abbot	3	12 locomotives built by LNER 1946		12
BL	St Phillips Marsh	12	NPT	Ebbw Jct	5	39 locomotives purchased by BR 1948		39
CDF	Cardiff Canton	5	PDN	Old Oak Common	8			
CHR	Chester	2	OXY	Oxley	15	3 locomotives purchased by BR 1957		3
CNYD	Croes Newydd	2	PPRD	Pontypool Road	3			
DID	Didcot	2	RDG	Reading	5		Total	666

Allocation of Stanier '8F' locomotives returned from the LNER and GWR 1946-48

Period	Ex-LNER, allocated to:	Ex-GWR, allocated to:
10/46- 1/47	Midland Division: Sheffield 1, Canklow 1	Midland Division: Saltley 5, Toton 2, Canklow 2, Royston 1
	Central Division: Rose Grove 1, Lostock Hall 1, Wakefield 8	Central Division: Lostock Hall 1
1/47- 6/47	Western Division: Shrewsbury 1, Crewe South 5	Western Division: Willesden 3, Crewe South 7, Shrewsbury 2
	Midland Division: Leicester 1, Kirkby 1, Derby 1, Canklow 1, Royston 5, Westhouses 4, Staveley 2	Midland Division: Kirkby 4, Derby 2, Toton 2, Canklow 3, Royston 6, Saltley 2
	Central Division: Huddersfield 2, Lostock Hall 3, Wakefield 8	Central Division: Huddersfield 5, Goole 4, Sowerby Bridge 5, Bolton 8, Bury 5, Lees 3
6/47- 1/48	Western Division: Crewe South 4 (26)*	Western Division: Crewe South 8
	Midland Division: Leicester (2), Staveley (2), Royston 1	
	Central Division: Aintree (2), Accrington (1), Rose Grove (6), Lostock Hall (2), Lower Darwen (1), Wakefield 7 (7), Huddersfield (2), Mirfield (3), Farnley Junction (4), Newton Heath (8), Agecroft (1), Bolton (1), Bury (2)	

* Numbers in brackets indicate ex-LNER 'O6'.

of Bolton putting in some electrifying work on the four-coach 17.16 Manchester Victoria-Bolton local service.

Oil Firing

In October 1946, 245 '8Fs' were proposed for conversion to oil burning in view of the near impossibility at the time of obtaining good quality locomotive coal. Twenty-six major depots were to be equipped for oil and it is a tragedy that there was subsequently insufficient foreign exchange available to buy the oil and the scheme collapsed. However, 11 '8Fs' were converted, the first being No 8696, which was also the last engine to be reconverted to coal burning in April 1949. The engine was tested with different types of oil burner on the Midland lines coal traffic early in 1947, and all concerned were delighted with the performance. A typical run is detailed below, but operating conditions (in one of the worst winters of the century) were appalling, with up to five hours being lost on some trips between Nottingham and Kettering.

Firing Instructor K. Stokes commented on the tests as follows:

1. Average fuel consumption 6-7gal/mile. Oil with a calorific value of 18,000BTUs compared with best coal of about 14,000BTUs, almost unobtainable in 1946.
2. The Burner Steam Pressure gauge was invaluable in balancing the steam and oil supply to the burner. With ideal atomisation, black smoke was almost non-existent and far better than that from the best managed coal burner.
3. Careful co-operation between Driver and Fireman could produce much more precise engine management than was possible with coal firing, with little blowing off.
4. Footplate conditions were much cleaner with no coal dust or ash, especially when running tender first. Steaming was as good as with coal, but was not impaired by the build up of clinker. Absence of ash and clinker gave a 30% improvement in availability by eliminating disposal duties. The absence of secondary air entering the firebox through the firehole was better for tubes and stays.
5. The fuel temperature in the tender was critical. This had to be 70°F minimum, otherwise poor steaming and oil consumption resulted. Ideally, 120-160°F was needed. The heater connection between engine and tender needed to be more reliable. It was essential to close the dampers as soon as steam was shut off to avoid rapid cooling of the firebox.
6. Best results (a consumption rate of between 5.2 and 8.7gal/mile) were obtained with the 6-groove, shouldered-lip burner. This was easier to light than the shoulderless-lip burner, and could be turned down to mark 7, even to mark 5 with care. It gave very little popping and the firedoor was never visibly hot.
7. Generally oil burning offered a vast improvement over coal burning; it was cleaner, more efficient, and steaming was just as good as with coal.

The locomotives converted to oil burning were Nos 8064/79, 8191, 8269/73, 8370/85/86, 8606/53/96. Most reverted to coal in 1948.

05.15 Nottingham-Wellingborough — 8 January 1947
Locomotive: Stanier '8F' 2-8-0 No 8696, oil fired (short lip without shoulders to burners)
Load: 45 wagons (coal)

	Booked time	Actual time	Boiler pressure lb/ sq in	Reg	Cut of %	Water	Oil in tanks gal	Burner position	
Beeston Sidings	5.15	5.48	225	1/3	50	Full	1,340	19	Signal check 6-0 to 6-1½
Mansfield Junction	5.26	6.21¾	227	0.4	40	Full	1,325	19	Signal check 6-8 to 6-14½
London Road Jun	5.34	29	—	Full	35	Full	1,300	28	
		36	220	Full	40	Full	1,290	32	
Edwalton		38½	225	Full	30	Full	1,285	35	
			225	Full	35	Full	1,260	35	
Plumtree		45	225	Full	35	Full	1,260	32	
Tunnel			227	Full	35	Full	1,250	32	
Widmerpool	6.5	55½	225	Full	35	Full	1,240	32	
Upper Broughton			222	Full	30-28	Full	1,235	32	
Old Dalby			222	Full	28	Full	1,210	35	
Grimston		7.14		Signal stop		Full	1,205	10	
		25				Full			
Melton	33	53				Full	1,190	20	Signal check 8.1 to 8.20
Brentingby (A)	40	8.22½				Full	1,160	10	
(D)	47	9.6				Full	1,140		
Saxby	57	9.23	224	3/4	30	Full	1,130	20	
Wymondham			225	F	40	Full	1,100		Signal check 9.32 to 9.34
Wissendine		41¾	225	0.4	45-25	Full	1,090	25	Adverse signals up to Oakham
Ashwell	7.10	52½	220	F	45-35	Full	1,075	25	
		57	220	1/3	25-35			18	
Oakham	7.18	10.10½		Cst			1,030	14	

Steaming was excellent on the ruling gradient of 1 in 200 up from London Road Junction to Old Dalby with the engine worked at 35% cut off and full regulator. Continuous signal checks were experienced after this point.

Two-thirds of the firehole door were red hot at Old Dalby after the heavy working up the bank but this is not so bad as the heating experienced with the lipless burner.

The burner flame could be maintained, when standing, with the oil regulator set at 10.

The sides of the firebox were sprayed with oil when standing with a low flame and this feature will be watched on future tests.

Water Treatment Experiments
Although the LMS had spent considerable sums installing water treatment plants, the real value of this work in terms of reduced boiler maintenance had not been fully quantified. In 1946 an experiment was mounted involving 50 '8Fs' stationed at Toton and Wellingborough, which were given overhauled boilers fitted with manual blowdown valves so that the sludge and suspended matter could be released from the boiler virtually as it was formed. The engines were to work only between Toton, Brent and Willesden under carefully monitored conditions, and were easily recognised by a large 'X' painted on the cabsides.

In the difficult weather and operating conditions of 1946/7 it only proved possible to reach a maximum of 83% of water treated and softened instead of the 95% required. Also, the method of preventing the formation of hard scale which the blow down could not remove was not discovered until after 1950. The trend was then towards individual TIA water treatment on the locomotives themselves. Under British conditions, the discipline required for effective lineside water treatment schemes was not attainable, and eventually, the experiment lapsed.

By 1947/48 the '8Fs' were infiltrating the Western Division in significant numbers. Mold Junction and Widnes had gained allocations early in 1948, whilst a visitor to Abergavenny in late 1947 found five on the shed; they were to do extensive work on the North and West route in subsequent years.

In Scotland the '8Fs' were tending to drift back to England, but in the autumn of 1948 three were surprisingly sent on loan to Corkerhill where freight locomotives were virtually unheard of. Equally unusual was the allocation of five '8Fs' to Carlisle Canal, now technically a London Midland shed (12B). The engines were frequently seen at Newcastle and Edinburgh until transferred elsewhere in 1952.

The 1948 Locomotive Exchanges described in detail elsewhere found the '8Fs' occupying a respectable position amongst the locomotives tested, but not the commanding one that many LMS supporters had expected. It would seem that the real success of the '8F' design lay in its rugged reliability rather than its thermal efficiency. The latter, although perfectly satisfactory, was not as good as that of some of the other competitors.

Globetrotters Return
In the spring of 1948, 39 locomotives were recovered from the Middle East and arrived at Birkenhead docks in various states of disrepair, having spent six hard years in the desert wastes of Iran and Egypt. They were all dragged to Crewe and stored in a very sorry state until the works could deal with them.

Ten engines, Nos 8012/16/18/20/39/45/46/61/77/94, had been requisitioned from the LMS and retained their old numbers; the others were renumbered within their original series, namely Nos 8246-63 (North British) and Nos 8286-92/94-7 (Beyer Peacock). They were returned to traffic at the rate of about eight per month between August and December 1949. Their initial allocation was to Crewe South, but most quickly moved elsewhere.

In 1948/9 the London Midland Region of British Railways began to receive surplus WD 2-8-0s which had been stored since the end of the war. The Scottish Region also had some, together with a batch of WD 2-10-0s which replaced the '8Fs' at Grangemouth and Motherwell. The '8Fs' at Perth and Edinburgh also disappeared, and by the spring of 1949 none remained on the Scottish Region except at Carlisle Kingmoor; however, Wellingborough's No 48003 was reported to have been seen heading north through Dunkeld on 8 January. The Central Division also lost its '8Fs' to both the Western and Midland Divisions — they were not to return in significant numbers until steam's final retreat to the Northwest in the 1960s.

Northwich depot acquired its first '8F' No 48340, in April 1949. Previously, Heaton Mersey engines had been stabled at this depot to work the ICI limestone hoppers to Peak Forest, but these trains were now to be worked from Northwich. The 2-8-0s were instantly very popular, and in marked contrast to the 'J10' 0-6-0s which covered the rest of the shed's freight work! The gusto with which the Northwich men and their '8Fs' tackled these 1,000-ton trains was to speak volumes for the reputation of the class, and had much to do with the eventual preservation of No 8233. Other depots to receive '8F' allocations in 1949 were Stafford, Nuneaton and Longsight, together with

Low Moor and Birkenhead (LMS) in the autumn.

On the Midland Division, Kirkby engines began to work through to Frodingham instead of handing over to LNER locomotives at Swinton Junction, and Swansea engines began to work fill in turns to Cardiff now that the LMS depot had been incorporated into the Neath Motive Power District. Another long-standing practice established since at least 1945 was that of a Swansea engine working to Burton via Stafford and the Lichfield spur, which continued through to the early 1960s. In the summer of 1950, '8Fs' went to Warrington, and Bescot gained an allocation at the expense of Swansea, part of a move to replace the '8Fs' at both Swansea and Shrewsbury by WD 'Austerities'. However, Stanier engines from the Central Division were drafted back to Central Wales by the end of the year.

On the Eastern Region, the LMS depot at Peterborough was closed and No 48074 found itself at New England for a time. Also on the ER, Colwick WD 2-8-0s took over from the '8Fs' on the mineral workings to Willesden via the GNR/LNWR Joint Line through Melton Mowbray, although Northampton '8Fs' were to be prominent on this line with iron ore traffic until its closure in the early 1960s. The late 1940s also saw the beginning of through workings from the Midlands to the Northeast, with Leeds engines working to Darlington and those from other North Midlands depots to Tees-side with traffic for the steel industry. As evidence of the strange things which could sometimes happen in these years, a concluding story relating to the Christmas traffic of 1949 is best left to Driver George Whyte of Edinburgh:

'We were standing at Tweedmouth, working back to Edinburgh, and I was amazed to see our train come in behind a shining Newton Heath '8F', just out of Darlington shops. Heaton turntable was under repair, and No 48707 had been "borrowed" to work north. We had a full load and old McCann, my driver, was beaming all over. What an engine! She ran like a coach and steamed her head off with the firedoors open. We had a marvellous run home over the frozen countryside. Joe said it was the best run he'd ever had, and the warmest!'

No 48707's record card shows that she was shopped in December 1949, but at which works is uncertain. Horwich is more likely than Darlington, but the possibility of Newton Heath using an ex-works engine to Leeds or York is very likely, with the North Eastern Region 'borrowing' her to work further north.

LMS DAYS

Right:
No 8000, now allocated to Wellingborough, heads a long, loose-coupled freight towards London through Elstree in 1938. The engine has yet to receive vacuum brakes, and the three-link coupling on the front bufferbeam should be noted. *Photomatic*

Right:
Vulcan built No 8035, then less than a year old and looking remarkably clean for a freight locomotive, heads a long mixed freight on the Midland Main Line at Elstree in 1937.
Wethersett Collection/ Ian Allan Library

Centre right:
The highly unusual combination of '8F' No 8111 (C39) and Cauliflower 0-6-0 No 8450 heads a local train near Old Milverton between Leamington and Coventry in 1939. Nos 8111 was allocated to Warwick shed at the time. *J. A. G. Coltas*

Below:
A scene which thoroughly captures the atmosphere of the Midland Division and its newly introduced '8Fs'; No 8006 (C35) makes a spirited passage through Kettering with a mixed train of coal and iron ore wagons on 16 April 1938.
M. F. Yarwood

Top:
No 8018 (C37) heads north through Berkhamstead with empty coal hoppers returning from the LMS Stonebridge Park power station to Toton yard, on 19 August 1939.
H. C. Casserley

Above:
No 8007 (C35) rolls a return Holwell Iron Works-Stanton Gate trip working past Nottingham MPD in the late-1930s.
Real Photos

Left:
Heaton Mersey's No 8017 (C36) winds a Great Rocks Junction-Northwich limestone hopper haul round the connecting spur between the CLC Stockport-Glazebrook line and the route to Chester at Skelton Junction, in April 1939. *W. Potter/ V. Forster Collection*

Above:
Northampton's No 8116 (C39) trundles a long train of mineral empties, probably destined for Toton, along the West Coast Main Line near Bletchley on 7 June 1939.
H. C. Casserley

Below:
Symbolic of the new order in LMS locomotive affairs; T. G. Hepburn's fine study of No 8035 (VF36) at Nottingham waiting to depart with a heavy coal train for the south, shows clearly the neat and business-like lines of Stanier's '8F'. 25 September 1937.
T. G. Hepburn/Rail Archive Stephenson

Left:
Locomotives for War; a posed publicity photograph taken at Toton in about March 1942. Featured are Nos 8133 (C41), 8001 (C35), WD 544 (NB42, Iran, Egypt and BR No 48261), 8105 (C39), 8198 (NB42) and 8199 (NB42). The WD engine, complete with air brake, is on loan to the LMS before conversion to oil firing and shipment abroad. *BR(LMR)*

Below left:
The typical industrial surroundings of the Nottinghamshire coalfield against the background of which the '8Fs' did so much of their work. No 8028 passes Royston with an up coal train shortly before the war. *Real Photos*

Above:
WD No 317 (NB40) nears Market Harborough on 7 June 1941. Still in early WD livery, she had been loaned to the LMS from November 1940 to January 1941, and again from April to June, awaiting shipping space to Egypt. She became Egyptian State Railways No 883 in 1944.
A. G. Wells

Below:
No 8196 (NB42) trundles a wartime ammunition train out of a loop 'somewhere on the LMS'. The clue to the cargo is in the reporting number 'FM'. *Ian Allan Library*

Above:
No 8318 (C44) rolls an Inverness-Perth freight homeward through coniferous forests surrounding the Highland Main Line near Pitlochry in September 1945.
C. Lawson Kerr/V. Forster Collection

Below:
Edinburgh's No 8160 (C43) heads a long, partially fitted, up freight near Kingsknowe on 19 June 1945.
J. L. Stevenson

SOUTHERN

Above:

No 8681, built at Brighton in 1944, is seen in works grey livery. Note the absence of relief valves on the front cylinder covers. The location is thought to be Brighton works. *'8F' Society Collection*

Below:

The last of the SR-built 2-8-0s for the LNER, Class 'O6' No 7675, is seen newly completed from Brighton in September 1944. Subsequently LNER Nos 3100 and 3524, and BR No 48729, she was withdrawn in December 1967. Note the blacked out cab windows, and black out tarpaulins. *BR (LMR)*

GWR

Above:
Familiar place, unfamiliar face: an unidentifiable '8F' heads an up freight along the sea wall away from Teignmouth, in about 1944.
D. J. Montgomery Collection

Centre left:
No 8469 (S45) of Pontypool Road drifts a train of Oxfordshire iron ore for South Wales along the Cotswold Edge at Bishops Cleeve in April 1945. The stains on the boiler are an indication of leaking top feed joints — the engine was then virtually brand new.
W. Potter/V. Forster Collection

Left:
No 8428 (S44) takes water at Reading West Junction with a westbound haul of timber, towards the end of the war. *M. W. Earley*

LNER

Above:
LMS No 8510, ordered by the Railway Executive Committee, built at Doncaster in June 1943 and on loan to the LNER. The engine had built up balance weights with cast iron inserts, with lead inserts on the driving axle, giving nil reciprocating balance. The solid tender wheels, were a feature of many LNER-built '8Fs'.
Ian Allan Library

Below:
A travel stained 'O6' No 3537 (DR46), heads an up goods along the East Coast main line near Darlington on 23 August 1947. The LNER is also having trouble with top feed joints. *Photomatic/A. Biwandi Collection*

POSTWAR LMS

Above:
With the war over, and peacetime austerity to follow, No 8195 (NB42) trundles a load of Nottinghamshire coal southwards through the Erewash Valley at Langley Mills on 7 May 1946. Traditional small, grease-lubricated, private owner wagons still hold sway, soon to be replaced by the BR 16-ton steel variety. *H. C. Casserley*

Below:
Recently transferred from the GWR, LMS No 8460 (S44) of Bury approaches Mytholmroyd on the Calder Valley main line with a hefty Trans-Pennine coal haul in 1947. *Wethersett Collection/Ian Allan Library*

Above:
No 8713 (ex-LNER 'O6' No 3508, BN44) of Rose Grove heads westwards from Sowerby Bridge with coal from Yorkshire, presumably destined for North Lancashire via Copy Pit. Twenty years later, the '8Fs' saw out the end of normal steam working on these duties.
D. J. Montgomery Collection

Below:
No 8281 (NB42) heads a Wellingborough-Brent mineral haul at Radlett in 1947. The 'X' on the cabside indicates that she is only to work between Toton, Brent and Willesden as part of the Water Treatment Experiment. The operating lever for the Manual Blowdown can be seen on the RH side of the firebox. Originally WD No 568, and destined for duty abroad, she entered LMS stock in December 1943. *Real Photos (15960)*

Above:
Generations apart: a contrasting combination of 'Super D' 0-8-0 No 9060 and '8F' No 8136 (C41) double-heads a train of mineral empties over Bushey troughs in the summer of 1947. Both locomotives appear to be at least skimming the water with their scoops.
F. R. Hebron

Centre right:
A recent arrival from the GWR depot at Croes Newydd, Crewe South's No 8422 (S43) heads an up semi-fitted freight through Rugeley in September 1947. *V. Forster Collection*

Right:
An up through freight, headed by No 8156 (C42) completes the descent of Beattock bank and rolls through Beattock station on the Caledonian main line on 22 July 1947.
J. L. Stevenson

5
Service Abroad

War Department Orders and Specification

When war broke out in September 1939, it was initially thought that many locomotives would be needed for service in Europe. Large numbers were to be requisitioned from the British railways, and many new heavy freight locomotives would also be required. The Stanier '8F' was the most modern locomotive available, and had the proven reliability and wide route availability which would be essential abroad.

The fact that Mr R. A. Riddles, the LMS Vice-President, was also Director of Transport Equipment for the War Department also certainly influenced the choice of the '8F' as the early Ministry of Supply standard design for overseas. In December, orders were placed for 240 locomotives for use in Europe — 100 (WD Nos 300-99) from North British, 100 (WD Nos 400-99) from Beyer Peacock, and 40 (WD Nos 500-39) from the Vulcan Foundry.

The LMS design was modified where possible, to allow the use of materials which were not also used in munitions production, and to include items necessary for operation under conditions which were very different to those in Britain. These were as follows:

1. Frames of $1^1/_{16}$in mild steel instead of 1in-thick high tensile steel.
2. Connecting rods shortened by 5in, piston rods and slidebars correspondingly lengthened to facilitate piston ring changing. This was applied also to later builds of '8Fs'.
3. Mild steel for coupling and connecting rods instead of manganese molybdenum steel.
4. Solid pins and plain bushes instead of needle roller bearings for motion bushes — this change was applied to all wartime construction.
5. Springs of carbon steel instead of silico-manganese steel.
6. Two live steam injectors. (WD-requisitioned locomotives and WD locomotives which worked on the LMS had an exhaust steam injector.)
7. Westinghouse automatic air brake. Steam brake retained for engine and tender. Side couplings, Flaman speedometer, steam heating, 'commode' handles for shunters, wheels turned to 'French' profile, water scoop omitted.

The first locomotive, WD No 300, emerged from the North British Co's Hyde Park Works in Glasgow in May 1940, and presented a strange appearance in grey livery with large yellow lettering, complete with air brakes, side couplings and other non-British features. Despite the speed with which the engines had been produced, events in Europe had moved even more quickly and already Hitler's Panzer units were poised to sweep across France. Within weeks the Dunkirk evacuation had occurred and the new locomotives were no longer needed. The Vulcan Fountry order was cancelled, and those from North British and Beyer Peacock reduced to 60 and 40 locomotives respectively. The new locomotives were loaned to the LMS — actually becoming part of LMS stock in 1940 — with the intention that they would become LMS property at the end of hostilities. Further service abroad was not then envisaged.

WD Nos 300-18 and some Beyer Peacock locomotives were completed to the full 'French' specification. These were sent to Crewe works where LMS livery was applied and their wheels were turned to British profiles. Additional modifications included the replacement of the right-hand live steam injector by an exhaust steam injector, and the removal of the air brakes (although the graduable steam brake was retained and a standard LMS driver's brake valve fitted), steam heating and shunter's commode handles. WD Nos 300-37 became LMS Nos 8226-63, and the Beyer Peacock engines, WD Nos 400-14, became LMS Nos 8286-8300. (LMS Nos 8226-8325 were allotted to WD Nos 300-59, 400-49, No 415 actually running trials as LMS No 8301 before shipment abroad.)

Twenty-five locomotives were loaned to the GWR in South Wales, whilst, as previously described, the remainder were put to work on the LMS, in LMS livery. Seven locomotives, which had been earmarked for service in Egypt early in 1941, were returned to the LMS for a few months whilst awaiting shipment, and these ran in WD livery as WD Nos 312/16/17/24/26/27 and 405. In February Beyer Peacock-built WD No 421 was sent to the Longmoor Military Railway as a training locomotive where it was named *Wolfe*, but it had been shipped to Iran by October.

Early in 1941, there was great concern about the security of British interests in the Middle East. Egypt was threatened from Italy, and there was anxiety about oil supplies from Iran where there was some German influence. Further north, it was essential to retain good relations with Turkey to ensure her neutrality. Early in 1941 some Beyer Peacock engines were sent direct to Egypt, followed by the despatch of WD Nos 338-59 to Turkey, and the recall of many locomotives from the LMS and GWR for service in Egypt. This was to herald the

Stanier '8F' locomotives built for War Department

Builder/works Nos	Running Nos	Built	Initial allocation	Final disposal
North British 24600-37	WD 300-337	May-October 1940	LMS 38 (GWR 13), Egypt 17, Iran 21	Lost 2, Egypt 16, Iran 1, Iraq 2, Italy 1, Israel 4, BR 9, scrapped by WD 3
North British 24638-59	WD 338-359	October 1940-March 1941	Turkey 22	Lost 7, Turkey 15
NB 24668/9 NB 24730/2	WD 360-361 WD 362-364	May-December 1941	Egypt 2, Iran 3	Egypt 2, Iran 1, Iraq 1, BR 1
North British 24673-707	WD 365-399	May-December 1941	Egypt 11, Iran 24	Lost 2, Egypt 16, Iran 2, Iraq 1, Israel 5, Italy 1, BR 6, Jordan 1, scrapped by WD 1
Beyer Peacock 6980-7000	WD 400-420	July-December 1940	LMS 15, (GWR 12), then Egypt 8, Iran 13 (1 not sent)	Lost 2, Egypt 6, Iran 1, Iraq 1, Israel 4, Italy 1, LMS/BR 1, BR 4, scrapped by WD 1
Beyer Peacock 7001-19 7034-43	WD 421-449	January 1941-January 1942	Longmoor 1 and LMS 1, on loan, then Egypt 14, Iran 15	Lost 6, Egypt 11, Iran 2, Iraq 1, Italy 2, BR 7
North British 24708-29	WD 500-521	October-December 1941	Iran 22	Egypt 5, Iran 2, Iraq 4, Israel 5, Italy 2, BR 3, scrapped by WD 1959 1
North British 24670-2	WD 522-524	May 1941	Turkey 3	Turkey 3
North British 24733-41	WD 540-548	January-February 1942	Iran 9	Egypt 2, Iran 2, Iraq 2, Israel 1, Italy 1, BR 1
North British 24742/3/6/9/ 52/5/8/61/4/7/70/ 3/6/9/82/5/8/91/ 4/7, 24800/3/6	WD 549-571	February-August 1942	Turkey 23 (only 2 sent)	LMS/BR 8264-81 =21, Turkey 2
	WD 572-622		Requisitioned from LMS	
North British 24809	WD 623	August 1942	Turkey 1 (not sent)	LMS/BR 8285=1
				Total: 208

introduction of the '8Fs' to operations in an entirely unfamiliar environment.

In June 1941, Germany attacked Russia and, in addition to the Arctic Convoys, Britain established a further supply route to her new-found ally via the Persian Gulf and the recently opened Trans-Iranian Railway to the Caspian Sea. British and Russian troops took control in Iran, and in September the War Cabinet directed the LMS to release 50 '8Fs' to meet the desperate need for locomotives on the new route. This also effectively entailed the recall of all the WD engines which were on loan to the LMS. A total of 51 LMS '8Fs' was actually requisitioned — this included one extra to compensate for WD No 407 (LMS No 8293) which was undergoing repairs following the Dolphin Junction accident. Whilst many WD engines were sent immediately to Iran, the requisitioned engines were shopped, fitted with over-hauled boilers if necessary, and prepared for overseas service at Crewe, Swindon and Eastleigh. Oil burning equipment was fitted, as were air brakes, graduable steam

	Nos	Built	First Allocation	Final Disposal
Crewe	8012-16	January-April 1937	Iran 13	Egypt 1, Iran 4, LMS 1943 1, WD 2 (scrapped 1954 and 1959) BR 1948 4, BR 1957 1
Vulcan Foundry	8028, 8030-2, 8034, 8038-49, 8051/2, 8058/9, 8061/6/8/9, 8071/2/7/8/9, 8080/5-8, 8091/3/4	July 1936-February 1937	Iran 38	Lost 4, Egypt 3, Iran 7, Italy 7 Israel 4, LMS 1943 7, BR 6

Total 51

Wartime Overseas Allocation

Destination	Allocated	Lost at sea	Arrived	Not sent
Turkey (1941)	25	7	18	—
Egypt (1941)	52	10	42	—
Iran (1941-2)	158	6	143	9
Turkey (1943)	24	—	2	22
	259	23	205	31 (LMS 1943)

Postwar allocation

LMS and/or British Railways	73
Turkey	20
Egypt	62
Italy	15
Israel	23
Iran	22
Iraq	12
Scrapped by WD	9
Lost at sea	23
Total:	259

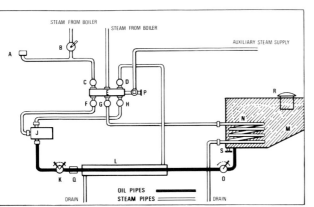

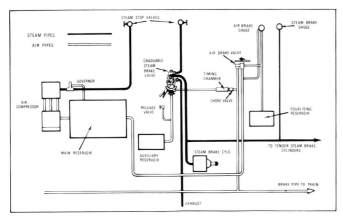

Fig 13
Arrangement of oil firing equipment.
Key: A Blower; B Main steam blower control valve; C Auxiliary steam blower control valve; D Preheater steam control valve; E Steam manifold; F Burner steam control valve; G Tender steam heater control valve; H Burner cleaner steam control valve; J Burner; K Oil supply control valve; L Preheater; M Oil tank in tender; N Steam heater in oil tank; O Oil supply stop cock; P Auxiliary steam supply stop cock; Q Sieve in pipe line; R Sieve in oil tank; S Sludge drain.

Fig 14
Air brake system — War Department '8Fs'.

brake valves and the LMS two-cone vacuum ejector in place of the single-cone type fitted to many of the locomotives.

So urgent was the situation in Egypt and especially Iran that 228 '8Fs' were shipped abroad in the space of only 15 months from January 1941. 23 engines failed to reach their destinations because of a series of maritime disasters. Ten were lost in the Mediterranean en route to Egypt, six on the voyage to Iran (four as deck cargo on the SS *Pentridge Hall* being cut loose during a severe gale in the Irish Sea), and seven en route to Turkey. Of the latter, four were lost when the *Berhala* was torpedoed near Freetown and the remaining three when the *Jessmore* was in collision west of Ireland. Locomotives in the holds of the *Pentridge Hall* were so badly damaged that they had to be returned to NBL for repairs. These engines — LMS Nos 8024/69/78/79/89/5/8/93 — together with the last batch built by NBL were not eventually needed in Iran and, after running in WD livery for a while, became LMS Nos 8264-85 in 1943.

Those locomotives sent abroad were to add an epic chapter to the history of the '8F' class, operating under conditions which were amongst the most hostile imaginable for a steam locomotive and, especially in Iran, climbing over gradients which made Shap or the 'Long Drag' to Ais Gill pale into insignificance. At the end of the war, many were scattered throughout the Middle East, and although only those in Turkey are still in service, long-stored survivors can be found in Iran and Iraq — gaunt reminders in this technological age of the struggle with steam to keep the 'back door' to Russia and the Western Desert open during those crucial dark days of World War 2.

Iran 1941-1963
The need to open up a second supply route to Russia was so urgent that 143 '8Fs' were pitched into a totally foreign

Fig 15
Gradient Profile of the Trans
Iranian Railway from Bandar
Shahpur to Bandar Shah.

*Reproduced by courtesy of
the* Railway Gazette
International

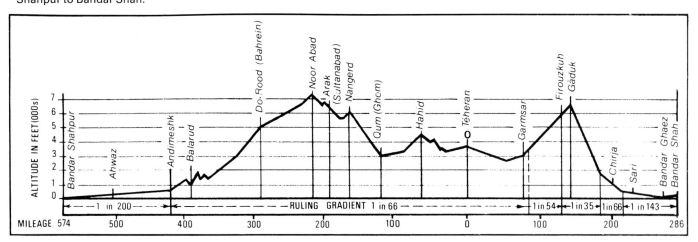

operating environment in the short space of only 12 months. The first batch of locomotives sailed in September, reaching Iran early in December, along with 70,000 tons of Welsh coal. With 190 Railway Operating Company, Royal Engineers working like Trojans, the engines were put into traffic at the rate of one every 36 hours.

From the Persian Gulf, the Trans-Iranian railway crossed 150 miles of featureless desert to Andimeshk. Over the next 200 miles came mountain country of extraordinary severity as the line climbed through gorges, over viaducts, and through spiral tunnels to a summit of 7,650ft at Noor Abad in the Luristan mountains. The gradient was at 1 in 67 for miles on end, with constant curvature. There was then a fall of nearly 4,000ft in 225 miles on similar gradients to Tehran, a total distance of 570 miles. Northwards, in the Russian operated sector (to which some '8Fs' were loaned), there followed 65 miles at 1 in 83 through the Elburz mountains, and a precipitous descent at 1 in 36 through spiral tunnels to the Caspian Sea at Bandar Shah. With daytime temperatures of 135°F in the desert, 70°F of frost in the mountains at night and terrible problems of water supply, the achievements with steam on this line were quite incredible.

The railway was completed in 1938, but was in no condition to take the traffic needed to supply Russia. Only two daily trains were run, plus the thrice-weekly Tehran mail — an average daily shipment of about 200 tons. By 1942, the Royal Engineers had raised this to 1,530 tons. South of Andimeshk, the '8Fs' working to the ports of Khorramshahr and Bandar Shahpur were diagrammed to take 850 tons. Over the 'Hill', they took 350 tons singly or 700 tons double-headed — no mean task on such gradients.

The first 27 coal burning '8Fs' were rushed to Persia to work south of Andimeshk — coal firing over the 'Hill' was an impossibility on a regular basis. This released the Iranian Ferrostaal 2-8-0s and 2-10-0s to work over the mountains, until supplemented from February 1942 by later '8F' arrivals which had been converted to oil-firing and fitted with air brakes before shipment. The '8Fs' entered traffic as follows:

Locomotives	Dates into traffic	Specification
41100-41127	Dec 41-Feb 42	Coal burning, vacuum and steam brakes. Ex-service on LMS and GWR. Three direct from manufacturers.
41128-41145	May 42-Dec 42	Coal burning, vacuum and steam brakes. Nos 41138-41 steam brake only. Some ex-service with LMS, some direct from builders.
41150-41246	Feb 42-Aug 42	Oil burning, air brakes, vacuum and steam brakes. Direct from builders or requisitioned.

Nos 41128-145 were put into service after May 1942 as the traffic increased, but mainly for shunting duties. Many of the coal burners were subsequently converted to oil-firing, but air brakes were also mandatory for working over the mountain sections.

As a totally British design, the '8Fs' stood up well to the Iranian conditions. They were very good mechanically — only one hot axlebox was reported amongst the 150 locomotives. They also stood up well to the fairly frequent derailments and minor collisions, the former often the result of their free running and steady riding on indifferent track! There were problems however, some associated with the locomotives themselves, but the majority due to the problems inherent in the operation of steam locomotives under such difficult circumstances. The wartime notes of Maj C. R. L. Rice, based at Tehran workshops reveal that the situation at times, was very dificult indeed.

One set of spares for every five locomotives had been promised, but only five sets materialised and improvisation on a grand scale was needed. For example, such unlikely practices as the use of unpicked tennis netting as the cord for injector cones, the casting of mudhole door joints in locally made moulds, and the cutting of firehole baffle plates from scrap steel plates were commonplace. There was a limit to what could be done by cannibalising one engine to keep another running, and when No 41142 was found to be minus every cab fitting this had to stop.

The Iranian water was poor and deposited large amounts of scale and dirt inside the boilers. These could not be cleaned properly because spare boiler tubes were not available for eight months. Washouts were needed at intervals of as little as 1,400 miles, and tube life was much less than under British conditions.

The water also caused gauge glass bottoms to corrode to knife-edge thickness after about 10 days service. A novel solution was the despatch of a bomber loaded with 10,000 glasses with a terse note that no more would be forthcoming! Feed water temperatures in the tenders were critical since these could reach 104-106°F and the failing point of the injectors was 103°F; tropical injector cones sent out from England cured this problem.

A problem found on the oil burning locomotives was that the superheater elements burnt out on the return bends. Designed for coal burning conditions, they were of only 0.08in thickness, whereas the elements on the Iranian Ferrostaal locomotives were 0.13in thick. The '8F' elements were shortened by 1ft to reduce the chance of them burning in the intense heat of the oil flame at the firebox end. A special unit had to be set up to carry out this work, but in the meantime a reserve supply of spares was set up by the blanking off of three elements on each locomotive.

The most serious problem was the failure of the British-converted oil burning locomotives to steam on the long gradients. The mixture of firebox air and oil was incorrect for perfect combustion at high outputs, when a serious deficiency of air arose. (WD No 387 had been tested successfully between Crewe and Wigan, but the Iranian steaming conditions were much more onerous!) The solution was to increase the free area of the air ports in the fire pan by 50%, as had been done on those coal burners which had been converted to oil in Iran and which always steamed well.

As evidence of the demanding nature of the locomotive work the following report by Capt R. Gardiner is given of No 41157 taking a 450-ton train between Tehran and Ghom:

'Anjivaland to Koupang is nine miles of intermittent 1 in 67 to 1 in 83 with severe curves. The engine was worked on full regulator and 40-50% cut off throughout, and steam was easily maintained with little smoking at the chimney top. Twice the engine actually blew off against the injector. I maintained only about 1in of water in the glass because of the danger of priming, and the water had to be fed in as quickly as it was being used. Fixing down the blastpipe cap allowed the engine to gain steam against the live steam injector, and for 20min the pressure was held at 215lb against the exhaust injector. The pressure never fell below 210lb. However, the tendency to prime on an engine only 125 miles after washout was disturbing, and stressed the need for constant water changing and washing out'.

Conditions in Iran were exceedingly harsh for both locomotives and their crews:

Driver W. F. Brain: 'Due to pressure of work, maintenance was difficult and the engines were often long overdue for washout. The class eights were small for the job, but somehow they kept going, blasting up the 1 in 67 gradients with the crew choking to death in the many tunnels, often struggling to maintain the water in the boilers because of the feed water temperatures affecting the operation of the injectors. Heat, sand, gradients, oil fumes — conditions were far worse than anything we had ever experienced in England'.

Despite all the problems, locomen were in general very pleased with the performance of the '8Fs' in this cruel environment:

Driver Don Speight: 'The "8Fs" and their crews worked together in every sense of the word. We spent almost all our waking hours at work — they were grand engines'.

Driver Ernie Rowe: 'How I remember the terrific heat in the summer of '42, booking on at Ahwaz "Loco" and battling across the desert expecting anything and everything in the way of trouble. With such a remarkable machine under us, we had few doubts about eventually winning through'.

Maj C. R. L. Rice: 'Within its class, the Stanier "8F" was undoubtedly a superb locomotive'.

The 'flavour' of the Trans-Iranian Railway is perhaps best illustrated by the recall of three incidents; firstly the derailment of the now preserved No 8233 (41109) by a camel, necessitating a long and difficult recovery without a crane; secondly, the occasion of a British driver, going 'hell for leather' through a sharp curve, taking a run at the 1 in 67 gradient ahead, with the Iranian banker in the rear braking hard to reduce the speed; the train stretched out, a coupling broke and half the train piled up against the tunnel entrance at the bottom of the bank. Lastly, how shortly after the American take-over in 1943, two '8Fs' (WD Nos 331 and 389) collided head-on on the single track to Khorramshahr. In thick mist, one train had completely missed a crossing point — the breakdown train was despatched before the accident happened!

Early in 1943, the United States Army Transportation Corps and their diesel locomotives took over main line operations in Iran south of Tehran. The period of steam operation with the '8Fs' and US 2-8-2s had been a short and glorious one, but the problems of operating an intensive steam service through such terrain were immense. In 1944, 50 '8Fs' were transferred by sea to Egypt and overhauled for further service in Italy and Palestine. Four locomotives (WD Nos 331/37/89, 406) were subsequently scrapped, including the two involved in the collision previously described. Many others were not repaired for several years largely due to the extent of the boiler repairs required. Washout periods were often extended in Iran with sometimes dire effects on the fireboxes. Two engines, WD Nos 508 and 583, were not repaired until they were returned to England in 1952. Of the overhauled locomotives, Italy and Palestine received 15 each, whilst five went to work on the Haifa-Beirut-Tripoli line until returned to Palestine in 1945. All 50 locomotives had been renumbered in the Middle East Forces 9350XX series, but this was soon replaced by the 1944 scheme in which 70,000 was added to the original WD numbers.

At the end of the war 93 '8Fs' remained in Iran. Subsequently 59 locomotives were moved by rail through Iraq, Syria and Turkey to Palestine and Egypt. On the metre gauge section to Baghdad, the locomotives were carried on special eight-axle articulated transporter wagons; in spite of this, the axle loading was still 2 tons over the official limit, and the trains were restricted to a maximum permited speed of 15mph. Each train carried four locomotives and tenders.

Twenty-two engines remained in Iran; these were certainly still at work in 1957 but had been replaced by diesel traction by 1963. As recently as 1977 a forlorn row of '8Fs' could be seen stored in a very neglected state at Ahwaz. Peeling paint on one cabside poignantly revealed the numbers '8014'. At the time of writing, circumstances would seem to preclude preservation, but could another Iranian '8F' eventually materialise to join No 8233?

Turkey 1941-1985

In 1939, the Turkish Railways had placed locomotive orders with British builders, which could not be fulfilled because of wartime restrictions. It was essential that good relations were maintained and, as a palliative, the Turks were persuaded to accept Stanier '8Fs' instead. WD Nos 338-59 appeared with right hand drive and air brakes in 1940-41 in black livery embellished with the TCDD star and crescent on the tender, and with the WD number on a small plate below the TCDD markings on the cabside.

Shipment took place early in 1941, but seven were lost at sea. WD Nos 522-24 were sent out in June as partial replacements. Although small by Turkish standards, the Turks liked the 'Churchills' and clamoured for more, WD Nos 552 and 554 following in June 1943. Being a normal export order, the engines were sent out in a dismantled state and were re-erected in the Turkish workshops at Sivas under the direction of LMS engineer Mr R. G. Jarvis in some secrecy, since Turkish neutrality had to be protected. A comprehensive workshop manual was also produced, copies of which are still doing useful service on at least one British preserved railway today.

Originally the engines were coal burners, although some may have been converted for oil burning later. The absence of drop grates made the engines unsuitable for extended main line work in a country where coal supplies were often of doubtful quality, and TCDD Nos 45151-70 have spent most of their lives scattered throughout Eastern Turkey on local trip and shunting work. The Turkish engines have remained the longest lived of the Stanier '8Fs'. Nine remained in service in 1985 — the only '8Fs' to achieve their intended operational lifespan of 45 years.

Italy 1944-1953

The Allied invasion of Italy began in September 1943. An armistice was quickly signed with the Italians, but the Germans wreaked vengence as they retreated northwards, systematically destroying the railway system and its locomotives. Major problems therefore abounded, the lack of locomotives being aggrevated by an acute shortage of coal. In 1944, 15 overhauled '8Fs' were transferred from Egypt to Taranto. WD Nos 70335/437/441, 514/20/48/85/89/94/95/98, 609/12, were oil burners; two coal burners, Nos 70334/408 were used on local work until converted for oil burning in 1946.

For three months from December 1944, five '8Fs' worked on the spectacular and severely graded Trans-Appenine line from Terni through Fabriano to Falconara. In conditions reminiscent of Iran, 900-ton block trains were hauled by five locomotives in any combination of British, American and Italian types (two at the head, three banking, with one spare to guard against failure) over the tortuous 10 miles at a gradient of 1 in 40 from Terni to Spoleto. Charlie Meacher vividly recalls the rather easier conditions between Falconara and Fabriano:

'Never faltering, the "8Fs" barked their way across this cavernous route of magnificent engineering. In the long tunnels we got on to the bottom footstep near the flow of air and hung on until that marvellous mountain breeze replenished our heaving lungs. The suffocating heat of the trapped oil fumes was almost unendurable.'

Mercifully, electrification was restored between Terni and Spoleto in February 1945 and such dramatic railroading became a thing of the past.

For the remainder of the war the '8Fs' worked turn and turn about with the American 2-8-2s and native Italian classes between Fabriano, Falconara and Ancona, and along the Adriatic coast to Rimini and Bologna. There were no speed records to be broken on the hastily repaired Italian railways, but the '8Fs' handled the 900-ton trains notably better than the native Italian locomotives. Rosters on the two coal burners were popular with footplate crews in that they presented an opportunity for scarce coal to be exchanged for local produce! Another comfort was the Thompson machine gun which was always handy in the cab.

At least two accidents involving '8Fs' are known to have occurred in Italy. One involved No 70548 which collided with a truck on a level crossing near Rimini in December 1944; the locomotive concluded its journey in a ditch with derailed wagons piled up around it. On another occasion, a member of the class was involved in a collision with a US 2-8-2 on the coast line. The American locomotive was apparently much more severely damaged than the British machine.

Injector performance remained a weak point with the '8Fs', and firemen lost much of the benefits from oil firing in constant adjustments to keep a decent level of water in the boiler. The FS (Italian State Railways) fitted the much more reliable Friedmann injectors to the engines, and many of them received the FS matt-black livery with brownish red wheels and frames.

Leave trains began at the end of 1944, running to Rome to connect with a sea passage to France. Few servicemen would understand the pent up emotion of one Midlands enthusiast as the familiar shape of the tender of No 70548 was seen backing on to his train at Rimini. The sight of No 70609 (alias LMS No 8072) standing on shed and still carrying a 16A Nottingham shedplate served only to intensify the sentiment!

From 1946, the 2-8-0s became FS Nos 737.000-015. The Italian crews were rather alarmed by their new mounts at first. The '8Fs' offered a degree of cab comfort which they had not previously experienced and also steamed so well that their safety valves were frequently lifting — a fineable offence in Italy for wasting fuel! Compared with the sluggish Italian designs they accelerated at unheard of rates, and came to be much appreciated.

In 1947, the '8Fs' were concentrated at Bari, in south eastern Italy where they worked northwest on main line freights to Foggia. In peacetime, greater attention had to be paid to axle loadings, and the '8Fs' were consequently unsuitable for many Italian lines. Being completely non-standard, the spares position dictated an early end for these locomotives despite their proven worth. All were withdrawn in 1953 and broken up shortly afterwards, many at Foggia shed.

Iraq 1945-c1973

At the end of the war, the railways of Iraq were still under British control, and between 1945 and 1948 12 surplus '8Fs' were transferred from Iran, travelling on metre gauge transporter wagons as far as Baghdad. Numbered 1421-32, the '8Fs' seem to have put in some good work on main line freight and important passenger trains, and also appear to have had a large influence on the design of the Krupp-built 2-8-0s introduced in 1956. The chassis of these locomotives was clearly almost identical to that of the '8F', although a large parallel boiler was employed rather than the taper variety. The '8Fs' remained at work until the early 1970s, but some long-stored examples were seen derelict at Baghdad in 1982 and may still survive.

Palestine and Jordan 1944-1974

After the removal of the Vichy French from Syria in 1941, it was decided to build a railway along the coast from Haifa through Beirut to Tripoli, thus completing the rail link from the Bosphorous to the Nile Delta.

Some very determined engineering by the Australian Royal Engineers saw the 140-mile line completed by December 1942. The single-track railway was blasted out of the coastal headlands and was not only picturesque, but also demanding in terms of gradients. Traffic was heavy; large tonnages of military supplies were sent north, while Syrian grain came south for shipping from Beirut for European relief. Robinson 'O4s' and diesels worked the line initially, but when these were concentrated in Egypt in 1944, five '8Fs' arrived from Iran after overhaul at 169 Workshops, Suez. By 1946, a total of 15 Stanier 2-8-0s were at work on this railway, and it is a pity that no photographs exist of them working along the Mediterranean coast where they were reliable and popular with their crews.

In 1945/6, a collection of 59 battle-scarred '8Fs' arrived from Iran at WD depots in Palestine and the Canal Zone. Maj W. Kirby recalls:

'The locomotives were covered in gritty sand which was very difficult to remove when mixed with Mazout oil spillage. Brass fittings had "disappeared" en route from Iran, and the boilers were in a very bad state, poor water and lack of regular washing out having taken a heavy toll. Fires from surplus Mazout had started below the fireboxes and spread to the axleboxes in some cases, causing the white metal bearing surface to run out, scouring the journals'.

The engines were dumped at Azzib, Sarafand and Jaffa until being taken into 193 Workshops at Jaffa for overhaul. After repairs, running-in trips were arranged over the Palestine Railways (PR) where, due to Israeli terrorist activity, the engines went out with machine guns prominently positioned on the cab roofs. About one engine per month was overhauled, after which they were put to work on the PR or sent across the Sinai Desert to the Canal Zone.

With the creation of Israel in May 1948, it was essential to move as many locomotives as possible to Egypt. Not all the ex-Iranian engines had been overhauled by then — hence the growing lines of incapacitated '8Fs' at 169 Workshops and elsewhere in the Canal Zone. Twenty locomotives remained within the boundaries of the new state and were absorbed by Israeli Railways where they were appropriately known as 'Class LMS' and continued working until replaced by diesels in 1958.

Of the 228 '8Fs' which went abroad on WD service, one remained unaccounted for until 1967. No 70372 had been abandoned at Tulkarm on the old main line between Haifa and Lydda in 1948 when this area became part of Jordan. Belated attempts were made to restore it, but these took place against the background of the 1973 Yom Kippur War. Too many parts were missing and regrettably this old warrior was scrapped in 1974.

Egypt 1941-1962

In 1941, the military situation in North Africa was potentially very serious. The British had driven the Italians out of Libya in 1940, but this had provoked a German/Italian offensive which threatened the whole of the Western Desert. The allies had a supply route some 230 miles long from the railhead of the Western Desert Railway at Mersa Matruh, 184 miles from Alexandria. There were no suitable seaports along this length and the whole route was vulnerable to air attack. Adequate supplies were essential, and in September 1940 New Zealand engineers began to construct the Western Desert Extension Railway to Tobruk. By June 1942, Belhamed, 15 miles from Tobruk had been reached, but the Fall of Tobruk caused a hasty evacuation back to El Alamein, 70 miles from Alexandria. Following the British victory at El Alamein in November 1942, 355 miles of railway were rapidly cleared and services restored to Tobruk with diesel traction in December. Later, as the water pipeline was extended westwards, steam working returned as far as Capuzzo, 43 miles short of Tobruk — two '8Fs' being allocated to El Hadra for the Western Desert passenger service.

It was into this new and hostile environment that the first '8Fs' were hastily thrust in the spring of 1941. Until June 1942, the Extension Railway was used seven days a week, day and night as 60-car, 2,000-ton trains wound their way through the desert wastes hotly pursued by the Luftwaffe. At one point 17 out of 23 '8Fs' on the railway were out of action due to cannon fire. Whilst the Me109s and 110s took 'pot shots' at the trains during the day, Ju88s and Heinkels bombed the trains and construction sites at every possible opportunity. Protection came in the form of anti-aircraft batteries mounted on the trains. More successful were the barrage balloons trailed from the leading wagon as the trains forged through the desert — they at least forced the cannon fire to take place from a greater distance where it was less accurate! Seven '8Fs' were equipped with armour protection consisting of walls of concrete 4in thick or steel plates to protect the boiler, cab and tender front. This added nearly 10 tons to the locomotive weight and caused severe rolling at speeds over 30mph, enforcing a 20mph speed restriction.

Life for the locomotives and their crews was just as hard as in Iran. Poor water caused tube failures on boilers only five or six years old, and many tubes had to be plugged until spares could be obtained. Temperatures in the desert were 130-135°F, whilst swirling sandstorms blew almost constantly out of the Sahara desert. Controls became too hot to touch, and sand caked on crewmen's faces making vision impossible. Trains stopped in the worst of the storms. Afterwards, fires would be re-lit, the motion and wheels would be hosed down with water via a long connection from the degging pipe, all moving parts would be oiled up and the train would set off into the pitch black desert night before the sandstorms returned at sunrise.

Under these conditions, motion wear was heavy, and complete remetalling was needed at 25,000-mile intervals. On a single round trip $^3/_{16}$in wear could develop on the crossheads. Substitution of bronze liners for the white metal bearing surface increased this to three trips, but the GC 'O4' with renewable slippers was a better maintenance proposition under desert conditions than the '8F'. Inevitably, the situation entailed heavy, hard and unpleasant work for the fitters under very hot conditions.

Water supply was a major concern. An '8F' used 60-80gal/mile, all of which had to be supplied by pipeline or tanker. Some steam-hauled trains carried 25,000gal of locomotive water. Coal supplies were also difficult, especially when coal became mixed with sand causing havoc with fire cleaning. According to one source sheets of glass were being taken out of the fireboxes[1]. Ultimately, all the '8Fs' in Egypt were oil burners.

The Western Desert line was fairly flat, apart from the start from Similla Junction where the line ascended the Fuka escarpment. Some brisk running was possible, one traveller noting a speed of 55mph behind an '8F' hauling a 510-ton train. With a 'Jimmy' inserted in the blastpipe the Egyptian crew tackled the Fuka bank in fine style. How did the '8Fs' fare overall? The New Zealand crews on the Western Desert Railway certainly thought highly of them.

Driver C. H. Gledhill: 'They were highly satisfactory, and most reliable prime movers. They passed the "acid test" working daily under the most ruggedly abrasive conditions'.

Elsewhere in Egypt, the largest freight locomotives were 2-6-0s, and when it was realised that the '8Fs' could time most Egyptian passenger trains as well, the Egyptian State Railways (ESR) hired all the '8Fs' displaced by diesels in the Western Desert. The engines were badly needed to handle the ever increasing military traffic in the Nile Delta operating from Gabbary depot, Alexandria. The ESR ultimately bought seven '8Fs' in 1942 (ESR Nos 850-56), 20 in 1943 (Nos 857-76), 13 in 1944 (Nos 877-89), and one in 1945 (No 890). One locomotive was damaged beyond repair in a collision, leaving 41 to be purchased by the ESR. Although the first '8F' arrivals in Egypt were painted in the early WD light grey livery with large yellow lettering, most engines were black with small 2in WD markings. All continued to carry their original smokebox numberplates. Those locomotives on loan to the ESR had their numbers painted on the cabsides in arabic numerals, the hire cost being £14,775 per locomotive.

The '8Fs' worked mainly from Cairo to Alexandria, Suez, Ismailia and Port Said, and on the Western Desert line to Daba, on both passenger and freight services. They were also used on the principal service across the Sinai Desert. In July 1942, the opening of the Firdan Bridge across the Suez Canal allowed the start of a Cairo to Haifa through passenger service. This route assumed greater significance after the opening of the HBT line in 1943. The US 2-8-2s were leaving Egypt in 1945 and ESR '8Fs' Nos 850 and 865 were specially overhauled at Abu Zaabal works to haul the 'Orient Express' — the 17.30 Cairo Main to Haifa via Ismailia, and the Firdan Bridge to Quantara, a distance of 120 miles. This was a heavy train, which was very popular with troops on leave and presented quite a severe test for a moderately sized locomotive. An example of No 850's work, timed by Capt P. Proud, is given in the accompanying table.

'The Orient Express' was a demanding duty, and there were times when the performance deteriorated dramatically. No 850 lost nearly seven hours on one trip in August 1945, persistently stalling due to a shortage of steam! In contrast, the '8Fs' did very well on the Cairo to Alexandria route where, with lighter loads, they took over from the Egyptian 2-6-0s, and had no difficulty in maintaining the 40mph schedules. The versatility of the '8Fs' had again been conclusively proved, and with further purchases from the WD in the 1950s, the ESR ultimately had 62 '8Fs' in stock. They were replaced by diesels in 1961/2.

Egyptian State Railways — 18.00 Cairo-Tel El Kebir 'Orient Express'

Locomotive: Stanier '8F' 2-8-0 ESR No 850
Load: 15 coaches, 685 tons

Distance miles		Sched Time min	Actual Time min sec	Average speed
	CAIRO		0.00	
0.8	Cabin 4	4	3.40	
3.0	Tawdeeb Cabin	7	8.15	33
4.1	Shubra	9	10.15	33
6.2	Mitnama BP	12	13.50	35
8.8	Qalyub Junction	16	17.45	39
12.4	Sudiyum BP	21	23.10	40
15.9	Qaha	26	28.20	41
20.6	Tukh	33	35.00	41
24.9	Sandanhur	39	41.20	42
27.9	BENHA	45	46.50	41
			0.00	(Dep 6 early)
2.8	Mimyet el Siba	7	7.30	35
7.3	El Azizya H.	13	15.55	38
18.2	El Zambalum	29	33.25	37
22.00	ZAGAZIG	36	40.30	(Arr 3 late)
			0.00	(Dep right time)
1.0	Cabin 5	4	4.00	
8.7	El Siva	15	17.55	39
14.8	El Mahgas BP	24	27.55	35
18.4	TEL EL KEBIR	30	34.20	

[1] Major E. Howell. Letter to author.

War Department Activities 1945-1959

In 1944, 50 surplus '8Fs' were transferred from Iran to the War Department in the Canal Zone. Thirty five were overhauled, after which 15 went to Italy, 15 to Palestine, and five to the HBT line. The remainder were set aside for later attention, four of these being scrapped, and two eventually returned to England for overhaul in 1952, whilst the others were put back into traffic either with the WD or on loan to the ESR.

By the autumn of 1946, with the addition of 59 surplus locomotives sent overland from Iran, the WD had 95 locomotives in the Middle East. Some of these were fit only for scrap, others were extremely run down after their exertions in Iran, and the remainder were either stored or on loan to local railways, the actual tally being: On loan to HBT 15, Palestine Railways 24, ESR eight, for scrap five, on WD lines or awaiting overhaul 43.

Not only could the WD not find work for such a large number of locomotives, it did not have the resources to overhaul them either, especially if heavy boiler repairs were needed. Following an inspection by Mr R. G. Jarvis, 39 locomotives were purchased by British Railways and brought home for overhaul in the spring of 1948. They arrived from the WD depots at Sarafand, Azzib, Jaffa and Suez in clusters of four (one engine in steam towing three others) and were shipped from Port Said aboard the well known Bel Line ships, specially fitted for transporting railway equipment. This operation had been preceded by a hurried evacuation of remaining WD equipment from Palestine on the declaration of the state of Israel in May 1948. As recorded, 24 '8Fs' were left in Israel, and in the summer of 1948 the locomotive position in Egypt was: ESR stock 41, and WD stock remaining in the Canal Zone 27 (11 were sold to the ESR from 1948-51, these being ESR Nos 841-9, 891/2).

The remaining WD engines were either stored awaiting attention, on loan to the ESR, or working WD military traffic on the ESR. All were under the jurisdiction of 10 Railway Squadron Royal Engineers whose headquarters was on the Adabiya to Ataka military railway. Overhaul facilities were available at 169 Railway Workshops, Suez, and it was here that a varied collection of cannibalised wrecks could be found, all of which were beyond immediate repair. The serviceable locomotives remained at work on the military railway itself, and also made forays on to the ESR, particularly to the docks and oil refinery at Suez. As a means of boosting morale, eight of the working locomotives were named after Royal Engineers who had won the Victoria Cross in the Crimean War. These were:

70320	*Lt W. O. Lennox VC*
70373	*C/Sgt H. McDonald VC*
70387	*Cpl W. J. Lendrim VC*
70395	*Capt H. G. Elphinstone VC*
70501	*Spr John Pirie VC*
70516	*Cpl J. Ross VC*
70574	*Cpl Leitcher VC*
70593	*Lt Graham VC*

The naming ceremonies were splendid affairs with full military ceremony and the engines looked magnificent. In Egypt, however, the political situation was becoming increasingly serious.

In 1950, agreement had been reached with the ESR to move military freight over the railway alongside the Suez Canal with WD locomotives and crews accompanied by an ESR pilotman. With national feeling turning against the British, WD activities were now largely confined to a zone stretching 15 miles on either side of the Canal. In October 1951, the treaty between Egypt and Britain was abrogated and running facilities over the ESR withdrawn. The British continued to run their trains, but Egyptian nationalist groups resorted to sabotage as part of their campaign to remove the British. Trains were attacked from boats in the Nile Delta, whilst nail bombs placed between the rail joints caused serious problems. In October 1951, No 70387 was derailed and badly damaged in the saltmarsh near Suez, presenting a very difficult rerailing operation. In January 1952 No 70574 was mined near Quantara, having the driving axle and a considerable portion of its framing blown out; in May No 70373 was similarly attacked, although with less serious consequences.

To the problems of security were added the problems of keeping the engines running. By 1952, a combination of long-term repairs and terrorist activity meant that there were only three locomotives working WD traffic, two were on loan to the ESR, and the remaining 11 locomotives were awaiting extensive repairs or scrapping. Britain had no intention of being driven out of the Canal Zone by terrorist activity, and it was decided to return five locomotives to Britain for overhaul prior to further service in the area. The five locomotives, but not their tenders, were returned to Derby for overhaul in 1952, being replaced by '04' 2-8-0s purchased from British Railways. In the meantime, a new number series (WD Nos 500-15) had been introduced for the 16 locomotives; by coincidence No 508 retained its original number.

No sooner were the '8Fs' on their way to England, than King Farouk was deposed and Colonel Nasser took control in Egypt, thus making the British position in the Canal Zone increasingly untenable. Of the 11 '8Fs' remaining, the bomb-damaged No 70574 never ran again and was scrapped in 1954. The remainder continued to do some work, but were soon put into store. Eventually they became ESR Nos 832-40 and 893 in 1954, bringing the total number in ESR stock to 62.

The five locomotives which returned to England (now WD Nos 500/01/08/11/12) were slowly overhauled from 1952-54 and sent to the Longmoor Military Railway (LMR) for storage. Five tenders were recovered from Suez in 1955, and the engines began to be used intermittently for training purposes. No 501 acquired the full 'Longmoor Blue' livery, complete with its name *Lt W. O. Lennox VC*, and was used rather more than the others.

In 1955, No 511 was named *Sgt J. Smith VC Bengal Sappers & Miners* before despatch to the Cairn Ryan Military Railway near Stranraer. In 1957 operations were considerably reduced at Longmoor and Nos 500/01/12 were sold to British Railways. Overhauled at Eastleigh, they went to Glasgow Polmadie as BR Nos 48773/4/5. After numerous further adventures, Nos 48773/5 survived to see out the end of steam in 1968, No 48773 becoming the only active survivor of the Stanier '8Fs' which served their country so well in foreign fields. Restored as LMS

No 8233, and owned by the Stanier '8F' Locomotive Society Ltd, she is still doing a useful job of work on the Severn Valley Railway.

WD No 508 was sent north to join No 511 at Cairn Ryan where there was little work for them; they worked the odd train of gas shells for dumping in the sea from Stranraer down to the military port of Cairn Ryan a couple of miles away. Both engines were offered for sale in 1959; curiously BR was apparently not interested despite serious shortages of freight power and the engines were cut up by Messrs J. W. Connel at Coatbridge later in the year.

So ended a remarkable chapter in the '8F' story. The engines had acquitted themselves extremely well in a variety of exceedingly hostile foreign environments. Although often small for tasks they were given, their sharp bark and solidly-engineered design marked them out as real 'drivers' engines' able to win through under the most adverse circumstances. We shall not see their like again.

Below left:
WD No 300, the first of the Stanier '8Fs' built for overseas service, as completed by the North British Locomotive Co Ltd, 17 May 1940. Features to note are air brake equipment, side couplings, air reservoir on running plate, live steam injector behind cab steps, WD grey livery and lettering.
BR (LMR)

Bottom left:
WD No 387, one of the first batch of British-built, oil burning '8Fs' completed by NBL in August 1941. This locomotive ran trials between Crewe, Wigan and Shrewsbury to test the oil burning system in September of that year. Note the cowcatcher, vacuum and air brakes, also the miniscule WD lettering. She became ISR No 41.155, moving to Egypt in 1944 and becoming ESR No 834 in 1956. *BR (LMR)*

Top right:
One of the last '8F' arrivals in Iran, WD No 547 (NB42) is swung on to dry land at Ahwaz by the Anglo Iranian Oil Co's crane. This operation used so much electricity that the town's supply had to be cut off during the exercise.
Imperial War Museum

Centre right:
1,000 tons for Joe. A Russian supply train, double-headed by two '8Fs' and banked by a third, sets out from Andimeshk into the foothills of the Luristan Range in 1942. 200 miles of climbing, much of it at 1 in 67, lie ahead to the 7,500ft summit at Noor Abad. *D. H. Cardew*

Right:
Andimeshk Loco Shed: Iranian Ferrostaal 2-10-0s are surrounded by Stanier products in the summer of 1942. *D. H. Cardew*

Top left:
Iran 1942: a freight train, double-headed by two '8Fs', charges across a viaduct, and into a tunnel to do battle with the next stretch of 1 in 67 amidst the rugged grandeur of the Luristan Mountains. *D. H. Cardew*

Above left:
Massive physical features combine to dwarf an '8F' as she passes the 'Company's Bathing Pool' at Balarud. This was a brief respite after the initial climb from Andimeshk, the real 'tug-of-war' is about to begin. Immediately behind the engine are two auxiliary water tanks, 1942. *D. H. Cardew*

Above far left:
A Russian oil train, hauled by two '8Fs', waits in the loop at Chamsangar as two '8Fs' blast out of the spiral tunnel in the hillside with a southbound freight for Andimeshk, 1942. *P. J. Howard*

Left:
The way ahead in the heat and desolation of the Iranian Highlands. A view from the cab of a hard-worked '8F' nearing Noor Abad Summit in 1942.
The late Capt Stanier, courtesy of P. M. Kalla Bishop

Top:
British and American soldiers survey Nos 41.110 and 41.107 locked in deadly embrace on the single line between Khorramshahr and Ahwaz on 2 February 1943. Neither of these North British-built machines ever worked again, but they were remarkably evacuated to the Canal Zone in 1946, being scrapped later in the same

year. Note that No 41.107's driver has managed to get her into reverse. *US Army (395835)*

Above:
Two '8Fs', Nos 41.177 and 41.180, double-head the up 'Tehran Mail' at Ghom in 1942. No 41.177 (BP40) moved to Egypt and Italy in 1944, being withdrawn as FS No 737.004 in 1953. No 41.180 (BP40) moved to Palestine in 1945/46 and became BR No 48292 in 1949, being withdrawn in April 1968. *E. J. M. Hayward*

A pair of wagons loaded

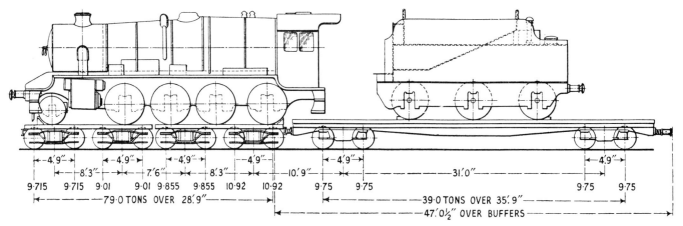

Diagram showing principal dimensions and weights of the loaded wagons

Left:
Special transporter wagons were needed to move the '8Fs' from Iran to Egypt over the metre-gauge section from Basra to Baghdad in 1946. An '8F' sits rather ungainly on a low-slung transporter wagon with four-wheel bogies to spread the load.
Railway Gazette International

Below left:
WD No 358, prepared for shipment to Turkey and photographed at the North British Locomotive Co's Hyde Park Works in 1941. The Turkish insignia and RH drive should be noted. Air brake equipment mounted on LH side of the locomotive. This locomotive became TCDD No 45154 and was withdrawn in 1977.
Mitchell Library

Above right:
Turkish '8F' No 45151 (NB40) pilots a Vulcan 2-10-0 on a heavy freight through forbidding terrain near Irmak in the early 1980s. Note the Westinghouse euipment mounted on the LH side of the engine, RH drive, shut off valves fitted to the top feed, and also the 'quality' of the coal in the tender.
L. A. Nixon/ A. Biwandi Collection

Right:
Falconara, Italy, 2 February 1945. WD No 70514 (NB41), later FS No 737.006, is seen with fitters and enginemen of 153 Railway Operating Company, Royal Engineers. To the right is FS No 685.524, originally a four-cylinder compound rebuilt in 1926 as a four-cylinder Caprotti simple, and also WD No 70612. (VF36, ex-LMS 8098, and later FS No 737.015.)
J. M. Proud, courtesy P. M. Kalla Bishop

Above:
WD No 9356 (ex-WD No 308, NB40), stands at Beirut in the company of an American 2-8-2 in 1944. Note the modified top feed with shut-off valves to allow the clacks to be examined with the engine in steam — a modification pioneered in Palestine. The engine has been converted to oil firing, but is not fitted with air brakes — she became part of Israeli Railways stock in 1948. *Maj E. Howell*

Below:
WD No 70596, ex-LMS No 8042 (VF36) leaves Beirut with the 08.15 train for Haifa. The coaches are Grand Indian Peninsula Railway broad gauge vehicles converted to standard gauge by 199 Railway Workshops Company, Royal Engineers in about 1945. No 70596 passed into Israeli hands in 1948. *K. R. M. Cameron*

Right:
WD No 70515 (NB41) is having its boiler washed out at Lydda shed, Palestine Railways, on 22 September 1945. This locomotive passed to Israeli Railways in 1948. Note the double cab roof, designed to reduce the heat in the cab. *R. E. Tustin*

Centre right:
A construction train on the Western Desert Extension Railway at Milepost 34 (from Similla Junction). Rommel had arrived in Libya, and the railway was being pushed forward rapidly. Locomotive No 9427 ex-WD No 427 (BP41). Note the 'locals' hopefully waiting with their cans for water spillage from the injectors — unless watched, they were not beyond slashing the feed bags! These trains loaded up to 2,000 tons and the New Zealand crews could be on duty for 21hr at a stretch.
C. H. Gledhill Collection

Below:
An '8F' passes the remains of a Ju87 Stuka dive bomber, downed near milepost 83. The lorry-mounted guns gave little protection against cannon fire, but there was more useful armament in the armoured box van, sixth from the engine.
C. H. Gledhill

Top:
Battle-weary '8Fs' from Iran, in varying degrees of disrepair, congregate at 400 Transportation Stores near 169 Workshops, Suez in 1947. Some returned home, others were repaired to run in Egypt, some were cannibalised, and the worst cases scrapped. *D. S. Currie*

Above:
With the desert wastes stretching for miles into the distance, an '8F' crosses the border between Egypt and Libya at Milepost 155¼, early in 1942. *C. H. Gledhill*

Right:
German prisoners help Royal Engineers to lift an '8F' boiler at 169 Workshops in 1946. The crinoline for the cladding plates can be clearly seen, also the shape of the ashpan designed to clear the trailing coupled axle. Also unmistakable is the presence of 'authority' in the left foreground! Boilers could be exchanged in the Middle East, but major overhauls could not be attempted.
D. S. Currie

Top:
Going home. WD No 70332 (NB40) and No 70584 (NB41), later BR Nos 48251 and 48263 respectively, are loaded on to the SS *Belnor* at Port Said in April 1948. A total of 39 engines was similarly repatriated. *D. S. Currie*

Above:
An immaculate WD No 70387 awaits her naming ceremony as *Corporal W. J. Lendrim VC* at Elphinstone Camp in the Canal Zone, about 1950.
Courtesy Col G. C. L. Alexander

Above right:

A scene at Geniefa between Port Said and Suez in August 1951. WD No 70387 *Corporal W. J. Lendrim VC* of 10 Railway Squadron, Royal Engineers, heads a military freight train on the ESR. Note the armed guard by the bufferbeam, the headlamp and its turbo generator mounted just in front of the cab.
G. F. Heiron

Right:

WD No 509 *Corporal J. Ross VC* (NB41), heads a northbound WD freight of Centurion tanks away from Suez, near Fayid, on 25 March 1952. The engine appears to have acquired the tender from an earlier batch of '8Fs' to judge by the large lettering. She subsequently became ESR No 832 in 1956.
G. F. Bannister

Right:

WD '8Fs' Nos 508 (NB41), 512 (C37), 511 (C37), 501 (NB40), and 500 (NB40), shipped to Britain for overhaul in 1952, stand at Derby works on 30 August 1953. No 500 in the foreground, later to be preserved as LMS No 8233, has been overhauled whilst work proceeds on the other extensively cannibalised survivors.
B. Hilton

6
'8Fs' Galore — The '50s and '60s

The late 1950s saw the British '8F' allocation at its greatest extent, with locomotives on every region except the Southern. With over 350 congregated on the Midland Division of the London Midland Region (LMR) and the remainder spread throughout the Western Division and on the other Regions, the 2-8-0s could be seen anywhere from Perth in the north, to Plymouth and Southampton in the south, Swansea in the west and Scunthorpe in the east.

From 1950, the distribution of the class remained substantially unaltered until the early 1960s, although some locomotives displaced on the Midland Division by BR Standard Class '9F' 2-10-0s had gone to the Western Region from 1954. Change came from about 1962 when increasing dieselisation on the Eastern and Midland Regions displaced the '8Fs' on to less important duties. They were transferred in increasing numbers on to the Central Division of the LMR and other routes in the North West, a process aided by the transfer of WD 2-8-0s from the Midland to the Eastern Region (ER) and completed towards the end of 1964. At the beginning of that year, the '8F' class was still virtually intact, but with the increasing spread of diesels on to freight work over the next few years, the 2-8-0s were to spend more of their time on lower category work or at sheds — on the ex-Great Central or ex-GWR lines in the West Midlands for example — where rationalisation was soon to make them redundant.

For much of the 1950s the '8Fs' were largely used on traditional mineral work, but the end of the decade saw the introduction of longer through workings and increased pressure on motive power, which caused the class to appear in some very unusual locations and on a much greater variety of duties — fitted freights, empty stock work, vacuum-fitted bulk tank hauls, and a surprisingly large amount of passenger work. The real worth and versatility of the class was very convincingly demonstrated in these years.

By the mid-1960s, a subtle retreat by the '8Fs' from their traditional duties on the Midland and Western Divisions of the LMR was well under way. This was especially rapid in 1965/66 with the end of steam on much of the Midland Division and on the Western and Eastern Regions. At the end of 1966, the 380 or so survivors — still over half the class — had withdrawn to the hill country and gritty industrial surroundings of the North for what was to be most emphatically, a very Grand Finale.

The Midland Division
In the 1950s, there were many more '8Fs' on the Midland Division of the LMR than there had been before the war,

and their presence had seen the banishment of the surviving 'Austin Seven' 0-8-0s to the Central Division, whilst the Stanier engines had an almost complete monopoly of the heavier work in this part of the country (the WD 2-8-0s were never allocated to the Midland in BR days).

Traffic patterns were very similar to those of the prewar years — coal was still the principal source of energy and much home iron ore was still used. The '8Fs' were busy taking Northamptonshire iron ore to the North East, coal from the North Midlands to London, the North West and South, steel from the Midlands to the capital and elsewhere. The heaviest coal trains to London and the Midlands were worked turn and turn about with the Garratts, but with the traffic reorganised around the maximum 2-8-0 load. The '8Fs' did the job much more efficiently, and also displaced the last double headed combinations of 0-6-0s on such work. Toton with 61 and Kirkby with 43 were undoubtedly the places to see 8Fs at work in these years, and the whole of the Midland from London to Leeds was indeed a very happy hunting ground for the class.

Nationalisation saw Midland Division locomotives working north of York to Teesside, and following the closure of Peterborough LMR depot in 1950, Toton and Rugby engines began to work through to March, whilst Sheffield and Kettering locomotives also ventured to Frodingham and Immingham with steel and coal traffic.

The arrival of the BR '9F' 2-10-0s saw the disappearance of the unmourned Garratts by 1958, and the '9Fs' worked turn and turn about with the '8Fs' on the Toton to Brent mineral hauls. The Wellingborough allocation of '8Fs' was somewhat reduced in consequence, but with the expansion of the Corby steel works, the Kettering allocation expanded whilst some surplus '8Fs' had been transferred to the Western Region. From about 1950 Cricklewood also had about 10 '8Fs' which worked to Toton and across London; by 1960 Kentish Town depot had gained four.

However, not every Midland depot had cohorts of '8Fs' at its disposal, indeed some allocations of 2-8-0s were very small and for one or two specific duties only. Bournville's sole example No 48523 spent years on the same diagram (the 16.45 Water Orton to Westerleigh Minerals and its return working), the Lancaster engines were seldom seen away from the Heysham to Leeds tank workings, and the small band at Coalville worked mostly on coal traffic to Wellingborough.

In 1957, the Midland line depots in the Leeds area became part of the North Eastern Region, whilst early in

Stanier '8F' allocations 1950-1964

Depot	Shed Code	4/11/50	1/1/56	5/11/60	1/1/64
Willesden	1A	43	29	21	18
Rugby	2A	16	9	16	16
Nuneaton	2B	12	18	30	19
Warwick	2C	2	2	—	—
Bescot	3A	10	27	14	21
Bletchley	4A	7	8	8	19
Northampton	4B	8	6	14	6
Crewe South	5B	26	20	23	11
Mold Junction	6B	17	5	6	16
Birkenhead	6C	10	11	8	21
Edge Hill	8A	4	5	11	10
Warrington	8B	7	12	7	5
Speke Jn	8C	15	11	9	11
Widnes	8D	8	7	11	6
Longsight	9A	8	9	7	1
Buxton	9D	19	14	10	8
Trafford Park	9E	4	3	5	4
Heaton Mersey	9F	20	27	19	25
Northwich	9G	13	16	22	20
Carlisle Canal	12B	3	—	—	—
Cricklewood	14A	7	10	10	—
Wellingborough	15A	50	29	19	12
Kettering	15B	15	22	17	24
Leicester	15C	7	14	—	—
Bedford	15D	1	1	—	—
Nottingham	16A	16	26	24	21
Kirkby	16C	43	34	48	41
Mansfield	16D	7	19	—	—
Derby	17A	11	9	14	10
Coalville	17C	5	—	3	6
Toton	18A	63	61	59	31
Westhouses	18B	24	18	3	15
Staveley	18D	12	20	18	23
Sheffield	19A	8	6	6	—
Canklow	19C	10	17	13	—
Leeds	20A	10	8	9	6
Stourton	20B	9	12	15	11
Royston	20C	19	24	24	23
Normanton	20D	18	12	—	—
Saltley	21A	13	10	15	12
Skipton	23A	3	—	—	—
Hellifield	23B	3	2	—	—
Lancaster	23C	3	4	—	3
Newton Heath	26A	18	—	8	10
Agecroft	26B	6	—	—	—
Bolton	26C	7	—	—	—
Belle Vue	26G	6	—	—	—
Aintree	27B	5	—	—	—
Carlisle Kingmoor	68A	5	8	8	13
Shrewsbury	84G	7	20	14	11
Chester Northgate	6D	—	2	—	—
Bidston	6F	—	2	1	—
Stockport Edgeley	9B	—	1	3	2
Burton	17B	—	3	4	13
Rowsley	17D	—	2	4	—
Hasland	18C	—	3	16	7
Bournville	21B	—	1	—	—
Annesley	38B	—	1	—	15
St Phillips Marsh	82B	—	8	7	—
Banbury	84C	—	3	—	—
Pontypool Road	86G	—	1	—	—
Swansea Paxton St	87K	—	11	—	—
Stoke	5D	—	—	6	5
Llandudno Jn	6G	—	—	3	3
Kentish Town	14B	—	—	4	—
Aston	21D	—	—	4	3
Mirfield	56D	—	—	9	8
Polmadie	66A	—	—	3	—
Old Oak Common	81A	—	—	3	—
Tyseley	84E	—	—	7	7
Llanelly	87F	—	—	22	20
Cardiff Canton	88A	—	—	1	—
Woodford Halse	1G	—	—	—	21
Stourbridge Jn	2C	—	—	—	8
Stafford	5C	—	—	—	2
Chester	6A	—	—	—	1
Patricroft	9H	—	—	—	14
Bury	9M	—	—	—	4
Carnforth	10A	—	—	—	2
Fleetwood	10C	—	—	—	8
Lostock Hall	10D	—	—	—	1
Farnley Jn	55D	—	—	—	4
Bristol Barrow Road	82E	—	—	—	1
Bath Green Park	82F	—	—	—	4
Gloucester Barnwood	85C	—	—	—	2
TOTAL		663	663	665	664

1958, the Sheffield district became Eastern Region territory, potentially opening up new fields of action for the 2-8-0s. By 1960, the Midland '8F' population remained at its 1950s level, with the '8F' still the prime mover of the prodigious freight traffic throughout the lines of the old Midland Railway system. One '8F', No 48616, had been withdrawn because of the Turvey accident, well outside any planned withdrawal scheme, but this was perhaps a portent of the great changes to come over the next five years as dieselisation and changes in traffic patterns gradually made the '8Fs' redundant.

The first major allocation of diesels to freight work occurred in April 1962 when BR Type 4 1Co-Co1 'Peaks' Nos D1-10 were concentrated at Toton. Freight traffic at this time was still very heavy, especially the flow of Northants ore which was keeping the '8Fs' very busy indeed. Within two years, the 2-8-0s and 2-10-0s had been replaced on almost all the principal Midland freight workings and were spending much more of their time on colliery trips and local work rather than working to Brent or Willesden. With the LMR take over of the Great Central line in 1958, increasing numbers of '8Fs' found their way on to this popular but doomed route.

The harsh winter of 1962/3 had seen steam again in command of many of the principal freight services, but at the end of 1962 No 48009 became the first '8F' to be withdrawn as part of a normal programme. Large numbers of Type 2 diesels running in tandem with brake tenders were beginning to threaten the '8Fs' in earnest. South of Wellingborough most trains were now diesel hauled, together with many of the workings between Toton and Northampton. It was salutary to find that by January 1964, the Toton '8F' allocation had dwindled to half its former size.

By the end of 1964, '8F' numbers on the Midland were down to rather less than 200 and steam was very rare south of Wellingborough where the only regular jobs for the class were the heavy coal trains to Goldington Power

Station on the Bedford to Cambridge line. Large numbers of 2-8-0s had been transferred to the North Western Lines and the sight of an '8F' barking vociferously up to Sharnbrook was becoming increasingly rare, although there were a surprisingly large number of '8F' forays up to London on fitted freight work. The closure of Cricklewood depot in December ended such exploits.

During 1965 Toton depot, once a haven of '8F' activity, became fully dieselised, although a fair amount of steam working remained from the north, south and west. Nottingham shed had closed in April, followed by Coalville and Kettering. In March Wellingborough had lost its '9F' 2-10-0s to Birkenhead, leaving the '8Fs' to see out the end of steam on the Midland Division. Their work was mostly of a mundane nature, but long-distance work was still to be had on the Goldington jobs and on the Blisworth to Frodingham and Pitsford to Barrow Hill iron ore workings. Diesels began to appear on the Goldington trains in February 1966, few of which were steam-hauled after April. Surprisingly an '8F' managed to get through to Limbury Road with coal in February, but by April there was no steam depot still open south of Leicester. By the autumn of 1966 Leicester, Burton and Derby sheds had lost their steam allocations, and steam working was virtually extinct on the Midland main line and on the Birmingham route. Those '8Fs' in reasonable condition survived to fight again in the North, but for many there was now only one inevitable journey remaining.

A vestige of steam operation remained in the North Midlands into 1967 at Westhouses and Kirkby. '8Fs' allocated to the North Eastern Region still worked in from the north but the days when the Erewash Valley re-echoed from end to end with the fierce bark and clonking big-ends of Stanier's '8Fs' were now gone forever.

In the late 1950s '8Fs' had begun to work pick-up and through freights over the Stratford-on-Avon and Midland Junction line from Bedford through Towcester to the Western Region at Stratford-on-Avon. The line was useful as a relief route and also had a fair amount of originating iron ore traffic. The principal '8F' jobs were the iron ore trains from Woodford Halse to South Wales, traffic which became quite heavy after the opening of the connection to the Stratford-on-Avon to Cheltenham line in 1960. Midland, Great Central and Western Region based '8Fs' could be seen on the line. Alas by 1965 rationalisation and a decline in iron ore traffic had sounded the death knell for this interesting route.

Another fated line worked latterly by the '8Fs' was the Great Central, administered by the LMR from January 1958. When Warwick shed closed in November, '8Fs' Nos 48012/18 transferred to Woodford Halse and the class began to appear on the Woodford to Annesley mineral traffic as understudies to the '9Fs'. By 1963, substantial numbers of '8Fs' which were surplus to requirements on the Midland Division had replaced the 'O1' and WD 2-8-0s at Annesley. In the meantime, Woodford '8Fs' were extensively used on traffic to South Wales, Banbury, and a variety of destinations in the London area via both the Great Central and Great Western routes. Determined attempts were then being made to divert as much traffic as possible away from the Great Central and in June 1965, Woodford Halse depot was closed. The remaining freights

and colliery trips in the North Midlands continued with '8F' power. Occasionally a 2-8-0 would probe the deserted and cavernous depths of Nottingham Victoria, but the end could not be long delayed.

Early in 1966, Annesley shed closed, whilst Colwick depot was transferred from the Eastern to the London Midland Region. Thirty-eight '8Fs' were sent to replace the Eastern Region freight types at Colwick which adopted the old Annesley code of 16B. Their stay was to be short. Within eight months the Great Central was closed as a through route and the shed had closed by January 1967. The engines spent most of their time on the Great Central, but also had some of the last remaining steam workings on to Eastern Region territory. With the end of steam at Colwick, and with Kirkby about to lose its last steam locomotives, the Midlands, for so long the natural home of the '8Fs', were virtually fully dieselised.

The Western Division
The '8Fs' undertook a much greater variety of work on the Western Division of the LMR and were not confined to purely mineral jobs. Until 1962, large numbers of ex-LNWR 'G2' 0-8-0s were also available for such work, although it would be fair to say that a Stanier 'Black Five' 4-6-0 and 45 wagons on fitted or semi-fitted work was much more typical of the West Coast freight scene than an '8F'.

There were around 250 '8Fs' stationed on the Western Division in 1950, the largest concentrations being at Willesden and Crewe South, with a scattering at most of the major depots in between. Willesden engines worked mainly to Toton via Northampton, and at one time had turns on the GN&LNWR Joint Line to Colwick. They also appeared on the heavy cross-London freight traffic, hauled a fair share of the general West Coast freight and appeared at Euston on heavy empty coaching stock work, particularly the overnight sleeper services. Rugby, Bletchley and Northampton engines had a wide range of other work in addition to West Coast duties — freight to the Midland Division and Eastern Region via Peterborough, workings over the Northampton to Wellingborough and Rugby to Leicester routes, and to the Western Region via Bletchley and Oxford. Much of this traffic was iron ore, but also included chalk from Dunstable and general merchandise. The Nuneaton allocation was principally involved in serving the Warwickshire coalfield and the Coventry industrial area. Most of this was coal traffic, but there were general freight and tank trains to a variety of destinations including Banbury, Liverpool, Birkenhead, Birmingham and Leicester.

The Crewe South '8Fs' were used on a great variety of duties and could be seen working heavy pick-up freights to the Cheshire saltfield and the Potteries, moving cattle to North Wales, slogging over the Pennines to Leeds, tackling the grades of the Shrewsbury line with traffic for the Western Region or heading over the West Coast Main Line on all sorts of duties. Some very complicated cyclical diagrams were operated; one '8F' set off with a trip to Birkenhead, then worked the 18.06 Stanlow to Colwick tanks arriving early the following morning. It then visited Water Orton before returning with the next evening's Colwick to Stanlow tanks, regaining Crewe on the following day with a further freight from Birkenhead.

Many ex-works Midland Division engines were returned on this diagram, but there were some rough trips with locomotives due for shopping in the reverse direction! Between 1950 and 1964 Warrington also had a fairly small '8F' allocation which spent much of its time on West Coast traffic, including some workings to London and Carlisle with fitted freights.

A clutch of '8F' depots in the North West served the industrial and chemical districts of Merseyside, Mid-Cheshire and Manchester. Speke Junction locomotives had long distance work over the Pennines, on fitted freights to Carlisle, and were much involved in special traffic to and from the docks. The Heaton Mersey allocation worked the heavy freight traffic on the Cheshire Lines, where small ex-Great Central 0-6-0s had been gradually replaced by the 2-8-0s after the war. A lot of Trans-Pennine coal was worked forward from Guide Bridge and other Manchester yards near the Pennines to a variety of destinations, whilst there was heavy work to be had on limestone trains to Peak Forest and other workings to the south over the old Midland route. The Northwich engines were always hard worked and enthusiastically driven, never more so than on the 1,000-ton limestone hopper workings from Tunstead. The '8Fs' had ousted all the remaining Eastern Region 2-8-0s from the Cheshire Lines by 1963, and saw out the end of steam in this area while still doing a vigorous job of work. The Longsight '8Fs' worked turn and turn about with 'Black Fives' on fitted freight work to London, and also across the Pennines to the West Riding. The Buxton engines travelled to many industrial areas on both sides of the Pennines with limestone from the Peak District, and led a hard life with heavy climbing in all directions, often under severe winter conditions. Stockport Edgeley gained a small allocation of '8Fs' in 1956, which was increased considerably in the 1960s, the 2-8-0s working to London on fitted freights, and to Merseyside and Buxton with mineral traffic and trip workings. Elsewhere on Merseyside, Liverpool Edge Hill was host to a few members of the class, and had 10 on its books by 1964. Widnes engines were heavily involved in chemical traffic throughout the North West. At Birkenhead, the allocation was gradually increased throughout the 1950s as oil refinery activities were expanded at Stanlow and the shed gained some responsibility for the iron ore hauls from the docks to the John Summers steelworks at Shotton, on what were nominally Bidston diagrams. The sight and sound of an '8F' in full cry pounding up to Heswall Hills with these heavy trains was an experience not soon forgotten. Redundant '9F' 2-10-0s from the Midland Division replaced the Birkenhead '8Fs' in 1964.

In the 1950s, the '8Fs' were not very common between Preston and Carlisle, although Shrewsbury and other depots would not hesitate to use them on fitted freight work in the event of a shortage of Class 5MT 4-6-0s. The Salop turn to Carlisle, returning with the 05.15 Carlisle-Bushbury was frequently thus worked, and the return train remained a regular '8F' turn into the last years of steam.

In 1953, Bidston gained two '8Fs' for the Shotwick iron ore jobs, and the expansion of the steel plant here saw two allocated to Chester Northgate in 1956. By 1960, the class had appeared at Llandudno Junction where they were often used on ballast traffic from Penmaenmawr. Mold Junction had a substantial allocation since at least 1950, so the 2-8-0s were no strangers to North Wales.

Early in 1958, Carlisle Kingmoor shed was transferred to the LMR. Its '8Fs' sometimes worked into Scotland, but their main duties were the anhydrite workings from Long Meg sidings to Widnes, together with main line work to Leeds and Crewe. Again, surplus '9Fs' replaced the '8Fs' here in 1964.

The '8Fs' reached the Potteries in 1960, when Stoke at last began to lose its large allocation of Midland '4F' 0-6-0s. There was heavy coal traffic from the North Staffordshire pits to Shotwick, Northwich and later to Ironbridge, sand from Oakamoor to the glass industry at St Helens, and further mineral workings to Mold Junction and the Midlands. Stafford shed also had occasional '8Fs' on its allocation.

In the Birmingham area, Bescot always had substantial numbers of '8Fs' engaged in the haulage of coal and steel traffic to and from other industrial areas. The '8Fs' also worked fitted freights to Carlisle and Crewe, and worked passenger excursion traffic in times of pressure. The other major '8F' base in the Midlands was Saltley. The engines here were employed mostly on mineral work to Leicester and Toton, Gloucester (via Bromsgrove and also Redditch), Bristol and later Banbury. They also put in very good work on the heavy transfer trips between Washwood Heath and Bordesley. A trip to Long Marston on Western Region territory usually saw them very hard worked in the interests of regional rivalry. In the 1960s came longer distance tank train work to the Southern Region via Banbury, and more work over the ex-GWR route to Gloucester and South Wales via Honeybourne.

Western Lines
In 1963, regional boundary changes saw the LMR taking over all ex-GWR territory north and west of Banbury. All LMR territory south of Crewe and west of Birmingham was designated as the Western Lines, the North Western Lines covering the area northwards, and west of the Pennines.

At the beginning of 1964, there were about 200 '8Fs' allocated to the Western Lines. They were noticeably fewer south of Crewe, with the Willesden allocation down to 18, but former WR territory was being ventured into in the west, albeit for a fairly short stay before the route rationalisation of the late 1960s.

On the West Coast route, steam-hauled freight trains remained fairly common until early in 1965, indeed there were complaints of a shortage of '8F' power at Willesden because of the time taken to overhaul them at 'foreign' works. However, Rugby shed closed to steam in May, followed by Willesden and Northampton in the autumn. Bletchley had closed in June, and in October steam was banned south of Northampton after an '8F' on a Derby to Wolverton stock special had run out of water, causing the fire to be dropped. In Northamptonshire, supplies of iron ore were beginning to run out and No 48678 worked the last Irthlingborough to Rogerstone ore train to Bletchley on 1 October, returning light engine. Some steam working remained from the Midland Division to Northampton on the Blisworth to Frodingham ore trains for a few months longer.

On former Western Region (WR) territory, the '8Fs' began to take over from WR classes and to supplement allocations of the class already at former WR sheds. The Tyseley and Stourbridge Junction engines had a good deal of local work together with main line freights to Oxford, whilst Oxley gained an '8F' allocation from October. Steam-hauled freight trains remained quite common on the ex-GWR routes to London until the end of steam on the WR in January 1966, when Banbury became the usual limit of steam working. '8Fs', '9Fs' and 'Black Fives' continued to work freights from Burton and the West Midlands this far south until the closure of Nuneaton shed in June; the closure of the Great Central connecting route into Banbury saw Banbury shed itself closing in October. Two Saltley turns for '8Fs' on coal trains from Washwood Heath survived until the end of the year, diesels taking over early in 1967.

In the West Midlands, Stourbridge shed closed in June 1966 and its turns on the Severn Valley branch to Alveley colliery and throughout the Black Country were dieselised or transferred to Oxley and Tyseley Sheds. A reasonable amount of steam working to the West Midlands remained at the end of 1965, about half the freights on the Derby line still being steam-hauled, but an influx of diesels early in 1966 saw the Bescot steam allocation reduced from 60 to 20, and the shed closed to steam in February. The remaining steam work in the West Midlands consisted increasingly of local trip work with very few main line turns. Tyseley closed in November, leaving Saltley to supply the remaining steam power. Oxley '8Fs' had diagrams to Shrewsbury, Buildwas and Donnington as well as work in the West Midlands itself, while a number of steam locomotives continued to work into the area from Crewe and the Potteries, and from Burton and Derby until the autumn of 1966.

After the end of through freight working on the Central Wales Line in 1964, the Shrewsbury allocation of '8Fs' was much reduced, dwindling to four early in 1966. However, after 1963 the Stanier engines were allocated to Wrexham, replacing the native GWR '28xx' 2-8-0s on the Brymbo branch and on freights to the West Midlands and Shotton. Another '28xx' preserve which fell briefly to the '8Fs' was Oswestry, where two were allocated in December 1964 for the ballast trains to the West Midlands and elsewhere. Within a matter of weeks, however, the shed had closed and the engines were transferred to Croes Newydd. A little further north Chester, traditionally a passenger depot, gained one '8F' in 1964, and eight in 1966 following the reallocation of Mold Junction diagrams when that shed closed in April.

North Western Lines

After 1963 the North Western Lines encompassed the old Central Division and the Western Division north of Crewe. Apart from the Newton Heath '8Fs', the Central Division had been 'G3' 0-8-0 and WD 2-8-0 territory from about 1951 onwards, but with '8Fs' becoming surplus on the Midland Division from 1962, and the transfer of WD 2-8-0s to the Eastern Region in 1964, there followed a steady influx of Stanier 2-8-0s into the North West in the years up to 1967.

In 1962, Sutton Oak and Patricroft sheds had gained '8Fs', and were followed in 1963 by Carnforth, Bury and Fleetwood. In 1964 Bolton, Agecroft, Gorton and Springs Branch acquired the Stanier machines, followed by Lower Darwen, Rose Grove and Lostock Hall in 1965. Early in 1965 Sutton Oak gained several '8Fs' from Birkenhead which had been displaced by '9Fs', whilst at the end of the year considerable numbers of displaced '8Fs' from the Midland Division invaded north Lancashire. Withdrawals notwithstanding, over 200 '8Fs' could be found on the North Western Lines in 1965, the same number in 1966, and early in 1967 the total had risen to nearly 250.

With the rationalised railway system of today, it is not easy to visualise the bustling railway system of the North West in the years 1964-68. There were large numbers of local trip and shunt workings, especially in the Manchester area with its complex system of routes and yards; with most of the older, smaller engines withdrawn, much of this work fell on the '8Fs'. On the main lines up to 1967, the 2-8-0s were busy on all the Trans-Pennine routes with coal and mineral empties, and engines from the Manchester area depots took a substantial share of the general freight traffic to the north via both the West Coast Route and via Blackburn and the Settle and Carlisle line. At Sutton Oak the glass industry at St Helens kept a small band of '8Fs' busy, and they handled much of the freight on Merseyside from Edge Hill and Aintree in these years.

Some depots kept their new '8F' allocation for only a matter of months before closure and the transfer of their duties to neighbouring sheds. Lancaster had closed in 1964 with Carnforth taking over its duties. The '8Fs' here worked latterly to the West Riding with tank and mineral trains, but in the 1950s they had travelled as far south as the West Midlands on oil traffic to Rowley Regis, being serviced at Oxley. Bury, Lower Darwen and Fleetwood depots all closed in 1965/6 with their allocations being absorbed by Bolton, Lostock Hall and Rose Grove. Throughout the fell country of the north, the sight of a grimy '8F' on a heavy mineral haul, leaking profusely, with big-ends knocking loudly, but still barking defiantly at the chimney top came to typify the atmosphere of the end of steam in Britain.

Passenger Workings

On reflection it is hardly surprising that the free running capabilities of the '8Fs' led to their use on passenger trains during the war and on summer weekends in the 1950s and 1960s when motive power was sometimes desperately short. They were also frequently awaiting a path with their freight trains at just the right moment to replace an ailing passenger locomotive, several epic substitutions being on record, especially on the Midland Division.

It must be said that the '8Fs' were not ideally suited to such work, although they could cope well with 55mph fitted freights, the practical speed ceiling with the 4ft 8½in driving wheels being in the region of 60-65mph. This was not enough for most passenger work (although some heroic attempts have been known) but it was adequate for excursion and Summer Saturday jobs — some of them over very long distances — where a spare powerful, free running locomotive was a god-send.

The '8Fs' were a good passenger locomotive on steeply graded, speed-restricted lines — hence their use on Trans-Pennine routes, in Central Wales and, for a time, in Scotland. Whilst incapable of the performance of a BR

'9F' 2-10-0 on such work, they were a willing machine which could cover the ground in reasonable order, with fair comfort for their crews. Few pre-nationalisation freight locomotives have acquitted themselves as well, or so frequently, on passenger work.

In LMS days, the 2-8-0s were largely confined to freight traffic, but were occasionally seen on excursions as recorded in chapter four. There was also at least one spirited effort on a Euston to Bletchley commuter service, with the 2-8-0 concerned sustaining 60mph on the 1 in 335 gradients up to Tring.

The desperate wartime motive power situation put an end to many traditional diagramming practices, and the '8Fs' were used quite extensively on regular passenger and troop specials in Scotland and Central Wales.

In the postwar era, as already recorded, some Lancashire & Yorkshire sheds used their 2-8-0s for suburban work, and in the 1950s, Longsight also made fairly regular use of them on the evening commuter trains to Buxton. They had no difficulty in maintaining the DMU timings on this steeply graded line.

On the Midland Division, on 27 March 1955 '8F' No 48177 was to be seen double-heading BR Standard Class 5MT 4-6-0 No 73011, short of steam, on the up 'Waverley'. 11 March 1955 found No 48132 assisting BR Standard Class 4MT 2-6-4T No 80045 on the 18.50 Bedford to London slow service. A heroic occasion was 12 September 1953 when No 48177 took over the 11-coach up 'Thames-Clyde Express' at Ampthill from failed 'Jubilee' No 45594 *Bhopal*. The '8F' stormed off into the late evening with coal and cinders raining down on the train. A speed of 72mph was attained after St Albans, and 1min gained on schedule to St Pancras. On 2 July 1955 the 'Thames-Clyde Express' headboard was again adorning an '8F' smokebox; No 48266 took over from another failed 'Jubilee' at Leicester, and kept time to Sheffield.

In Lancashire and Yorkshire, the '8Fs' were popular machines for all manner of relief and excursion work. Leeds area engines often worked to Wetherby races, Scarborough, Bridlington and Cleethorpes. '8Fs' from a variety of West Riding depots could be seen clambering westwards over the Pennines to Belle Vue, Morecambe, Blackpool, Southport and Rhyl as late as 1963. Central Division depots eagerly appropriated Western and Midland Division engines for Summer Saturday work, and in 1959 the LMR authorities felt obliged to issue an edict that '8F' and '9F' locmotives were to be used on passenger work only in extreme emergencies. Quite often, there were no other large locomotives left on the shed! The '8Fs' do not seem to have suffered in any way from hustling their merrymaking passengers on day trips to the coast; indeed, some of this work was very much in the long distance category. The regular Sheffield to Blackpool trains, and the Newcastle-Cardiff/Bournemouth reliefs on the Great Central, involved substantial distances. As late as July 1961 No 48439 turned up at Newcastle on an excursion from Leeds, whilst the Lancashire 'Wakes Weeks' could always offer the spectacle of '8Fs', sometimes double-headed, on specials from Blackburn, Burnley, and the towns of the Oldham branch.

Midland Region services to the West of England often saw '8Fs' manfully filling the gaps in the motive power provision on busy Summer Saturdays. On 5 September

1959, No 48101 was seen on the 08.05 Newquay to Newcastle, and was seen again the following year on a 10.05 Bournemouth to Derby service.

The situation was not quite so fraught on the London Midland Region's Western Division, but there was still a fair '8F' involvement in passenger work. No 48713 of Rugby was seen on 10 March 1952 performing on the Warwick to Rugby service with a two-coach auto set, whilst Market Harborough engines had fairly regular work on the GN/LNWR Joint Line Saturday workmen's service to Norton. In the Midlands, Bescot engines worked excursions from the Black Country to Stourport in the 1950s. In 1960, the depot was not averse to turning out '8Fs' to cover Stanier 2-6-0 failures on the Summer Saturday services to Yarmouth. As late as 29 August 1961 two '8Fs' turned up at Euston on relief trains from Birmingham.

In the grim winter of 1962-63, '8F' No 48389 and 'Crab' 2-6-0 No 42940 could be found with one coach, providing a service through the snow drifts between Ashbourne and Buxton — an emergency facility which could not be provided today! A very unusual pairing of '8Fs' took place on 27 April 1963 when several Stourbridge 2-8-0s were used to pilot a series of Bulleid Pacific-hauled Southampton to Birmingham football excursions up the 1 in 50 gradient of Old Hill bank between Stourbridge and Birmingham Snow Hill. In Central Wales, there was quite a long tradition of '8F' haulage on the midday trains in both directions in summer. The line was also busy with specials for troops and rugby internationals. Usually, a smaller engine such as a WR '22xx' 0-6-0 or a 2-6-4T was harnessed with the '8F' to provide steam heat, but some reports of unassisted '8Fs' indicate some very frosty return journeys on cold February Sundays! The troop specials were often worked forward to Crewe or Stafford, and it is hoped that for the faster stretches the crews had the benefit of balanced locomotives.

Two Central Wales '8Fs' received the supreme accolade for a freight locomotive of hauling the Royal Train from Aberystwyth to Pembroke Dock on 8 August 1955. Nos 48309 and 48707 were specially fitted with carriage warming equipment for the occasion. The politics and practicalities of the decision to use LMR freight locomotives for such a prestigious working over what was Western Region territory, must have been most interesting! The '8Fs' worked the heavy Royal Train over the steeply graded branch to Carmarthen and down to the shores of Milford Haven most successfully. The only other known appearance of '8Fs' on Royal Train duty was again in 1955 when Nos 48409 and 48709 were involved with the empty coaches in the Nottingham area.

On the Western Region the '8Fs' were not used on passenger work as much as the native '47xx' and '28xx' 2-8-0s, but they did work a lot of empty coaching stock and parcels trains in the West Country from 1955 onwards. A similar pattern could be discerned on the Somerset & Dorset line, although the through passenger trains had disappeared from this line before the '8Fs' appeared in any numbers. They did do some piloting over the Mendips on the occasional heavy excursion to Bournemouth, but it was not until shortly before the line's lamentable closure that they appeared regularly on S&D passenger work in 1965/66.

Some interesting work was done substituting for failed diesels in the early 1960s. On 26 July 1963 No 48478 worked the 06.30 Birkenhead to Paddington between Leamington Spa and Banbury, and four days later, No 48387 arrived at Paddington with the 07.10 from Shrewsbury, having relieved an ailing diesel at Princes Risborough. Earlier in the year, the unlikely combination of '8F' No 48179 and 'Western' diesel-hydraulic No D1000 *Western Enterprise* had been seen heading out of Leamington for the climb to Hatton with a Paddington to Birmingham express.

Stanier 2-8-0s were not common in Scotland after 1949, but the three at Carlisle Canal shed sometimes worked to Edinburgh over the Waverley route. St Margarets depot was always hard pressed for power, and on 4 July 1951 turned out No 48708 for the 11.30 Edinburgh to Thornton Junction passenger service. More intriguing, was the appearance of Kingmoor '8Fs' on Glasgow Fair Saturdays to work extra and sometimes even regular services between Buchannan St and Oban. This went on from 1949 to at least 1954. The engines were certainly seen leaving Glasgow, but it is not known if they got through to Oban. They would have been an excellent engine on the steep gradients of this popular route.

With the onset of dieselisation, the appearance of '8Fs' on passenger work became rarer after 1963. Some moments of glory remained however, and on 2 November 1963 commuters on the 07.22 Peterborough to King's Cross were surprised to make their way to Hitchin behind Toton's No 48221, Brush Type 4 (now Class 47) diesel No D1714 having failed en route. On 18 February 1966 Wakefield's No 48537 rescued the Hull portion of the up 'Yorkshire Pullman' following a diesel failure at Brough. During 1964, '8Fs' could still be seen at Scarborough and Bridlington, and as late as 1965 they were still working to Blackpool with excursions from the North Lancashire towns. On a warm evening in 1967 (the last summer of main line steam in the North West), No 48080 was standing at Weaver Junction with the 19.15 Northwich to Warrington freight when a Brush Type 4 diesel expired alongside with the 16.15 Euston to Barrow. The 2-8-0 worked the diesel and its 13-coach train on to Wigan, attaining 60mph before the climb to the Manchester Ship Canal bridge, and made a noisy and most impressive start from Warrington. Only six months earlier a rundown '8F' from Crewe South, purloined from the Whitchurch pick-up goods, had been spotted flailing down Wrenbury Bank at the head of another inoperative Type 4 on the 'Pines Express'.

The last years of steam also gave the '8Fs' the opportunity to display their prowess on numerous enthusiasts' specials. One of the most sporting efforts was on the RCTS 'Eight Counties' tour of 26 March 1966. No 48467 came on at Leicester, and with a six-coach train got very close indeed to even time by Loughborough (12½ miles). She was doing 65mph at Barrow-upon-Soar and reached a maximum of 72mph before Loughborough.

The various 'Farewell to Steam' specials in 1968 involved some very spirited running by Nos 48033, 48476 and 48773, and it was surely unjust that no '8F' was used on any part of the official BR Farewell trip on 11 August. It is highly unlikely that such heroic exploits will ever be seen again.

Eastern Region

After the transfer of its own '8Fs' to the LMR in 1947, the Eastern Region was without an '8F' allocation, although New England shed did briefly acquire No 48074 following the closure of Peterborough LMR shed in 1950.

BR days saw increasing through working of LMR '8Fs' on to ER territory, especially on the heavy coal, steel and merchandise traffic from the Midlands to March which brought '8Fs' from Rugby and a variety of Midland depots to the Fens. The engines were very occasionally borrowed to work on to Norwich or Ipswich, the last recorded instances on special freights being as late as 1964.

Scunthorpe steelworks and the coal export facilities at Immingham brought work for the '8Fs' with iron ore from Ashwell and other Midland sources routed via Syston, Toton and the Doncaster avoiding line. Leicester and Wellingborough engines, together with those from Toton and Canklow were often involved, Royston engines sometimes worked to the area with coal, whilst transfer steel traffic was handled by '8Fs' from Toton, Bescot, and by the early 1960s, from Woodford Halse and Annesley. Frodingham shed would frequently be host to several visiting '8Fs' at weekends, and the ER crews thought highly of them, preferring them to the WD or 'O4' 2-8-0s.

Northampton engines had regular diagrams to Doncaster in the late 1950s with iron ore traffic off the GN/LNWR Joint Line from Welham Sidings. About three workings per day were involved, joining the East Coast main line at Newark. The traffic ceased about 1962. Further south, '8Fs' from the Midland Division also penetrated Eastern Region territory on freights to Ripple Lane yard on Midland's London, Tilbury and Southend section, although such visits were increasingly scarce after electrification of the line in 1962. It was not unknown for Doncaster or Peterborough sheds to borrow an '8F' to work up the East Coast main line to London, but it was a rare occurrence.

In 1958, the ER absorbed the LMR Sheffield district, and '8F' workings into South Humberside became much more common, especially between Rotherham and Immingham on oil and coal traffic. The LMR take over of the Great Central at the same time eventually saw the 'O1' 2-8-0s at Annesley replaced by '8Fs' in 1962. The Stanier engines worked through from Woodford Halse and Annesley on iron ore and steel traffic. Earlier, in 1956, '8F' No 48078 and 'O1' No 63725 had been exchanged for several months between Toton and Annesley for boiler tube corrosion tests.

From about 1960, Nottingham area '8Fs' began to work through to Grantham, and later to Lincoln with freights from the East Midlands. Towards the end of 1961, Brush Type 2 diesels were introduced to the Sheffield area, and in August 1962, the ER withdrew four Staveley '8Fs'. They were reinstated as LMR stock, and many Staveley '8Fs' were replaced by redundant WD 2-8-0s from Mexborough in 1963. The dieselisation of Staveley in the spring of 1964 saw six '8Fs' withdrawn, and some others transferred to the LMR.

Although the ER lost its steam allocation in April 1966, LMR locomotives continued to work on to its territory for some time afterwards. The Ashwell iron ore trains were frequently '8F' hauled even as late as July, whilst occasional freights from Scunthorpe to Healey Mills and

Chesterfield, Avenue Sidings together with other services from the Midlands via Newark also produced members of the class. Locomotive variety was plentiful at this time. '8F' No 48436 of Shrewsbury was observed heading the 4.28am Doncaster to York service on 5 November 1965, and a variety of Manchester area and even Fleetwood engines appeared on turns between Scunthorpe and Chesterfield. The last steam workings to the Scunthorpe area were on the ballast trains from Wakefield to Santon, which produced a variety of '8F' types. No 48174 headed the final steam trip on 6 April 1967.

After the LMR gained control of Colwick depot in January 1966, '8Fs' began to work tank services to Hull, and to Scunthorpe on Colwick diagrams. As late as November there was still a regular Colwick to Barnetby mineral working, but this ceased with the closure of the shed at the end of 1966.

The last '8F' workings on to the ER seem to have been trips by Royston engines with coal trains for Keadby Power Station and to Immingham with export coal which continued almost until the end of steam on the North Eastern Region in the autumn of 1967.

North Eastern Region

The '8Fs' had always been relatively common on North Eastern Region (NER) territory as far as York which being a major route centre attracted 2-8-0s from the North and West Midlands on through freight workings across the Pennines. In the 1950s, '8Fs' were increasingly seen north of York either on through freights or as a result of being borrowed for work on NER territory. Traffic in coal and iron ore to Teesside was fairly frequently hauled throughout by the Stanier engines. Further south, Leeds engines would sometimes work north over NER territory to Darlington and Teesside via Harrogate and Wetherby.

In 1957, the Leeds area depots became part of the NER. Leeds, Stourton, Royston and Normanton engines could thenceforward be seen venturing more frequently on to NER territory. A feature of the allocation at these sheds was the number of engines which spent the whole, or at least most of their working lives either at the same depot, or in the area, although the Normanton '8Fs' were replaced by WD 2-8-0s in 1957. Also, comparatively few '8Fs' were withdrawn from NER depots.

The Leeds engines worked regularly over Ais Gill summit to Carlisle on general freight work, and could frequently be recognised by the bufferbeam-mounted snowploughs that they often carried for much of the year. Hellifield and Skipton also had small '8F' allocations at various times. The Leeds area saw a good many '8Fs' from a variety of North Western depots which arrived on Trans-Pennine coal, oil and general merchandise freights via both the Calder Valley and Standedge routes and from Heysham.

Normanton, Royston and Stourton depots had '8F' allocations since before the war when their main duties took them to Toton with coal for the south. In BR days their activities were more varied; they undertook more trip working in north Nottinghamshire and South Yorkshire, and worked northwards to York and Teesside. Royston engines ran over the remaining sections of the Hull & Barnsley line after 1960, and visited both Hull and Immingham with export coal. Wakefield often had a small

'8F' allocation. Its engines worked widely across the Pennines with coal traffic, and often into ER territory with colliery trips on the Dearne Valley line and elsewhere. '8Fs' from these Yorkshire depots also saw a fair amount of excursion work to East Coast resorts and Wetherby races.

Mirfield and Low Moor gained '8Fs' in June 1958, and in September 1959 the ex-Great Northern depot at Ardsley found itself with an allocation again for the first time since the LNER 'O6s' departed in 1948. Farnley Junction, the ex-LNWR shed in Leeds, had to wait until 1963 before it had any '8Fs' on its books, but it will be obvious that the class worked a very great deal of Trans-Pennine coal, merchandise, parcels and empty stock throughout much of the BR period.

After 1963, locomotives travelling to and from overhaul at Darlington provided another source of '8F' forays on to NER territory. The last '8F' to be repaired there was No 48392, which was outshopped in February 1966, shortly before the works closed.

By 1965, the '8Fs' were concentrated at Holbeck, Stourton, Farnley Junction, Royston and Mirfield. The 2-8-0s were still very busy working across the Pennines to and from Healey Mills yard, while freight traffic over the testing Settle to Carlisle line was still largely steam hauled. Quite a few 2-8-0s found themselves taking over from failed diesels on Liverpool to Newcastle services, and it was to be almost two years before the steam predominance on freight services in the area was broken. Wakefield and Normanton largely used WD 2-8-0s at this time, although a solitary '8F' returned to Wakefield in 1966/67.

As 1966 drew to a close, there were signs of the inevitable change in motive power. Healey Mills Type 4 diesels were beginning to appear on Pennine freight work to Stockport and elsewhere, and Farnley Junction shed closed on 26 November, '8F' No 48088 being the last engine off shed to work the 21.45 Stockport parcels. The NER's remaining '8Fs' still appeared in unusual places; Stourton's No 48126 worked to Darlington with coal on 27 October whilst, as already stated, Wakefield and Royston engines continued to make forays on to ER territory.

Western Region

Shortly after Nationalisation, the Western Region inherited all the former LMS network south and west of Shrewsbury, including the Central Wales '8F' allocations at Shrewsbury and Swansea Paxton Street. The LMR made a determined effort to regain its '8Fs' by having them replaced by WD 2-8-0s. The move was not popular with the footplate staff and the unbalanced WD locomotives were unsuitable for the passenger work that the '8Fs' often tackled. After six months of vociferous protest, the Stanier engines were back early in 1951, and remained the only members of the class on the WR until some fairly sensational happenings two years later.

In 1953, the WR management was viewing its forthcoming allocation of BR Standard Class 9F 2-10-0s with some alarm; with much short-haul freight work it felt that there was not scope for effective utilisation of such large locomotives, and it sought authority to build a further batch of '38xx' 2-8-0s, fine engines in themselves, but of a design which in basics, was then nearly 50 years old. Two outline proposals for a BR Standard 2-8-0 were schemed out but not proceeded with as it was felt that the general need was for a freight locomotive of '9F' capacity. A compromise was reached by allocating more '9Fs' to the LMR which released a number of displaced '8Fs' to the WR with the evident proviso that they should be Swindon built examples!

Nos 48420/75 appeared on loan to St Phillips Marsh in the summer of 1954. No 48475 soon moved to Ebbw Junction where it was used in the normal 2-8-0 links to London, whilst No 48420 had a wide range of action on all types of main line freight work to Plymouth, London, Banbury and on the North and West route. The WR deliberated on its new acquisitions for some 12 months before six '84xx' series were transferred to Banbury and St Phillips Marsh, followed by nine more in August. The Banbury engines enjoyed a wide range of action to Birkenhead, London, Bristol and on the iron ore traffic to Bilston and South Wales. However, the coal trains from the Warwickshire coalfield remained Nuneaton turns.

It would be fair to say that the '8Fs' enjoyed a mixed reception on the WR. They were much more popular than the despised WD 2-8-0s, but Western men never regarded them as being in any way the equal of their beloved '28xx'. Nevertheless, they were a versatile machine which was given a very wide range of action throughout the region. They were not used on passenger work to anything like the same extent as on the LMR, but the Old Oak allocation was well used on fitted freight, parcels, milk and empty coaching stock work to the West Country on busy Summer Saturdays. By 1956, enough confidence had been gained in the '8Fs' for the '84xx' series to be fitted with GWR Automatic Train Control (ATC) equipment as they passed through Horwich Works on programmed overhauls, gaining GWR type vacuum ejectors giving 25in vacuum in the process.

In the meantime, the GWR's Robinson ROD 2-8-0s were disappearing and attempts were being made to transfer WD 2-8-0s elsewhere. '8Fs' began to settle at such unlikely places as Newton Abbot, Worcester and Pontypool Road. They were often to be seen working the heavy mineral traffic between the West Midlands and South Wales, and the Pontypool Road allocation increased noticeably in 1956 as the last of the LNWR 'Super D' ('G2') 0-8-0s in the area were pensioned off. Hereford gained its first '8F' in April 1957, and with the Shrewsbury allocation augmented, the 2-8-0s put in much work on the North and West route.

During 1958, and in later years, some mixing of the original Central Wales and new ('84xx') allocations took place. Twelve engines were loaned to the LMR at the old GWR shed at Chester West in the summer of 1958, most of them moving on to Tyseley in the following April. By this time the '8Fs' were spread throughout the WR and could be seen working over most of the main lines except into Cornwall, although forays here by the Bristol allocation would have been quite possible.

In August 1959, the LMS depot at Swansea was closed and its '8F' allocation transferred to Llanelly. Although still usually working on the Central Wales line, the engines began to appear more frequently on WR routes in South Wales, especially after Cardiff Canton acquired

three in September 1959. More remarkable, was the allocation of No 48172 to Carmarthen for a month in August 1960. In June 1961, the class became more firmly associated with the West Midlands when Stourbridge Junction received an allocation for heavy freight work to and from the 'Black Country'.

More new ground was broken in October when two '8Fs' were sent to Bath Green Park as replacements for the ageing S&D 2-8-0s. The slightly inferior braking qualities of the '8Fs' were no longer an impediment on the shorter trains traversing the Mendips in the line's closing years, and there was no disputing the vigorous way the Stanier engines tackled the 1 in 50 gradients of this unique railway. Surprisingly, not until June 1962 did Bristol Barrow Road acquire a solitary '8F', No 48474, which was soon replaced by No 48431. For many years the depot had been visited by 'foreign' '8Fs' working to the West Country from the North Midlands.

From 1957 the WR had gained control of the Midland's main line to the West of England south of Barnt Green, and from 1963 the LMR acquired the WR territory north of Banbury and Craven Arms. This meant that for the last two years '8F' activity on the WR was confined to depots in South Wales and the Bristol area. By the summer of 1963, steam activity in the West of England was virtually at an end, but No 48423 of Birkenhead did manage to reach Plymouth with a special freight on 22 September, Laira's only other steam locomotive by this time being a '45xx' 2-6-2T. With dieselisation, some of the WR-allocated '8Fs' had been transferred to depots in the West Midlands which came under LMR control from 1963. A major change came in July 1964 when through freight traffic ceased on the Central Wales Line. Many '8Fs' were initially placed in store at Llanelly, some were transferred to the North Western Lines and a few were withdrawn. The Bath Green Park allocation was considerably augmented, spelling the end for the S&D 2-8-0s, whilst Neath gained a couple of '8Fs' for a brief period before they returned to Llanelly where they joined others working the pick up freight to Craven Arms and some other WR freight traffic in South Wales which was then due for imminent dieselisation. No 48039 of Buxton reached Taunton after working chemical tanks to Bridgwater on 20 September, and also at this time '8Fs' were appearing on the Llandarcy to Llanwern tank workings; by the end of the year the WR allocation of the class was down to six at Bath and five at Llanelly.

During 1965, '8Fs' continued to reach Gloucester, Bristol and South Wales from the Midlands on general freight work. A coal dispute in South Wales saw a marked increase in '8Fs' working in from Yorkshire during June. They were serviced at Neath and the return light engines were frequently borrowed by the WR to cover diesel failures. '8Fs' also still reached the London area of the WR via the Great Central route and from the West Midlands via Oxford and High Wycombe. However, the Central Wales pick-up duty ceased in the summer of 1965, and by the autumn steam had been banished from South Wales. Steam traction was to be cleared from the whole region by the end of the year.

In January 1966, the WR officially withdrew its steam locomotives and closed its last steam depots. One enclave of steam working remained for a few months longer at

Bath Green Park where the Somerset & Dorset line, closure temporarily postponed, struggled on with a meagre service until March 1966. The allocation at Bath consisted of only eight locomotives, including four '8Fs', which sometimes had to be used on the surviving passenger trains, and only No 48309 had carriage warming equipment! Elsewhere on the region, there may have been occasional '8F' forays to Oxford from Banbury into the spring of 1966, and certainly steam remained fairly plentiful on the West of England line at this time. Numerous '8Fs' were seen working through to Gloucester from the LMR, and some even got through to Bristol at the end of 1965. On 31 January, No 48074 was seen at Honeybourne with the Thames Haven to Rowley Regis tanks, normally an English Electric Type 3 diesel working, whilst on 29 April, No 48651 was sent out from Worcester to rescue a failed 'Hymek' diesel on the 11.15 from Paddington. Occasional steam workings to Gloucester continued into the summer of 1966 by which time many sheds in the West and North Midlands had closed to steam; and the possibilities for such incursions were very much reduced. It was quite fitting that Stanier locomotives should have been amongst the last steam locomotives to work on the WR.

Scottish Region
After 1950, the '8Fs' were not often seen in Scotland, and until 1957 there was no '8F' allocation in the country itself. Carlisle Canal shed had lost its '8F' allocation in 1952, although Kingmoor engines continued to work north of the Border.

The Canal engines worked to both Newcastle and Edinburgh, where St Margarets depot was not above purloining them for its own duties in times of stress. Occasionally '8Fs' may have also appeared in the Scottish capital from the East Coast route up to 1950 as a result of being overhauled at Darlington. No 48544 was reported to have been seen at Tweedmouth in 1951.

The Kingmoor allocation appeared on a wide range of main line freights to Glasgow, sometimes Edinburgh and occasionally to Grangemouth or Perth. Both the Caledonian and Glasgow & South Western routes were used, but essentially the '8Fs' were intermittent visitors and Scotland remained firmly 'WD' 2-8-0 and 2-10-0 territory. The '8Fs' were sometimes used on the limestone workings from Shap Quarry to the steelworks in Lanarkshire, and it may have been these workings that produced a spare '8F' at St Rollox on busy Glasgow Fair weekends for the odd extra service bound for Oban. In July 1953 No 48464 was spotted at Aberdeen, presumably having worked in from Carlisle, and in March 1958, No 48612 was seen on Haymarket shed.

In 1957, BR purchased a final three '8Fs' from the War Department, BR Nos 48773/4/5. This purchase coincided with the introduction of a new service of iron ore trains between Glasgow's Terminus Quay and Ravenscraig steel works, for which '8F' power was required. The three 2-8-0s from Longmoor were despatched to Glasgow Polmadie. They spent much of their time double-heading with 'WD' 2-8-0s on the ore trains, and on a wide variety of the heavier trip workings in the Glasgow area. They also worked on main line freights to Carlisle and Ayr, and spent a lot of time on the coal traffic between the Clackmannan coalfield and the Glasgow area.

The three Polmadie engines led rather chequered careers; they were withdrawn at the end of 1962 following the introduction of the Clayton Type 1 diesels. However, this was one of the worst winters in memory, and within a month they had been reinstated whilst many of the diesels were in store. The engines were finally withdrawn in July 1963, and this marked the official end of the Stanier '8F' allocation in Scotland. In November 1963, the three engines were retrieved from the scrap road at Horwich, overhauled and reinstated at Carlisle Kingmoor. Two of them were to survive until the end, one to be preserved as LMS No 8233.

Over the next four years, the '8Fs' continued to make sporadic visits to Scotland from Carlisle, although the Kingmoor stud had been replaced by '9Fs' in 1964. It is strange that the Stanier 2-8-0s were not more extensively used in Scotland, especially after their good work there during the war. They would have done very well on many heavily graded Scottish routes.

Forays on to Southern Territory
For many years the only regular '8F' visits to the Southern Region were with the often heavy transfer freights across London from the LMR to the yards at Feltham and Norwood Junction via the West London Line. Willesden and Cricklewood engines were officially involved, but visiting locomotives from a wide range of depots were often used. Pathing was tight, and some spirited contests with Southern electrics were not unknown. The workings ceased with the closure to steam of Willesden depot in the autumn of 1965.

Towards the end of the 1950s, there were occasional forays of WR-based '8Fs' on through freights to the Eastleigh and Southampton area, but quite unprecedented was the appearance of No 48403 at Exmouth Junction on 18 February 1956. Following a derailment at Westbury, she had been diverted via Yeovil and the South Western route to Exeter. In 1957, Eastleigh works had rather surprisingly overhauled Nos 48773/4/5 newly purchased from Longmoor; the engines ran light to Polmadie — at least as far as Willesden.

As the 1960s dawned, regional boundaries were no longer quite so rigid and longer through locomotive workings became the rule. The development of the Fawley oil refinery saw '8Fs' working through from the Midlands to Eastleigh and sometimes to Totton or Millbrook with heavy tank trains. Saltley engines were usually involved, but Toton locomotives appeared on such trains as the 20.40 Fawley to Rotherham. From about 1963, many of the principal oil services were dieselised with Type 3 diesels working in tandem. However traffic to Southampton docks ensured that the '8Fs' continued to work into the area on a great variety of freight traffic until the end of steam working on the Western Region early in 1966. The 04.15 Basingstoke to Oxley was a favourite turn for returning straying '8Fs' and other LMR power to their native region.

After 1962, Bath Green Park '8Fs' could sometimes be seen at Bournemouth on freight and passenger work off the Somerset & Dorset line. On 1 August 1964, No 48737 was used to work the Bournemouth West portion of an express from Waterloo forward from Bournemouth Central. By this time, Eastleigh had begun to overhaul LMR locomotives in lieu of Horwich and Derby works,

'8Fs' travelling to and from overhaul working SR freight services. The Southern in fact became quite adept at using other regions' motive power in these years and on 22 December 1964 No 48374 was borrowed by Feltham to work a fertiliser special from Alton to Farringdon. Six months later, the incredible happened when No 48408, just out of Eastleigh works, was used to work a series of local trains, culminating in a Basingstoke to Waterloo commuter working on 17 June and the 17.09 Waterloo to Basingstoke return!

In 1965, '8Fs' also had a fairly regular working on a Severn Tunnel Junction to Chichester freight train,

returning with the 05.58 Chichester to Washwood Heath. Their Southern Region swan song however, was undoubtedly on 4 June 1965 when Willesden turned out No 48544 to work a Newcastle to Hove pigeon special. The Southern declined to replace the LMR locomotive, and she made a brave sight forging down the Brighton main line at the head of 20 bogie vans!

Eastleigh continued to overhaul a few '8Fs' until early in 1966, and the last '8F' appcarance on Southern Region territory was probably that of No 48706 which worked into Bournemouth with one of the 'Somerset & Dorset Farewell' specials early in March.

MIDLAND DIVISION

Right:
No 48338 (H44), heading a long train of mineral empties back to the North Midlands, is checked at Wing Sidings on 26 September 1959. The Fireman, trying to 'keep the engine quiet', is manipulating the water regulator for the live steam injector, under the driver's seat. *P. H. Wells*

Below:
A period scene in the Erewash Valley. Pit mounds mark the skyline as No 48313 (C43) heads iron ore empties southwards near Stapleford and Sandiacre on 3 May 1958. *D. Swale*

Right:

The rough and tumble of colliery trips was all part of the day's work for Nottinghamshire '8Fs'. No 48317 (C44) battles with a heavy Kirkby-Staythorpe coal haul on the Mansfield Colliery Branch near Blidworth and Rainworth in March 1962. *J. Cupit*

Centre right:

No 48319 (C44) rolls a southbound coal haul from Toton through the layout at Wigston, south of Leicester, on 22 August 1959. *M. Mensing*

Below:

No 48355 (H44) pounds away at the 1 in 176 gradient as she approaches Elstree tunnel with a down Class 7 freight on 14 September 1963. Steel-bodied mineral wagons are prominent in the consist, and before long there will be a change in the motive power as well.
B. Stephenson

Above:
Wellingborough MPD — so long the home of a substantial number of '8Fs' — is prominent in the background as No 48467 (S45) rolls southwards with a substantial ballast special. 19 April 1963.
C. P. Boocock

Centre left:
Midland Steam Finale; No 48225 (NB42) shouts defiance at the surrounding countryside as she tackles the grade to Wymington Tunnel with a substantial train of slack for Goldington Power Station on 3 November 1965. *K. Fairey*

Left:
No 48271 (NB42) leaves Derby with a mixed through freight for the south on 27 March 1965.
J. S. Hancock

Above:
Westhouses' No 48204 (NB42) climbs past Chinley North Junction's distinctive signals, heading for Cowburn Tunnel and Edale with the 08.15 Gowhole-Blackwell colliery empties on 22 April 1965. *J. Clarke*

Below:
No 48475 (S45) of Tyseley, climbs away from Ettington towards Stratford-upon-Avon with a westbound partially-fitted freight in March 1964. *T. E. Williams*

Right:
Burton's No 48117 (C39) heads a down express freight out of Basford tunnel on the Great Central main line north of Nottingham on 17 July 1965. *J. Cupit/ V. Forster Collection*

Centre right:
No 48166 (C43) attacks the 1 in 176 of Ashby bank, south of Leicester, with an Annesley-Woodford minerals haul on 26 October 1963. *M. Mitchell*

Below:
Requiem; A vintage scene at Ambergate Station South Junction on 12 February 1966. No 48098 (C39) heads a train of Midlands iron ore for the Lancashire Steel Co's works at Irlam on to the Peak Forest route. Barely 12 months' steam operation remained in Derbyshire at that time. Today the Peak Forest route is closed and Ambergate stands on the single track Matlock branch. Steel making at Irlam is also no more. *B. Stephenson*

WESTERN DIVISION

Above:
Bletchley, 26 September 1953. No 48685 (B44) 'gets the road' on the up slow with a Toton-Willesden coal haul.
B. K. B. Green/V. Forster Collection

Below:
The West Coast scene of the 1950s; No 48648 (B43) heads southwards from Nuneaton with an up through freight in the summer of 1953. *K. Robey*

Above:
No 48551 (D45) makes for Oxford through Verney Junction with a load of Northamptonshire iron ore destined for South Wales on 27 February 1960.
S. Rickard

Below:
This picture has appeared before, but it evocatively tells what the '8Fs' were all about. It is probably a Saturday afternoon in 1962 as an enthusiastic pair of Northwich men set No 48521 (Dn44) storming up the 1 in 90 to Peak Forest near New Mills South Junction with return limestone hoppers for Tunstead. They have probably been going at it like this since Cheadle Heath, and it wouldn't have been done on one firing! *A. H. Bryant*

Left:
Manchester London Road, 2 June 1954. Longsight's No 48501 (D44) comes off the MSJ&A route and heads southwards with a cross-Manchester freight. In the background a 2-6-4 tank marshals stock whilst a 'Royal Scot' heads a London express.
*B. K. B. Green/
V. Forster Collection*

Left:
Nuneaton's No 48289 (BP40) winds an up express freight away from Llandudno Junction on 7 September 1962.
V. Forster Collection

Below:
Mold Junction's No 48447 (S44) rolls under the Town Walls at Chester with a long train of tank wagons from the ICI plant at Amlwch on 20 August 1951. *P. M. Alexander*

Above right:
Industrial Midlands; No 48339 (H44) gets hold of a Washwood Heath-Bordesley trip working and prepares for the climb past St Andrews as she passes Saltley station on 26 April 1958. *M. Mensing*

Right:
No hint of the forthcoming electrification in this scene on the West Coast main line at Hanslope on 11 May 1961. Life-long Willesden resident No 48624 (A43) heads a train of Stonebridge Park hoppers back to Toton. Withdrawn in 1965, she spent 17 years or so in Woodham Brothers' Barry Scrapyard before being rescued for preservation at Buxton by the 48518 Preservation Society. Numerous '8Fs' exchanged their Stanier tenders with 'Jubilees' for the Fowler 3,500 gallon variety in the late 1950s, regaining the Stanier version in the mid-1960s as a result of passenger locomotive withdrawals. *K. Fairey*

Right:
Nearing the end; No 48056 (VF36) wheels a long train of mineral empties under a forest of overhead wires out of Willesden Down Yard on 27 March 1965. Steam at Willesden had just six months left, but at least the '8Fs' retained many of their old jobs to the last. In the background 'Black Five' No 45392 sneaks into the picture with empty stock from Euston. *D. A. Idle*

Top:
Warrington's No 48543 (D45) is rather off the beaten track as she rolls a heavy trip freight through Handsworth and Smethwick on former Western Region territory in the West Midlands on 31 December 1964.
J. H. Cooper-Smith

Left:
Kirkby's No 48541 (D44) raises the echoes as she sets about the 1 in 126 climb from Nuneaton to Stockingford tunnel with a heavy Ashby-Birmingham freight on 6 November 1965. *J. H. Cooper-Smith*

Above:
Llanelly's No 48707 (B44) rolls down Gresford Bank with a freight for Chester on 1 June 1964. Following the end of through freight on the Central Wales Line she moved a month later to Bath Green Park, and then to Lostock Hall in September. The steam heating connection fitted for her Royal Train duty in 1955 can be seen on the front bufferbeam. *D. Cross*

Above:

Traction change; A scene that was to be repeated with increasing frequency as the diesel onslaught engulfed the railway in the mid-1960s. D5278 arrives at Northwich with limestone from Peak Forest, as No 48632 (B43) heads through the station with a return set of hoppers on 19 July 1967. Fortunately steam lasted at Northwich for a further eight months, No 48632 being active on the very last day. *C. T. Gifford*

Right:

No 48141 (C42) darkens the sky as she roars past Springs Branch, Wigan, taking a run at the climb to Boars Head with a Northwich-Shawfield Covhop special in September 1965.
E. F. Bentley

Right:

One of the last '8Fs' to be overhauled at Crewe in August 1966 — Northwich's No 48151 (C42) — is run in by Crewe South shed on a coal special to Carlisle, seen here tackling the 1 in 75 at Shap Wells, banked by Fairburn Class 4MT 2-6-4T No 42210. After withdrawal in January 1968, No 48151 spent over 10 years incarcerated at Barry before being purchased privately for preservation. She is currently being overhauled near Wakefield.
J. S. Hancock/
V. Forster Collection

PASSENGER SERVICES

Below:
The 'Thames-Clyde Express' headboard sits well on the smokebox of No 48266 (NB42) as she rolls the down express into Trent, following a 'Jubilee' failure at Leicester, on 2 July 1955. *J. Kent*

Bottom:
Stourton's No 48652 (E43) climbs through Scholes on the now closed Cross Gates-Wetherby line with a race special from the Huddersfield area on 7 April 1958. *M. Mitchell*

Above:
No 48308 (C43) romps through Kirkham with a Northwich-Blackpool excursion made up of a spare Northwich-Manchester suburban set, about 1961. *J. Davenport*

Right:
No 48508 (D44) gets away from Banbury with a summer Saturday Newcastle-Cardiff relief train in the late 1950s. The engine worked through from York at least as far as Oxford! *V. Forster*

Below right:
Southern Region stock predominates in the make up of the 10.05(SO) Bournemouth-Derby, seen leaving Bromsgrove for the climb of the Lickey incline behind Saltley's No 48101 (C39), banked by two 94xx pannier tanks. It would appear that the 2-8-0 had worked through from Bath. 6 August 1960. *T. J. Edgington*

Above:
Regal Progress; Two immaculate '8Fs', Nos 48309 and 48707, wind the heavy Royal Train through the Cambrian Mountains from Aberystwyth up to Tregaron, photographed near Trawscoed on 8 August 1955. The two engines worked the train over the now closed branch to Carmarthen and down to Pembroke Dock in the heart of Western Region territory. *I. Higgon*

Top:
Black Country Spectacle; Stourbridge's No 48417 (S44) pilots SR 'West Country' 4-6-2 No 34039 *Boscastle* up the 1 in 50 of Old Hill bank with a Southampton-Birmingham Snow Hill football excursion on 27 April 1963. *M. Mensing*

EASTERN REGION

Above:
**No 48750 (D46) eases a
haul of coal from the East
Midlands to East Anglia
under the East Coast Main
Line, and approaches
Peterborough East station
on 21 October 1961.**
P. H. Wells

Right:
**Pontefract (Baghill) in the
late-1950s. No 48205
(NB42) creeps into the
picture with an iron ore
train from the East
Midlands to the North East
as 'Jubilee' No 45685
Barfleur leaves with the
08.10 to Sheffield.**
P. Cookson

Below right:
**No 48140 (C42) passes
Appleby (Lincs) with an
Immingham-Rotherham
tanks haul in July 1962.**
J. J. Foreman

Top:
No 48119 (C39) heads a heavy train of steel and coal south of Staveley on the Rotherham-Chesterfield line on 12 June 1965. *J. S. Hancock*

Above:
No 48150 (C42) heaves a heavy southbound coal haul off the Sheffield avoiding line and across the layout at Tapton Junction, Chesterfield, on 29 April 1963. *D. Booth*

Above:

Holbeck's No 48104 (C39) sets a spanking pace through Cotehill, taking a run at the 'Long Drag' up to Ais Gill with a Carlisle-Leeds through freight in the early-1960s. *R. Leslie*

Left:

No 48621 (A43) of Mansfield double-heads 'Black Five' No 44891 (Newton Heath) into York with the afternoon Clifton Sidings-Manchester Red Bank stock and parcels train on 3 August 1957. *R. A. Panting*

Below left:

No 48067 (VF36) wheels round the curve at Leeds Whitehall Junction, with a 15-coach rake of empty stock being taken to Carlisle for work on the 'Starlight Specials'. 7 September 1961 *G. W. Morrison*

Above:
No 48340 (H44) takes the west to south curve at Wakefield Kirkgate with Hartford North-Woolley Colliery empties, about 1967. It was unusual for Northwich engines to work beyond Godley Junction with such traffic, and the engine may be a substitute for a failed Wakefield WD 'Austerity' 2-8-0. *L. A. Nixon*

Right:
No 48744 (D46) drifts an eastbound express freight towards Mirfield on 20 July 1962. *D. Ian Wood*

Below right:
Severe surroundings of blackened Pennine gritstone form a typical background as No 48158 (C43), complete with buffer beam snowplough, heads an up freight through Bingley Junction, Shipley, in the late 1960s. *H. Weston*

SCOTTISH REGION

Top:
Carlisle Kingmoor's No 48758 (Dn45) completes the climb of the Clyde Valley and nears Beattock Summit with limestone empties returning from the Lanarkshire steelworks to Shap Quarry. August 1960.
P. H. Groom

Above:
Polmadie pairing; Class '8F' No 48774 (NB40) and WD 'Austerity' 2-8-0 No 90549 pass Glasgow's Terminus Junction with iron ore from Glasgow Docks to the Lanarkshire steelworks. 26 April 1960. *W. A. C. Smith*

WESTERN REGION

Above:
No 48475 (S45) — recently allocated to Bristol St Phillips Marsh — climbs Hemerdon bank, east of Plymouth, with a Tavistock Junction-Bristol express freight, banked by 2-6-2T No 3186 on 5 July 1955. *R. C. Riley*

Right:
No 48475 again, this time caught wheeling a down empty stock train along the Exe estuary at Dawlish Warren on 9 August 1956. *T. E. Williams Colln/ NRM, York*

Below right:
No 48417 (S44) rolls downhill from Colwall to Great Malvern with a load of South Wales coal destined for the industries of the 'Black Country' on 31 May 1958. *A. A. Vickers*

Above:
Great Western lower quadrant signals and the South Shropshire hills frame this photograph of No 48409 (S44) drifting through Craven Arms with a train of mineral empties for South Wales on 5 June 1964. Alas, this scene is very much rationalised today. *D. Cross*

Below:
No 48459 (S44) approaches Birmingham Snow Hill with an up express freight for the south in August 1961. Despite the multitude of lamp brackets on the locomotive, of both GW and LM pattern, the position of the top headlamp should be noted! Incredibly, not a rail remains today to remind us of this once busy scene in the centre of Birmingham. *B. A. Haresnape*

120

Above right:
A long mineral haul, headed by Old Oak Common's No 48431 (S44) threads the layout at Oxford on 11 September 1960. No 48431 was withdrawn from Bath in the spring of 1964 and spent eight years in Barry scrapyard before being rescued for use on the Keighley and Worth Valley Railway in 1972.
M. Mensing

Centre right:
No 48412 (S44) provides merry music as she makes a spirited attack on Hatton bank, having eschewed the services of a banker, on 9 April 1960. The GWR vacuum ejector giving 25in of vacuum instead of the standard 21in is prominent in its forward-mounted position on the left-hand side of the boiler. *T. E. Williams Colln/ NRM, York*

Right:
Traction change on the Somerset & Dorset. At least the S&D was never a diesel railway, but the 1960s saw the steady replacement of the S&D 2-8-0s by '8Fs'. A scene at Midford on 19 July 1963 — S&D 2-8-0 No 53808 (now preserved on the West Somerset Railway) heading a Writhlington Colliery-Bath coal train waits for No 48737 (D45) to clear the single line section from Bath with empties for Norton Hill colliery. *D. Cross*

Above:
A mid-1950s scene on the Midland's West of England main line; Toton's No 48637 (B43) powers a long haul of North Midlands coal past Berkeley Road South Junction towards Bristol on 15 April 1956. *D. S. Fish*

Below:
Ashley Hill Bank, Bristol, about 1957. With headlamps lit, No 48402 (S43) is caught by the fast fading light of a winter's afternoon as she attacks the 1 in 75 with northbound minerals, banked in the rear by a '41xx' tank. *G. F. Heiron*

Above:
Summer in Central Wales; No 48354 (H44) takes water at Builth Road with the 12.25 Shrewsbury-Swansea (Victoria) as No 45190 coasts into the picture with the 12.20 from Swansea on 25 August 1962.
B. J. Ashworth

Centre right:
Clambering into the mountains of Central Wales, a Stanier '8F' barks defiantly as she tackles the tough, curving approach to Knucklas viaduct with the heavy 15.15 Class H freight from Coleham to Llandilo Junction, on 11 April 1961. *D. Cross*

Right:
Rugby's No 48005 (C35) is wandering far away from home passing Haresfield with a southbound throught freight on 19 October 1963.
E. J. S. Gadsden

Above:
No 48669 (B44) shatters the Cotswold stillness as she forges up the 1 in 100 from Honeybourne to Chipping Campden with oil tanks returning from the West Midlands to Fawley on 7 March 1964. *G. England*

Below:
Bustling up the GW/GC Joint Line near Beaconsfield is No 48650 (E43) at the head of an up freight from Woodford Halse to the capital on 9 November 1963. *B. Stephenson*

Above:

With closure and abandonment less than 12 months away, No 48309 (C43) makes a spirited attack on the notorious 1 in 50 out of Bath Green Park towards Devonshire Tunnel on the Somerset and Dorset line, with the LCGB 'Wessex Downsman' special of 4 April 1965. *B. Stephenson*

Below:

Traction change on the Western Region; the last months of steam between Birmingham and Gloucester find a diesel-dominated scene at Bromsgrove on 16 June 1966. Two English Electric Type 3 (or Class 37) diesel bankers return from Blackwell to assist the 'Hymek'-hauled up freight on the left as '8F' No 48336 (H43), having descended the Lickey with wagon brakes pinned down, draws forward from its train to take water. *A. A. Vickers*

SOUTHERN REGION

Above:

A cross-London freight from the Midland Division, headed by Wellingborough's No 48386 (H45) approaches Feltham yard on 22 March 1951.

J. F. Russell-Smith/National Railway Museum

Below:

No 48629 (B43) comes up the Brighton main line and approaches Clapham Junction with a Norwood Junction-Willesden transfer freight on 3 May 1963. Note the star under the number on the cabside, indicating a 50% reciprocating balance.   *B. Stephenson*

Above right:
No 48706 (B44) departs from Bournemouth Central with the stock of the GWS 'Farewell' special on the Somerset & Dorset Line which it has just worked from Bath. 5 March 1966.
P. W. Gray/V. Forster Collection

Right:
Stranger at Waterloo; No 48408 (S44) stands alongside 'Battle of Britain' 4-6-2 No 34063 *229 Squadron*, having arrived with the 08.21 from Basingstoke following overhaul at Eastleigh. 17 June 1965.
H. A. Gamble

Below:
Willesden's No 48544 (D45) gallops down the Brighton Main Line near Clayton Tunnel with a mammoth 20-vehicle Newcastle-Hove pigeon special on 4 June 1965.
S. C. Nash

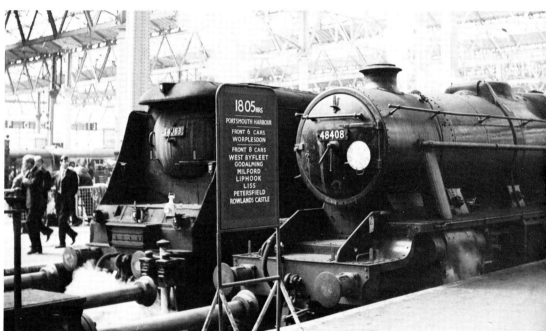

7

Retreat to the North

As 1967 dawned, 382 '8Fs' remained in service, the heaviest concentration of the class being on the North Western Lines where 252 were in traffic. A further 10 months useful service remained for the 40 engines on the Eastern Region in the West Riding, but steam was in its death throes on the LMR's Midland Division and was soon to disappear in the West Midlands and North Wales. The last '8F' to be overhauled had left Crewe Works in November 1966, and with the end of steam overhauls in February 1967, the surviving engines were consigned to the scrap heap as soon as major repairs were needed. A fair number of '8Fs' had received intermediate overhauls of various sorts in 1966 and many of these locomotives were stored, waiting for the remainder to fall by the wayside.

The 2-8-0s were still in command of a great variety of freight work. They could be seen challenging the northern fells over both Shap and Ais Gill, much of the freight traffic on all the Trans-Pennine routes was still steam worked, whilst perhaps 80% of traffic on the Cheshire Lines was still hauled by steam, most of it in the hands of the '8Fs'. Although the ICI hopper trains had been dieselised in 1964, steam substitutions were quite frequent. Local freight throughout Lancashire and on Merseyside was still very much an '8F' domain, and on the Eastern Region engines from Royston were still working to York, and the North Midlands and South Humberside with Yorkshire coal, while Leeds engines ran to Heysham and Carlisle. Further south, the picture was a good deal less rosy; the Colwick engines were not in traffic in 1967, and Kirkby had only a handful left for local trip work. In the Potteries there was still a fair amount of steam working, but in the West Midlands there were very few main line turns for the '8Fs'. Oxley and Stoke engines still worked the steeply graded branch to Ironbridge with power station coal, and the 2-8-0s could be seen on main line freights between the West Midlands and the Wirral. At Wrexham they were still busy with local trip work and the Chester allocation maintained a small '8F' presence in North Wales.

In February, Kirkby's 31-year association with the '8Fs' ended and the Midland Division of the LMR, where the class had really made its reputation, became fully dieselised. In the West Midlands, diesels had been creeping in steadily since the beginning of the year and the route rationalisation carried out from 4 March saw Oxley and Saltley depots closed. One of the last long-distance steam workings into the area was the Ellesmere Port to Nuneaton tanks on which No 48459 performed the last honours on 4 March. Also, from this date the working of

Stoke '8Fs' into the area with North Staffordshire coal came to an end. Oxley continued to be visited by Crewe South engines for tyre turning and other repairs for a little while longer, but these light engine movements had ceased by the autumn.

Although No 48285 had got through to Holyhead with a fertiliser special on 18 February, steam had virtually disappeared from North Wales after Easter. The Wrexham allocation was stored by May, and in June the Chester engines were rendered redundant. A major retreat came in the autumn with the closure of Crewe South, Stoke and Birkenhead depots, when '8F' activity south of Preston and in the Potteries and Cheshire was much reduced. Their work on the heavy Trentham to Shotwick coal hauls and sand workings from Oakamoor was now at an end, as were their occasional visits to Shrewsbury.

Early in October, the Eastern Region rid itself of its last steam locomotives when Holbeck and Royston depots were closed to steam. This greatly reduced the steam workings in the West Riding and over the Settle & Carlisle line, but Newton Heath, Patricroft and Bolton '8Fs' continued to tackle the 'Lancashire Alps' to Blackburn and the 'Long Drag' to Ais Gill with Brindle Heath to Carlisle freights. On the ER, Normanton remained as a servicing point for LMR motive power working in to the West Riding, but as the year closed the amount of steam hauled freight over the Standedge route declined noticeably.

On the North Western lines, more Brush Type 4 diesels arrived from the Western Region and new deliveries of Type 1 and 2 diesels continued. The new English Electric Type 4s of the present day Class 50 were also beginning to roll off the production lines. Springs Branch, Wigan, closed in December and steam was by then becoming very rare on the West Coast Main Line south of Preston although isolated workings were to survive almost to the end. Early in January 1968 the new diesel depot at Carlisle opened, and with the closure of Kingmoor shed, steam working over Shap and Ais Gill ceased; the sharp, throaty bark of a hard worked '8F' attacking the Cumbrian hill country was now a thing of the past. All these changes had seen the withdrawal of 110 '8Fs' in just six months, and with other classes even more drastically decimated, the retreat of steam in the autumn of 1967 was on a massive scale.

In January 1968, 138 '8Fs' remained in traffic at Edge Hill, Speke Junction, Northwich, Heaton Mersey, Stockport Edgeley, Buxton, Newton Heath, Patricroft, Bolton, Lostock Hall and Rose Grove depots. No steam turns remained north of Carnforth (apart from bankers) or south of Hartford on the West Coast Main Line; there was still a good deal of steam working on Merseyside, and Cheshire Lines freight traffic was still about 50% steam hauled. A great variety of freight and trip working in the Bolton and Manchester areas remained steam worked. The mineral traffic between North West Lancashire and Healey Mills still gave the '8Fs' work via Todmorden and over the gable of Copy Pit, but steam hauled freight over Standedge was confined increasingly to special freights and diesel substitutes. Some demanding long distance trains survived, the heavy 10.30 Northwich to Whitehaven soda ash Covhops remained an '8F' duty until the shed closed in March, and '8Fs' still appeared romping along the West Coast with fitted freights from Heysham. Buxton 2-8-0s could still be seen forging up the 1 in 90 to Peak Forest against the magnificent backdrop of the South Pennine hills with the Gowhole trips or wandering across the lonely limestone plateau to the quarries and limeworks at Hindlow.

However, signs of steam's approaching demise were ever more apparent. As locomotives developed defects, they were laid on one side in forlorn groups awaiting the inevitable journey to oblivion at Buttigiegs of Newport, Cashmores of Great Bridge, Cohens of Kettering, Drapers of Hull and elsewhere. Because of their mechanical condition, some locomotives were incapable of making a last journey and were cut up at the sheds. No 48469 was disposed of at Bolton in this way, and No 48375, the victim of a collision with runaway No D398 on the Copy Pit incline in July 1967, was similarly dealt with at Rose Grove. The surviving locomotives continued unkempt, filthy, with oil caked on motion and running gear and steam leaks in profusion, run down but still capable of surprisingly good performances in the hands of determined crews.

Buxton and Northwich sheds closed their doors to steam in March, and were followed by Edge Hill, Speke Junction, Stockport Edgeley and Heaton Mersey in May. Steam hauled freight on Merseyside and over much of the Cheshire Lines was virtually at an end, together with the remaining steam work over Standedge. Many enthusiasts made the pilgrimage to the Peak District to see off the Buxton locomotives, and at Northwich the vociferous activities of Nos 48036 and 48632 on the ICI trip workings were memorable, concluding with a piece of pure nostalgia when No 48632 was allowed to work a set of limestone hoppers into Winnington works. The sight and sound of that begrimed entertainer storming over the Weaver Viaduct for the last time ensured the formation of the Stanier '8F' Locomotive Society and the eventual preservation of No 48773. In the meantime, the lines of dumped locomotives grew to unprecedented proportions — only a few of the inhabitants of closed depots survived by transfer to pastures new.

Steam working in the Manchester area ended on 30 June when Newton Heath, Patricroft and Bolton closed, bringing to an end, amongst other things the spectacle of an '8F' charging the 1 in 25/30 gradient on the Chequerbent branch, west of Bolton, with all of six wagons! No 48033 worked the LCGB 'Two Cities Limited' special in a most energetic manner, providing a last chance to travel behind steam over many lines in the

south Manchester and Liverpool areas, and then it was back to steam's last hunting ground at Lostock Hall, Rose Grove and Carnforth. Most of the '8Fs' congregated at Rose Grove with a small contingent at Lostock Hall, spending their last weeks on traditional mineral work between Healey Mills and Fleetwood, the trips to Padiham power station, as Stansfield Hall bankers and on local trains from the Lancashire pits to Whitebirk power station. Typical '8F' jobs were:

06.53(SO), 07.43(SX)	Farington Jn-Cudworth	7N82
08.15(SX)	Parkside-Whitebirk	7N87
11.30	Bickershaw-Whitebirk	8P12
14.10	Wyre Dock-Burnley	7P80
16.40(SX)	Wyre Dock-Preston	7P33
18.40(SX)	Preston-Healey Mills	7N99
21.45(SX)	Preston-Cudworth	7N68
02.15(MSX)	Rose Grove-Ribble Sidings	
08.55	Whitebirk-Bickershaw	8F43
10.52(SX)	Burnley-Wyre Dock	8P21
13.10(SX)	Rose Grove-Wyre Dock	6P32
14.30(SO)	Darwen-Heysham oil	4P21
18.40(TThO)	Darwen-Heysham oil	4P21

Other possible '8F' workings were:

06.05(MX)	Bamfurlong-Carnforth	6P03
10.50	Ribble Sidings-Heysham	6P03
11.23(SX)	Ribble Sidings-Carnforth	5P23
19.10(SX)	Ribble Sidings-Carnforth	6P16
15.05(SX)	Heysham-Warrington	5F16
16.50	Heysham-Burnden Jct	5J32

With the withdrawal of the last '9F' 2-10-0 in mid-June, the '8Fs' became BR's last surviving steam freight locomotives, and took over the Carnforth duties double-heading Type 2 diesels as far as Hellifield with the heavy Heysham to Leeds tank workings. Sometimes, these trains were steam worked through to Leeds, the '8F' returning with the empties. Other '8F' work involved several trip workings from Lostock Hall, and they sometimes appeared on parcels and ballast trains.

And so to the last week of steam, when hundreds of enthusiasts invaded North Lancashire. Copy Pit incline resembled the gatherings at Shap in years gone by as the careworn '8Fs' gamely blasted their way up the 1 in 68 gradient through the Cliviger Gorge against a background of gritstone scarps, gaunt mill chimneys and factory buildings of the industrial revolution. The depots, especially those at Rose Grove and Carnforth, were packed with enthusiasts who were rarely disappointed by the '8Fs' and their game crews. Whether struggling with the 1 in 40 on the Padiham branch, climbing to Copy Pit or forging up Hoghton Bank east of Preston, they went out in style with fireworks at the chimney top, big ends ringing, followed by the repetitive wheel beats of 16- and 21-ton loose-coupled mineral wagons — a sound almost totally foreign to BR today.

The Author's last encounter with a steam hauled freight train on the evening of Friday 1 August was not quite so dramatic, but nevertheless poignant. We had been following No 48423's progress on the 18.40 Preston to Healey Mills, and getting ahead of it waited at Rishton reservoir for a final photograph at sunset. The sunset died as a seemingly endless succession of DMU excursions passed on their way back from Blackpool to the West Riding. Photography was nearly out of the question when at last our objective could be heard approaching. Coupling rods ringing, exhaust shooting skywards, the flickering light from the firedoors playing on the woolly exhaust trail, rattling wagon wheels and wrenching couplings, our grimy entertainer crossed the reservoir and disappeared into the cutting accelerating eastwards on what was almost certainly her last assignment.

The end came on Sunday 3 August when a bewildering succession of enthusiast specials criss-crossed industrial Lancashire. No 48476 double headed BR standard Class 5 No 73069 on the RCTS Farewell special from Manchester to Blackburn via Oldham, Rochdale and Bolton. No 48773, the last engine to work off Rose Grove shed, double headed No 44781 with the LCGB Farewell from Blackburn to Carnforth, returning light engine to Burnley. A week earlier she had performed very well single handed on the SVRS/MRTS Farewell trip, and early in September quietly slipped away from her less fortunate sisters and headed for preservation on the Severn Valley Railway.

During the autumn of 1968, the remaining steam locomotives congregated at Lostock Hall and Rose Grove. Connecting rods and motion dismantled, coal removed from their tenders, begrimed and rusting they waited for the final journey to Messrs T. W. Ward of Sheffield and elsewhere.

Stanier '8F' allocations 1966-1968

Depot	Shed Code	1/1/66	1/1/67	7/1/68	4/8/68
Oxley	2B	7	12	—	—
Stourbridge Jn	2C	12	—	—	—
Saltley	2E	18	13	—	—
Bescot	2F	22	—	—	—
Crewe South	5B	10	7	—	—
Stoke	5D	18	17	—	—
Nuneaton	5E	19	—	—	—
Mold Jn	6B	12	—	—	—
Croes Newydd	6C	11	8	—	—
Shrewsbury	6D	4	1	—	—
Edge Hill	8A	12	13	18	—
Speke Jn	8C	18	16	5	—
Northwich	8E	14	21	17	—
Springs Branch	8F	12	19	—	—
Sutton Oak	8G	8	9	—	—
Birkenhead	8H	1	1	—	—
Aintree	8L	12	8	—	—
Stockport Edgeley	9B	8	17	7	—
Newton Heath	9D	18	19	13	—
Trafford Park	9E	7	12	7	—
Heaton Mersey	9F	21	27	24	—
Patricroft	9H	14	18	13	—
Agecroft	9J	10	—	—	—
Bolton	9K	11	15	9	—
Buxton	9L	9	13	7	—
Carnforth	10A	3	5	—	—
Fleetwood	10C	7	—	—	—
Lostock Hall	10D	11	15	8	6
Rose Grove	10F	15	23	20	20
Lower Darwen	10H	4	—	—	—
Lancaster	10J	3	—	—	—
Leicester	15A	14	—	—	—

Depot	Shed Code	1/1/66	1/1/67	7/1/68	4/8/68
Annesley	16B	39	—	—	—
Derby	16C	9	—	—	—
Nottingham	16D	2	—	—	—
Kirkby	16E	33	9	—	—
Burton	16F	20	—	—	—
Westhouses	16G	20	1	—	—
Leeds	55A	7	7	—	—
Stourton	55B	15	6	—	—
Farnley Jn	55C	2	—	—	—
Royston	55D	21	23	—	—
Wakefield	56A	1	1	—	—
Mirfield	56D	4	3	—	—
Bath Green Park	82F	4	—	—	—
Chester	6A	—	5	—	—
Widnes	8D	—	1	—	—
Colwick	16B	—	16	—	—
TOTAL		543	381	138	26

Stanier '8F' allocations as at 4 August 1968

Depot	Locomotive Nos
Lostock Hall	48253, 48294, 48476, 48723, 48765, 48775
Rose Grove	48062, 48167, 48191, 48247, 48278, 48340, 48348, 48393, 48400, 48410, 48423, 48493, 48519, 48665, 48666, 48715, 48727, 48730, 48752, 48773

Distribution of Stanier '8F' 2-8-0 locomotives 1965-1968

	1/1/64	24/4/65	1/1/66	1/1/67	7/1/68	4/8/68
Western Lines (LMR)	199	192	133	63	—	—
North Western Lines (LMR)	168	212	219	252	138	26
Midland Division (LMR)	195	166	137	26	—	—
North Eastern Region	52	51	50	40	—	—
Eastern Region	23	—	—	—	—	—
Western Region	27	11	4	—	—	—
Total:	664	632	543	381	138	26

Schedule of Stanier '8F' withdrawals 1960-68

Locomotives withdrawn		Locomotives in service	
Year	Total	Date	Total
1960	1	1/1/61	665
1962	8*	1/1/63	661
1963	—	1/1/64	664
1964	26	1/1/65	638
1965	95	1/1/66	543
1966	162	1/1/67	381
1967	231	1/1/68	150
1968	150	4/8/68	26

*Includes four locomotives withdrawn from Staveley and later reinstated as LMR stock. Three locomotives were withdrawn from Polmadie and later reinstated as LMR Stock in 1963.

Below:
Storm clouds on New Year's Eve proclaim tempestuous weather ahead for the '8Fs'; the sun fleetingly breaks through the cloud bank to highlight a 2-8-0 battling up the 1 in 100 to Blea Moor near Helwith Bridge, with a heavy coal haul bound for Carlisle on 31 December 1966. *B. Wrigglesworth*

Above:
West Riding Twilight; No 48540 (D44) trundles a train of coal empties between Cudworth and Darfield, two months before the end of steam working from Royston. 1 August 1967. *M. Mitchell*

Right:
Downpour at Diggle; in typical Pennine weather, No 48205 (NB42) tops Standedge Summit and drifts past Diggle Junction with a train of westbound carflats on 27 May 1967. Signs of rationalisation following the closure of the slow lines and original Standedge tunnels are evident on the right. *M. Mitchell*

Right:
A grimy No 48340 (H44) has nearly 1,000 tons on the drawbar as she nears Winwick Junction with the 10.30 Northwich-Whitehaven soda ash

Above:
No 48727 (B44) raises the echoes all over the town as she thunders across the Weaver Viaduct at Northwich, with a heavy trip working for Winnington Works on 3 February 1968. *Author*

Below:
An impressive backdrop of Peak District summits frames the scene as No 48775 (C36) battles against a heavy train, 1 in 91 gradient, and a strong westerly wind setting a Gowhole-Buxton trip working on the move from a signal check at Chinley South Junction on 27 January 1968. Wrong line working was in force to Peak Forest because of repairs to Dove Holes Tunnel, and the train is about to set back over the cross-over. The Pilotman can be seen in the foreground.
D. E. Gouldthorpe

Top right:

A scene repeated all too often in 1968. No 48036 has made her last run on the Wallerscote trip working and stands over the ashpit at Northwich on 2 March. This nomadic machine was delivered in immaculate finish by the Vulcan Foundry on 25 August 1936 at a cost of £6,515, and allocated to Wellingborough. She moved to Heaton Mersey on 19 June 1943, Cricklewood on 24 July 1943, Normanton on 4 September 1943 and to Kirkby on 11 October 1947. Then came Bury on 30 March 1948, Rugby on 17 December 1949, Nuneaton on 17 June 1950 and Newton Heath on 11 November 1950. After 14 years at Willesden from 9 December 1950, she went to Crewe South in January 1965, back to Willesden in February, returning to Crewe in May before reaching Northwich in March 1967. Upon withdrawal, she had run about 800,000 miles and was 13 years short of her 'standard life' of 45 years. *Author*

Above right:

Last weeks of steam on the Cheshire Lines. Heaton Mersey's No 48319 (C44) swings a trainload of Yorkshire coal bound for Garston on to the line to Stockport and Liverpool at Woodley Junction in April 1968. *R. Elsdon*

Right:

No 48033 (VF36) bursts through the closed station at Fallowfield, on the now abandoned Great Central line from Manchester Central to Guide Bridge with the LCGB 'Two Cities Limited' special of 23 June 1968. *David Birch*

Top:
No 48060 (VF36) pounds vigorously into the rise from Preston up to Coppull as she passes Farington Junction with a Heysham-Garston express freight on 8 March 1968. *I. C. Simpson*

Above:
The crisp, frosty air of an early April morning finds No 48448 (S44) storming towards the summit of Hoghton bank, east of Preston, with train 7N82 — the 06.53 Farington-Healey Mills empties on 5 April 1968.
I. C. Simpson

Right:
Thunder in the Pennines as two '8Fs' — No 48410 (S44) leading and another banking vigorously in the rear — heave a heavy train of coal for Wyre Dock up the 1 in 68 eastern ramp of the Copy Pit incline, west of 'the other Portsmouth' on 18 May 1968. *M. Taylor*

Below right:
Traction contrast at Preston, on 10 June 1968. Brush Type 4 (now Class 47) diesel No D1621 heading the 09.00 Perth-Birmingham is checked by No 48115 (C39) getting away with the 13.10 Rose Grove-Wyre Dock coal train. Increasing use of the Brush Class 47s and the final deliveries of the English Electric Class 50s completed the elimination of steam traction by 4 August. *D. Cross*

Below:
Grand Finale. The cosmopolitan scene at Blackburn on Sunday, 3 August 1968. Enthusiasts and members of the general public mill around, paying their last respects to the steam locomotive, as No 48773 (NB40) prepares to double head 'Black Five' No 44781 to Carnforth with the LCGB 'Farewell' special. *T. A. Haynes*

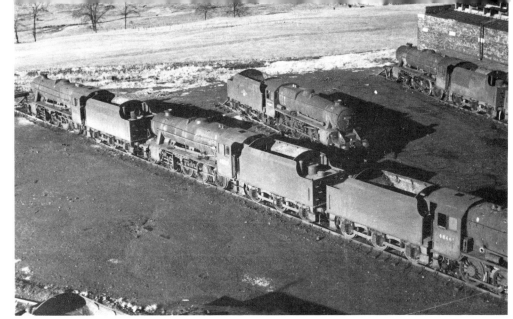

Right:
Requiem. Tenders emptied, connecting rods removed, silent and cold, Stanier '8Fs' and one 'Black Five' await the final call at Rose Grove in November 1968.
F. Hughes

Below right:
Active Preservation 1: No 48773 was purchased at the end of regular steam operation by the Stanier '8F' Locomotive Society Ltd and restored on the Severn Valley Railway to her earlier guise as LMS No 8233. Here she pilots the preserved Ivatt Class 4MT 2-6-0 No 43106 at York with the 07.30 Bridgnorth-Urlay Nook special on 11 August 1975, before participating in the Stockton and Darlington Railway 150th Anniversary Celebrations.
D. C. Williams

Below:
Active Preservation 2: After eight years in the Barry scrapyard of Messrs Woodham Brothers, No 48431 (S44) was rescued for preservation on the Keighley and Worth Valley Railway. She is seen heading an Oxenhope train at Ingrow in the summer of 1983. *H. Malham*

Appendices

1
Accidents

The '8Fs' lived in a rough and tumble world of loose-coupled freight working in which accidents of a minor nature were inevitable. Derailments could be expected on indifferent track in goods yards and colliery sidings. Controlling loose-coupled trains was always a tricky business, much depending on the skill of the driver and the state of the rail. Numerous '8Fs' have over-run loops, sometimes narrowly avoiding precipitous drops with no greater consequence than a few spilt wagons and some superficial damage. Occasionally, there occurred that event which all footplatemen fear — a full scale runaway — but this was rare. Comically, a few '8Fs' have had to be ignominiously rescued from turntable pits, and the odd item of damage sustained in shed collisions was all part of being one of 666 locomotives at work on a very busy system. Sometimes, however, distinctly more serious incidents did occur.

On 2 June 1941, No 8293, on loan to the GWR, was nearing Dolphin Junction, Slough with the 01.30 Old Oak Common to Severn Tunnel Junction freight. The train passed the distant signal at clear, but the signalman inadvisedly decided on a change of plan and returned the home signal to danger. With an unfitted 62-wagon train, the driver had no chance of pulling up from 30mph in the 400yd sighting distance. The '8F' ran past the signal and collided head on with 'Castle' class 4-6-0 No 4091 *Dudley Castle* which was crossing its path moving from the up main to the up slow line with the 18.20 Plymouth to Paddington. The combined speed of the two trains was about 30mph, but the heavy freight train had the greatest momentum and the 'Castle' was driven back about 4yd, causing severe telescoping in the coaches of the express. Five passengers were killed, and six seriously injured, including the driver of the '8F'. Both locomotives were extensively damaged, the '8F' particularly so with the front end stove in and the tender reared up against the cab. The first '8F' to be withdrawn, but eventually repaired, she was out of traffic until March 1942, missing an overseas draft to Iran in the process.

Another signalman's error was the cause of a spectacular incident on 4 October 1949. No 48644 was heading the 1,047-ton, 13.35 Wellingborough to Brent coal train, running on the up slow line under permissive block regulations. The train was allowed to pass Sharnbrook under clear signals when it should have been slowed and warned as the section ahead was already occupied by the 12.40 Wellingborough to Brent. The driver had only 550yd warning on sighting the preceding train on Oakley viaduct, and a collision at about 30mph

ensued in which the engine and 14 wagons plunged over the parapet and on to the valley floor 25ft below. A mass of wreckage piled on top of the engine and both members of the crew were regrettably killed. The rerailing operation was complicated. First, the engine had to be righted, and then raised on to a platform of sleepers before being lifted back on to the viaduct by two cranes.

A serious accident occurred on the Longmoor Military Railway on 13 October 1956, on the single line between Longmoor Downs and Liss Forest Road. WD No 512 (later BR No 48775) was heading the 08.40 Liss to Longmoor passenger train which should have crossed a works special at Liss Forest Road, but instead continued towards Longmoor without stopping. In the ensuing head on collision, the 350hp diesel shunter on the works train came off very much the worst, but more seriously, it was telescoped backwards on top of the box van at the head of its train. Six sappers were killed and eight injured as a result, and the '8F' suffered considerable front end damage.

On 9 February 1957, Driver John Axon and Fireman Ron Scanlon of Stockport were in charge of Warrington's No 48188, about to leave Buxton with the 11.05 freight to Arpley. The outward trip had been uneventful, except that the steam pipe joint leading into the Driver's Brake Valve had been blowing, and this had been tightened by a fitter at Buxton. With a 650-ton train, a banker was taken for the 2-mile climb at 1 in 66 to Bibbingtons Sidings. Shortly after leaving, the brake valve joint began to blow again.

Nearing the Bibbington distant the joint failed completely, allowing scalding steam at 225lb pressure to escape into the cab. The crew were in a terribly unfortunate position, nearing the summit at 15mph with the bank engine pushing behind, its crew unaware that anything was wrong. Doubly unfortunate was the fact that the engine was working on full regulator, and the handle had to be taken right across the quadrant and slammed shut to close it. With the chaotic conditions in the cab and high pressure steam billowing around, this was impossible.

John Axon told his fireman to jump off and pin down as many wagon brakes as he could, while he courageously remained on the engine in the forlorn hope of regaining control, a remote possibility on a 7-mile falling gradient of 1 in 58/79 with no steam brake. No 48188 and her train were travelling at 55mph when they overran the preceding 08.45 Rowsley to Stockport freight in Chapel-en-le-Frith station; Driver Axon was posthumously awarded the

George Cross for his bravery in remaining on the engine, an action which was in the very highest traditions of the railway service.

The cause of the accident was the failure of the brazing on the collar of the pipe leading into the brake valve. The joint was secured by a large nut which had been successively overtightened to keep it steam tight, until eventually the brazing gave way and the collar was separated from the pipe, causing the joint to fail completely.

A driver's error was responsible for the accident at Turvey on 17 June 1960 which resulted in the withdrawal of No 48616, which was heading a very heavy train of prefabricated track sections on the now closed Bedford to Northampton line. Because of the sparsity of traffic, only one line was in use, the other being used partially for wagon storage. At Turvey the '8F' was allowed on to the disused down line for the purpose of crossing a troop special. The driver set off under the mistaken impression that he was 'right away'; not for nothing was this line known as the 'Northamptonshire Alps', and it was very difficult to stop on the steep falling gradient once the mistake had been realised. The '8F' ploughed into a line of stored coaches, scattering lengths of track in all directions, ending up covered by a mass of debris. She was recovered and sent to Derby for overhaul, but when the frames were stripped down they were found to be so badly out of alignment that the 17-year old engine became the first '8F' to be withdrawn in peacetime — well ahead of any official programme of withdrawal.

Some accidents did have a comical side and two brief incidents must suffice. On 12 January 1961, the 12.40 Greenford to Leamington parcels train headed by a GWR 'Hall' class 4-6-0 collided head on with an '8F' on the 18.50 Washwood Heath to Morris Cowley freight on the single line section near Morris Cowley station. As a result, Morris Minor car bodies from the freight train were strewn all over the track in gay confusion. Later the same year, on 2 November No 48674 was proceeding sedately 'wrong line' between Four Oaks and Sutton Coldfield stations on a ballast special. Someone had forgotten to clip the catch points in the engine's favour and she gently ran through them, heeling over at a drunken angle on the embankment. She spent the next week propped up precariously, threatening a suburban greenhouse, until recovered on the following Sunday.

Right:
No 48188 lies amidst the wreckage at Chapel-en-le Frith station as clearing-up operations begin following the accident of 9 February 1957. *Alan H. Bryant*

Below right:
WD No 512 (C37) and a 350hp diesel shunter stand firmly locked together, following the head on collision on the Longmoor Military Railway near Liss Forest Road on 13 October 1956. The '8F' was an oil burner at this time and the oil burner controls may be glimpsed through the fireman's window. Also visible is the oil heater below the footplating above the trailing and driving axles, and alongside the firebox, the linkage for the manual blowdown fitted to many WD '8Fs'. The live steam injector on the fireman's side was also a WD requirement.
E. C. Griffith/Rail Archive Stephenson

Chaos at Dolphin Junction, 3 June 1943. Nos 8293 and 4091 *Dudley Castle* are firmly locked together, whilst a mountain of wreckage has piled up against the '8Fs' tender. *BR*

2
Liveries

LMS Livery

Comprehensive details may be found in Messrs Jenkinson and Essery's *Locomotive Liveries of the LMS* (Roundhouse Books 1967). Basic livery details:

Plain black locomotive and tender.
Vermillion (bright red) bufferbeams and inside frames.
White cab roof interior with wood grained sides to waist level. This was probably not fully applied in the later war years when a plain buff colour was substituted.
No '8F' received the 1946 livery.
Smokebox numbers were usually 4½in high in the Midland style, but some engines had the 1936 block pattern numerals.
Tenders were officially lettered LMS in 14in high letters at 60in spacings between centres, but in practice, there was considerable variety in lettering and numbering:

Lettering style	Locomotive Nos
12in gold numerals and letters, unshaded	8000-11
10in gold numerals shaded black 1936 block style with block pattern smokebox plates	8012-95

12in numerals, chrome yellow insignia, shaded red	8126-75
	8226-63
	8264-85/93
	8301-99
	8490-95
	8705-8772
10in numerals, chrome yellow insignia, shaded red	8176-8225
	(probably block style smokebox numbers)
	8400-79
	8500-59
	8600-8704
12in chrome yellow insignia, plain unshaded letters	8096-8125

Nos 8400-79 had numbers painted on front bufferbeams in GWR style, with no smokebox numberplates. Transfers supplied by LMS for tenders and cabsides.

Nos 8500-59 had block style front numberplates when Doncaster or Darlington built.

Nos 8705-72 were originally LNER locomotives. LMS

insignia applied at sheds, often ran without smokebox numberplates at first. No 8759 not renumbered until 1948.

Postwar repaints could usually be recognised by the high position of the cabside numbers, with the power classification underneath.

War Department Livery

1 Locomotives completed by April 1941

Light grey engine and tender.

12in numerals and 14in letters on tender sides in golden yellow, later darkened to 'gamboge'.

Tender letters at 51in centres from central arrow 10in high.

Smokebox numbers in block style 4½in high. White at first, later black.

2 Later locomotives and those requisitioned

Black engine and tender.

2in letters and numbers in matt golden yellow.

Smokebox numberplates as in 1. These were frequently retained throughout.

Most had 2in numbers on front and rear bufferbeams, some had rear numbers on tender backplate, either side of water capacity plate.

Abroad, black livery was applied but with a great variety of lettering and numbering styles:

Egypt — 9000 was added to the original WD numbers. Locomotives purchased by the ESR were renumbered from 832 upwards.

Iran — Locomotives numbered 41.100-41.246.

1944 — Locomotives still with Middle East Forces renumbered from 9350, but this scheme was superseded later in the year by the addition of 70000 to the original WD numbers.

1952 — Locomotives remaining in WD hands were renumbered in a new series starting at 500 — only WD 508 by chance, retaining its original number.

Depot allocation codes were frequently carried on the cabsides in Iran and Egypt.

3 10 Railway Squadron Royal Engineers c1950

Certain locomotives were named and given a special livery of:

Lined black locomotive and tender.

White tyres and burnished handrails, motion, and smokebox hinges.

14in 'WD' on tender, sometimes with regimental crest in between the letters.

Number on front bufferbeam as W ↑ D 70320, etc.

36in numbers on cabside.

4 Longmoor Military Railway c1955

Normal livery was unlined black with 8in block numbers on cabside.

WD 501 *Lt W. O. Lennox VC* received the full Longmoor lined blue livery with white tyres. Lining in red, LMR on tender in 14in letters, small 6in numbers on cabside. W ↑ D 501 on front bufferbeam.

British Railways Livery

Black locomotive and tender.

Signal red bufferbeams and inside frames.

Buff colour for interior of cab roof and sides down to waist level.

Cast smokebox numberplate with 4½in numbers in BR-style, but some locomotives had numberplates cast in the Midland Railway style.

Cream numbers on cabside. 2in Power Classification below windows and 8in numbers below. Some works — Eastleigh and Darlington for example — used 10in numbers.

Star on cabsides beneath numbers to indicate those locomotives with 50% reciprocating balance.

British Railways emblem carried centrally on tender. This was the 'cycling lion' at first, but the later modified design was applied from 1957.

Some early repaints in 1948 carried the 'M' suffix before the number, others had the BR number in the 1946 LMS style and 'British Railways' on the tender.

3
Selected Locomotive Histories

8000 Built Crewe 19 June 1935. Cost £7,053. Standard life 45 years. Class 7F. 13 July 1935 to 18A Toton. 30 November 1935 reclassified '8F'. 10 October 1936 to 15A Wellingborough, 12 June 1943 to 16C Kirkby, 10 May 1958 to 18A Toton, 24 June 1958 to 21A Saltley, 20 September 1958 to 16A Nottingham, 12 March 1960 to 21A, 22 June 1963 to 17B Burton, November 1964 to 16C Derby, Stored 28 June 1965 to 21 December 1965, December 1965 to 16B Annesley, September 1966 to 9B Stockport Edgeley. 18 March 1967 Withdrawn. September 1965 Scrapped Cashmores, Great Bridge. Best mileage 1936 — 33,387, least 1952 — 17,310. Modifications: 1938 Vacuum brakes, 1952 new Piston Head Fastenings, 1961 AWS.

8014 Built Crewe December 1936. 9 January 1937 into traffic at 18C Hasland. 9 December 1939 to 15A. September 1941 requisitioned by WD. November 1941 converted to oil firing, air brakes, shipped to Iran as WD 590, Iranian State Railways No 41.232. December 1944 deleted from LMS stock. 1948 sold to Iran. 1963 (?) withdrawn. 1977 stored at Ahwaz with LMS livery visible. 1985 still stored in war zone?

8034 Built Vulcan Foundry August 1936, No 4711. September 1936 into traffic at 18A. October 1941 requisitioned. December 1941 despatched to Iran, No WD 593, oil and air brakes. ISR No 41.199. 1945/46 transferred by rail to Palestine/Egypt, WD No 70593. 1952 WD No 513, named *Lt Graham VC RE* on Adabiya-Ataka military railway. 1956 sold to Egyptian State Railways, ESR No 838. 1961/62 withdrawn.

8044 Built Vulcan Foundry November 1936, No 4721. 10 October 1936 to 18A, 11 February 1939 to 19D Heaton Mersey. October 1941 requisitioned. December 1941 despatched to Iran, WD No 598, oil firing and air brakes, ISR No 41.196. 1944 sent to Egypt by sea. MEF No 9371, later WD No 70598. 1944/45 sent to Italy, Falconara depot. 1946 sold to FS No 737.013. 1950 to Bari. 1953 withdrawn and subsequently scrapped.

8087 Built Vulcan Foundry January 1937, No 4764. 13 February 1937 into traffic at 20D Normanton. 14 January 1939 to 20C Royston. 11 February 1939 to 19D. November 1941 requisitioned, WD No 619. Lost overboard from SS *Pentridge Hall* in Irish Sea en route to Iran. June 1942 deleted from LMS stock.

8151 Built Crewe September 1942. Cost £8,355. 5 September 1942 into traffic at 12A Carlisle Kingmoor. 13 February 1943 to 31D Grangemouth. 5 February 1949 to 15A. 9 April 1949 renumbered 48151. July 1955 to 19C Canklow. January 1963 to 41E Staveley. April 1964 to 8A Edge Hill. March 1966 to 8E Northwich. 28 December 1967 last day's work on Over & Wharton trip. 13 January 1968 withdrawn with cracked piston valve liners, sent to Woodham Brothers, Barry. 1975 purchased for preservation, currently under restoration near Wakefield. Best mileage 1945 — 50,045, least 1957 — 20,459. Modifications: 1951 blowdown to ashpan, 1953 sandgun removed, 1960 AWS.

8226 Built North British Loco Co (NBL) No 24600 12 June 1940, as WD No 300. Air brakes, French specification, WD grey livery. September 1940 on loan to LMS, standard equipment as No 8226. October 1940 loaned to GWR at Severn Tunnel Junction (STJ). September 1941 returned to WD, sent to Iran. January 1942 ISR No 41.116, coal burner, vacuum brakes. 1945/46 sent by rail to Palestine/Egypt. Overhauled by WD, expecting sale to Lebanon. April 1948 returned to England, sold to BR as No 48246. Cost of purchase and repairs £10,137. 10 December 1949 into traffic at 5B Crewe South. 18 February 1950 to 6B Mold Junction. 18 July 1961 to 6C Llandudno Junction. June 1964 to 5D Stoke. 29 January 1966 withdrawn, April 1966 scrapped Cashmores, Great Bridge. Best mileage 1955 — 28,682, least 1960 — 24,600. Modifications: 1952 blowdown to ashpan, 1954 sandgun removed, 1960 AWS.

8229 Built NBL No 24603 June 1940, WD No 303. French specification, WD livery. October 1940 on loan as LMS No 8229, allocated to 4A Shrewsbury. (On loan from 17A Derby.) July 1941 returned to WD, September 1941 to Iran. February 1942 ISR No 41.139, coal burning and steam brake only. 1945 sold to Iraq, 1946 IqSR No 905, 1947 No 1425, class TD. At work until the early 1970s.

8233 Built NBL No 24607 June 1940. WD 307, French specification, WD livery. August 1940 on loan to LMS. December 1940 LMS livery and standard fittings to 18A Toton. March 1941 on loan to 20A Holbeck. June 1941 to 18B Westhouses. September 1941 returned to WD — to Iran. December 1941 ISR No 41.109, allocated to Ahwaz. Coal burning, vacuum and steam brakes. August 1942 derailed by camel. 1944 reallocated to Tehran, converted to oil. 1946 transferred by rail to Egypt, WD No 70307, on loan to Egyptian State Railways. 1948 returned to 169 Workshops, Suez with damaged firebox, almost scrapped. 1952 WD No 500, returned to Derby for overhaul. 1954 to Longmoor Military Railway. 1957 purchased by BR for £5,500, overhauled at Eastleigh, BR No 48773. September 1957 to 66A Polmadie. December 1962 withdrawn. January 1963 reinstated. July 1963 withdrawn — to Horwich for scrapping. October 1963 reinstated and overhauled. December 1963 to 12A Kingmoor. January 1964 to 9B Stockport Edgeley. June 1964 to 9L Buxton. September 1964 to 9K Bolton. June 1966 overhauled, Crewe. July 1966 to 9 April 1967 stored. June 1968 to 10F Rose Grove. 4 August 1968 withdrawn. 9 August 1968 purchased for preservation as LMS No 8233 on Severn Valley Railway by the Stanier '8F' Locomotive Society Ltd. Modifications: 1966 AWS.

WD 372 Built NBL No 24680, June 1941. September 1941 sent to Iran. ISR No 41.113, coal and vacuum brakes. 1946 converted to oil and transferred to Palestine as WD No 70372. 1946-47 worked in Palestine. 1948 abandoned and lost at Tulkarm on old Haifa-Lydda main line closed on Partition in 1948 when Tulkarm became part of Jordan. 1972 Rediscovered. Preservation proposed. Yom Kippur War intervened and locomotive scrapped in 1974.

8261 Built NBL No 24635 October 1940. WD No 335. November 1940 on loan to LMS as No 8261. December 1940 loaned to GWR at Newport and Severn Tunnel Junction. July 1941 returned to WD. September 1941 to Iran. May 1942 ISR No 41.142 coal and steam brake only. 1944 WD 70335. 1946 sent by rail to Palestine, converted to oil. 1948 sold to Israel as 'LMS' class, at work until 1958.

48292 Built Beyer Peacock No 7036 November 1941, WD No 442. Oil burning, air, vacuum and steam brakes. Sent direct to Iran, ISR No 41.180. 1946 by rail to Palestine/Egypt. Repaired by RE workshops, WD No 70442. April 1948 returned to England, purchased by BR. Cost, including repairs, £7,583. 1 October 1949 into traffic as No 48292 at 5B Crewe South. 2 April 1955 to 9G Northwich. 7 July 1955 to 5B. 10 June 1961 to 6C Birkenhead. 11 July 1961 to 5B. July 1965 to 8C Speke Junction. March 1966 to 9H Patricroft. 11 July 1966 to 30 October 1967 stored. November 1967 to 9F Heaton Mersey. 20 April 1968 withdrawn. August 1968 scrapped Drapers, Hull. Best mileage 1959 — 30,111, least 1960 — 18,294. Modification: 1960 AWS.

8340 Built Horwich January 1944. Cost £10,944. 24 January 1944 into traffic at 29A Perth. 10 August 1946 to 5B. 21 January 1950 to 1A Willesden. 18 November 1950 to 9G Northwich. February 1965 to 8H Birkenhead. April 1965 to 8L Aintree. 5 September 1966 to 27 May 1967 stored. June 1967 to 8E Northwich. March 1968 to 10F Rose Grove. March 1968 to 9K Bolton. July 1968 to 10F. 3 August 1968 withdrawn. December 1968 scrapped Wards, Beighton. Best mileage 1944 — 43,480 (ran 90,230 miles to first classified repair), least 1955 — 17,237. Modifications: 1953 blowdown to ashpan, 1960 AWS.

8431 Built Swindon March 1944. Cost £12,514. 10 March 1944 into traffic, Derby on loan to GWR at Newton Abbot (NA). April 1945 to Gloucester (GLO). 29 March 1947 returned to LMS at 20C Royston. 5 November 1949 No 48431. 11 September 1955 transferred to Western Region stock at 83A Newton Abbot. October 1955 to 82B St Phillips Marsh. January 1960 to 81A Old Oak Common. November 1962 to 82E Bristol Barrow Road. January 1964 to 82F Bath Green Park. 20 July 1964 withdrawn. 1965 to Woodhams, Barry. 1971 purchased for preservation. Restored as LMS No 8431 on Keighley and Worth Valley Railway. Best mileage 1957 — 26,334, least 1949 — 18,544. Modifications: 1953 sandgun removed, 1955 WR ATC and vacuum ejector fitted.

8435 Built Swindon April 1944. 17 April 1944 into traffic at Penzance (PZ). June 1945 to Laira (LA). 3 May 1947 to LMS at 25E Sowerby Bridge. 13 September 1947 to 23B Aintree. 11 October 1947 to 24B Rose Grove. 5 February 1949 No 48435. 12 March 49 to 25G Farnley Junction. 12 November 1949 to 2D Nuneaton. 4 August 1962 to 1A. 6 April 1963 to 6C Birkenhead. June 1965 to 10F Rose Grove. 20 May 1967 withdrawn. September 1967 scrapped Cashmores, Great Bridge. Best mileage 1950 — 25,940, least 1947 — 16,712. Modifications: 1955 sandgun removed, 1960 AWS.

8510 Built Doncaster June 1943 No 1956. Cost £11,754. June 1943 LMS Derby on loan to LNER, into traffic at Tyne Dock (TDK). February 1944 to Heaton (HTN). June 1947 to March (MAR). 5 June 1947 returned to LMS. 28 June 1947 to 25A Wakefield. 13 August 1949 to 25D Mirfield. 15 October 1949 to 8A Edge Hill. 25 October 1952 to 8C Speke Junction. 25 April 1953 to 6C Birkenhead. 13 June 1953 to 6B Mold Junction. 17 October 1953 to 17A Derby. 18 October 1965 to 21 December 1965 stored. December 1965 to 16B Annesley. December 1966 to 10D Lostock Hall. 28 January 1968 withdrawn. 4 October 1968 scrapped Buttigiegs, Newport. Best mileage 1951 — 27,755, least 1952 — 16,356. Modifications: 1952 sandgun removed.

8543 Built Darlington January 1945 No 1949. Cost £11,754. 13 January 1945 into traffic at Aberdeen (ABN). October 1945 to St Margarets (STM). 8 March 1947 returned to LMS at 17A Derby. 27 September 1947 to 17C Coalville. 20 August 1949 No 48543. 11 November 1950 to 15A Wellingborough. 8 November 1952 to 18A Toton. 20 September 1958 to 18B Westhouses. 29 February 1964 to 8B Warrington. March 1965 to 9G Gorton. June 1965 to 9D Newton Heath. 26 February 1966 withdrawn. May 1966 scrapped Wards, Beighton. Best mileage 1954 — 28,654, least 1957 — 12,228. Modifications: 1962 AWS, tube cleaner pipe to outside smokebox.

8600 Built Eastleigh January 1943. Cost £12,159. January 1943 running in from Eastleigh. 6 February 1943 into traffic at 1A Willesden. 18 June 1948 No 48600. 28 September 1963 to 1G Woodford Halse. 29 February 1964 to 16G Westhouses. October 1966 to 16B Annesley. November 1966 to 8C Speke Junction. 26 November 1966 withdrawn. May 1967 scrapped Drapers, Hull. Best mileage 1960 — 30,802, least 1947 — 19,110. Modifications: 1948 rebalancing to 40% reciprocating masses, 1953 sandgun removed, 1961 AWS.

8616 Built Brighton October 1943. 16 October 1943 into traffic at 16C Kirkby. 24 January 1948 to 20G Hellifield No 48616. 13 September 1958 to 18A. 23 May 1959 to 14A Cricklewood. 17 June 1960 damaged beyond repair in Turvey accident. 19 November 1960 broken up at Derby. Total mileage — 388,181, first of class to be withdrawn in peacetime. Best mileage 1956 — 30,061, least 1947 — 16,121. Modifications: 1948 snow damage repairs, 1950 50% reciprocating balance, 1952 sandgun removed.

8624 Built Ashford December 1943. 11 December 1943 into traffic at 1A Willesden. 13 November 1948 No 48624. 24 July 1965 withdrawn, delivered to Woodhams, Barry. 1981 purchased for preservation by the 48518 Preservation Society, now undergoing restoration at Buxton. Best mileage 1960 — 31,742, least 1945 — 19,727. Modifications: 1953 sandgun removed, 1961 AWS.

8707 Built Brighton June 1944 as LNER 'O6' No 7653. Cost £12,093. June 1944 into traffic at Mexborough (MEX). 1946 LNER No 3102. 1947 LNER No 3502. 8 November 1947 to LMS on loan from LNER at 23B Aintree. 19 February 1949 to 25A Wakefield. 13 August 1949 to 26A Newton Heath. 17 December 1949 No 48707. 27 January 1951 on loan to Western Region at 84G Shrewsbury. 10 February 1951 on loan to 87K Swansea Paxton Street. December 1951 to 84G. 19 April 1953 transferred from E&NER stock to LMR stock. 17 July 1955 transferred to WR stock. 8 August 1955 worked Royal Train Aberystwyth to Pembroke Dock with No 48309. August 1959 to 86C Cardiff Canton. December 1959 to 87F Llanelly. July 1964 to 82F Bath Green Park. September 1964 to 10D Lostock Hall. 8 April 1967 withdrawn. Scrapped Cashmores, Great Bridge, 1967. Best mileage 1952 — 37,143, least 1949 — 14,512. Modifications: 1953 sandgun removed, 1955 carriage warming apparatus fitted. (With No 48309 for Royal Train.)

NB: Details extracted from Locomotive History Cards may not necessarily list all modifications undertaken. Details of annual mileage were not religiously kept after about 1960.

4
Bibliography

General

Engines of the LMS, 1923-1951, J. W. P. Rowledge; Oxford Publishing Co, 1975.
Stanier 8F 2-8-0, Bond/Tyler/Wilkinson; D. Bradford Barton, 1978.
Locomotive Liveries of the LMS, Essery/Jenkinson; Roundhouse Books, 1967.
The 1948 Locomotive Exchanges, C. J. Allen; Ian Allan 1950.
What Happened to Steam — LMS 7F & 8F 2-8-0s, P. B. Hands.
Locomotives of the LNER, Part 6B; RCTS, 1983.

Mechanical

Master Builders of Steam, H. A. V. Bulleid; Ian Allan, 1963.
Locomotive Panorama Vol 1, E. S. Cox; Ian Allan, 1965.
BR Standard Steam Locomotives, E. S. Cox; Ian Allan, 1966.
Chronicles of Steam, E. S. Cox; Ian Allan, 1967.
Living with London Midland Locomotives, A. J. Powell; Ian Allan, 1977.
Stanier 4-6-0s at Work, A. J. Powell; Ian Allan, 1983.
Working with LMS Steam, H. C. H. Burgess; D. Bradford Barton, 1983.
A Breath of Steam, W. G. Thorley; Ian Allan, 1975.
Locomotive Management, Hodgson/Lake; Tothill Press, 1954.

Handbook for Steam Locomotive Enginemen, British Transport Commission, 1957.

Footplate

Both Sides of the Footplate, K. Stokes; D. Bradford Barton, 1983.
Firing Days at Saltley, T. Essery; D. Bradford Barton, 1980.
Through the Links at Crewe, P. Johnson; D. Bradford Barton, 1980.
Wellingborough Footplate Memories, G. Bushell; D. Bradford Barton, 1983.
London Midland Fireman, M. F. Higson; Ian Allan, 1972.

Abroad

War Department Locomotives, R. Tourret; Tourret Publishing, 1976.
Heavy Goods Engines of the War Department — Stanier '8F' 2-8-0, J. W. P. Rowledge; Springmead Railway Books.
190 in Persia, R. M. Robbins; R. M. Robbins.
Paiforce, HMSO, 1948.
Middle East Railways, H. C. Hughes; Continental Railway Circle.
Great Preserved Locomotives, Stanier '8F' No 8233, A. Wilkinson; Ian Allan, 1984.